D1498101

MASADA

MASADA

FROM JEWISH REVOLT TO MODERN MYTH

JODI MAGNESS

PRINCETON UNIVERSITY PRESS

PRINCETON AND OXFORD

Published by Princeton University Press
41 William Street, Princeton, New Jersey 08540
6 Oxford Street, Woodstock, Oxfordshire OX20 1TR

press.princeton.edu

LCCN 2018952836
ISBN 978-0-691-16710-7

British Library Cataloging-in-Publication Data is available

Editorial: Rob Tempio and Matt Rohal
Production Editorial: Sara Lerner
Text Design: C. Alvarez-Gaffin
Jacket Design: Faceout Studio, Spencer Fuller
Jacket Credit: (front) Aerial view of the archaeological site
of Masada and the Roman ramp built by Lucius Flavius Silva during
the First Jewish Revolt / Alamy. (back) Ruins of Masada fortress in Judaean
Desert / Alamy. (flaps) Topographic map of Masada and its surroundings /
Courtesy of Hillel Geva and the Israel Exploration Society
Production: Jacqueline Poirier
Publicity: Jodi Price and Amy Stewart
Copyeditor: Karen Verde

This book has been composed in Minion Pro

Printed on acid-free paper. ∞

Printed in the United States of America

1 3 5 7 9 10 8 6 4 2

To my parents with love

CONTENTS

ACKNOWLEDGMENTS

I did not plan to write this book. Rob Tempio at Princeton University Press persuaded me to do it, and I did not agree easily, because I had other commitments. Now, however, I am glad I wrote this book, and I am grateful to Rob for his persistence. Of the many individuals and institutions that provided support, thanks are due above all to my department and the administration at the University of North Carolina at Chapel Hill. To write this book while serving as president of the Archaeological Institute of America, UNC granted me a three-semester leave. The first semester (fall 2016) was covered by an internal award: a Pogue Senior Faculty Research and Scholarly Leave. The other two semesters were funded by a National Endowment for the Humanities Public Scholar Award (2017), which I feel especially fortunate to have received in view of proposed federal budget cuts. When in Israel, I conduct much of my research at the W. F. Albright Institute of Archaeological Research in Jerusalem—one of the American Overseas Research Centers (ORCs) also threatened by federal budget cuts. I hope my book demonstrates the value of funding agencies such as the NEH and ORCs which support scholarship in the humanities.

This book is the product of an education that began as an undergraduate at the Hebrew University of Jerusalem. There, as I mention in chapter 9, I had the privilege of studying with Yigael Yadin and other distinguished faculty at the Institute of Archaeology. One of these was Gideon Foerster, who, after Yadin's death, involved me in the publication of the military equipment from Yadin's excavations at Masada, and who invited me to co-direct the 1995 excavations in the Roman siege works. My familiarity and fascination with Masada, Qumran, and other sites around the Dead Sea began when I worked as a field guide and naturalist at the Ein Gedi Field School in 1977–1980.

Over the years my research on Masada has benefited from the advice of many friends and colleagues, including Kenneth Atkinson, Andrea Berlin, Sidnie White Crawford, Gwyn Davies, and Hanan Eshel (now deceased and sorely missed). Also missed are Israel Shatzman, with whom I studied at the Hebrew University, and Kenneth Holum, director of the Combined Caesarea Expeditions on which I worked from 1989–1992, both of whom passed away while this book was in the final stages of preparation. I am especially grateful to Ken Atkinson, Gwyn Davies, Stephen Goranson, Bob Susick, and two anonymous reviewers for reading and commenting on this manuscript, although I alone am responsible for its contents. During a visit to Jordan in November 2017, Győző Vörös, director of the excavations at Machaerus and his family, treated me like Hungarian royalty and shared the spectacular photo of Machaerus and Masada included among the illustrations here. I am indebted to the Israel Exploration Society for permission to reproduce many of the other illustrations in this book, and I thank Todd Bolen and Leen Ritmeyer for granting permission to use their images.

I continue to enjoy the unconditional love and support of my husband Jim Haberman (who prepared the illustrations for this book), my parents, my brother and sister and their families, and our adopted nephew, Mike Miller. I considered dedicating this book to Hanan Eshel or Yigael Yadin or my dear friend Tsvi (Harvey) Schneider, also deceased and greatly missed. But above all it is my parents, Herbert and Marlene Magness, who deserve the recognition and the *nachas*. May they live in good health to 120!

Map 1. Map of the Hasmonean kingdom.

Map 2. Map of Herod's kingdom.

MASADA

PROLOGUE

THE FALL OF MASADA

Two thousand years ago, 967 Jewish men, women, and children reportedly chose to take their own lives rather than suffer enslavement or death at the hands of the Roman army. They were the last holdouts of the First Jewish Revolt against Rome, which had ended officially three years earlier, in 70 CE, with an unimaginable disaster: the destruction of Jerusalem and the second temple. During the revolt, these families found refuge atop Masada, a remote fortress on a mountain overlooking the Dead Sea. Now, however, they were besieged by an overwhelming Roman force, and it was clear that the fortress would fall. At this critical moment, the rebel leader, Eleazar Ben-Yair, gathered the men together and convinced them to commit mass suicide. The ancient Jewish historian Flavius Josephus, who lived at the time of the revolt, reports Ben-Yair's speech as follows:

> Long since, my brave men, we determined neither to serve the Romans nor any other save God, for He alone is man's true and righteous Lord; and now the time is come which bids us verify that resolution by our actions. At this crisis let us not disgrace ourselves; we who in the past refused to submit even to a slavery involving no peril, let us not now, along with slavery, deliberately accept the irreparable penalties awaiting us if we are to fall alive into Roman hands. For as we were the first of all to revolt, so we are the last in arms against them. Moreover, I believe that it is God who has granted us this favor, that we have it in our power to die nobly and in freedom—a privilege denied to others who have met with unexpected defeat. Our fate at the

break of day is certain capture, but there is still the free choice of a noble death with those we hold most dear. For our enemies, fervently though they pray to take us alive, can no more prevent this than we can now hope to defeat them in battle . . . For not even the impregnable nature of this fortress has availed to save us; nay, though ample provisions are ours, piles of arms, and a superabundance of every other requisite, yet we have been deprived, manifestly by God Himself, of all hope of deliverance. For it was not of their own accord that those flames which were driving against the enemy turned back upon the wall constructed by us; no, all this betokens wrath at the many wrongs which we madly dared to inflict upon our countrymen. The penalty for those crimes let us pay not to our bitterest foes, the Romans, but to God, through the act of our own hands. It will be more tolerable than the other. Let our wives thus die undishonored, our children unacquainted with slavery; and, when they are gone, let us render a generous service to each other, preserving our liberty as a noble winding-sheet. But first let us destroy our chattels and the fortress by fire; for the Romans, well I know, will be grieved to lose at once our persons and the lucre. Our provisions only let us spare; for they will testify, when we are dead, that it was not want which subdued us, but that, in keeping with our initial resolve, we preferred death to slavery. (*War* 7.323–27, 331–36)[1]

So persuaded, each man killed his own wife and children. Then the men gathered together and drew lots, determining which ten of them would put the others to death. The ten remaining men drew lots again, and one man killed the other nine before taking his own life, as Josephus describes:

Finally, then, the nine bared their throats, and the last solitary survivor, after surveying the prostrate multitude, to see whether haply amid the shambles there were yet one left who needed his hand, and finding that all were slain, set the palace ablaze, and then collecting his strength drove his sword clean through his body and fell beside his family. (*War* 7.397–98)

What a gripping story! But how did the Jews atop Masada reach this point, and how do we know about these events?

Nowadays Masada, a UNESCO World Heritage Site, attracts more tourists than any other archaeological site in Israel except Caesarea Maritima, which benefits from a more accessible coastal location near Tel Aviv. Most visitors come from Jerusalem via a highway along the western shore of the Dead Sea, arriving on the mountain's east side. Others make the trip from the west, by way of the town of Arad and arriving at the Roman ramp. In the summer months, thousands of youth from abroad form a continuous line, climbing the mountain before sunrise by way of the Snake Path. After the sun comes up, many more tourists pack the cable car for a ride to the top. All these visitors share one goal: to stand on the very spot where a small band of Jewish rebels made their last stand against the mighty Roman Empire.

Josephus's account of the mass suicide at Masada is so compelling that after Israel was established in 1948, the slogan "Masada shall not fall again" became symbolic of the modern state. The example of Jews putting up a heroic resistance to the death instead of going meekly to their slaughter had great appeal in the wake of the Holocaust and at a time when Israel's population felt embattled. For many years, the Israel Defense Forces (IDF) held induction ceremonies atop Masada. However, times have changed, and so have perspectives on Masada. For one thing, even those who embrace the mass suicide as a symbol of modern Israel must reconcile it with Judaism's prohibition against taking one's own life (although according to Josephus's account, only the last man died by his own hand). More important, in today's post-Zionist era the story of Masada has become a less compelling model for Israelis. And scholarly views have changed as well. For example, we shall see that many scholars now believe Josephus's description of the mass suicide (the only ancient account of this episode) is fabricated—that it never happened!

In this book we examine the story of Masada, using it as a lens through which to explore the history of Judea in the late Second Temple period (mid-second century BCE—first century CE)—roughly the same period covered by Josephus in his account of *The Jewish War*. This turbulent era witnessed the reign of Herod the Great as well as Jesus's ministry and death and culminated with the destruction of the Jerusalem temple. Through the story of Masada, we become acquainted with the major Jewish sects of this period: Pharisees, Sadducees, and Essenes. It may be that some Essenes—the same group that deposited the Dead Sea Scrolls in the caves around Qumran—joined the Jewish rebels atop Masada. Examining Herod's fortified palaces at Masada provides us with an opportunity to explore Herod's other major building projects, including Caesarea Maritima and the Jerusalem temple. For the history of this period we rely mainly on Josephus, a controversial figure regarded in Jewish tradition as a traitor. We also devote attention to Masada's modern history, and in particular to the excavations conducted there by Yigael Yadin, who served as chief of staff of the IDF and was arguably Israel's most famous archaeologist. Yadin's expedition helped cement Masada's status as a symbol of the modern State of Israel.

CHAPTER 1

THE SIEGE OF MASADA

(72–73 OR 73–74 CE)

In 72 or 73 CE, 967 Jewish refugees holding out atop Masada watched helplessly as thousands of Roman soldiers surrounded the base of the mountain, cutting off all contact with the outside world. Our story of Masada begins at this critical moment: the siege of the fortress three years after the fall of Jerusalem. In this chapter we examine the Roman siege works and become acquainted with Josephus—the only ancient author who describes the siege of Masada.

THE SIEGE OF MASADA

When the First Revolt erupted in 66, bands of Jewish rebels took over some of Herod the Great's fortified palaces, which had been occupied and maintained by garrisons since the king's death seventy years earlier. Three were still in Jewish hands after the revolt officially ended in 70: Herodium (near Bethlehem), Machaerus (to the east of the Dead Sea), and Masada. The Roman legate (governor) of the newly established province of Judea, Lucilius Bassus, set out to subdue these last holdouts. Limited information from Josephus and archaeological evidence suggest that Herodium was taken quickly. The rebels at Machaerus capitulated before the Romans commenced their assault, although Josephus describes skirmishes between the two sides. The Roman circumvallation (siege) wall and ten or eleven siege camps are still visible surrounding the base of Machaerus, as is a massive stone assault ramp that was never completed.[1]

In 72 or 73, the Roman troops arrived at the foot of Masada, the last fortress held by Jewish rebels. In the meantime, Bassus had died and was replaced as legate by Flavius Silva:

> In Judea, meanwhile, Bassus had died and been succeeded in the gov-ernorship by Flavius Silva, who, seeing the whole country now sub-jugated by the Roman arms, with the exception of one fortress still in revolt, concentrated all forces in the district and marched against it. This fortress was called Masada. (Josephus, *War* 7.252)

Silva was a native of Urbs Salvia in Italy, where two inscriptions have been discovered recording his dedication of an amphitheater in 81 or later, after he finished his term as legate of Judea.[2]

The Roman campaign to Masada took place in the winter-spring of 72–73 or 73–74.[3] Although today many visitors are under the impression that the fortress held out against the Romans for three years (after 70), the siege lasted no longer than six months and almost certainly was much shorter—perhaps as little as seven weeks from beginning to end.[4]

The Roman Army

The Roman army was so effective because its soldiers were highly trained career professionals—mostly legionaries and auxiliaries—who enlisted for a lifetime of service.[5] Legionaries were drafted from among Roman citizens and served primarily as heavy infantry. At the time of the siege of Masada, there were approximately thirty legions in the Roman army, each consisting of about five thousand soldiers.[6] Auxiliaries were con-scripted from among non-Roman citizens, who were awarded citizen-ship at the end of their term of service. Auxiliaries usually operated as light infantry, cavalry, and archers, that is, the more mobile troops who protected the flanks of the heavy infantry in battle. Auxiliary units were organized into regiments numbering five hundred or a thousand soldiers each.

Approximately eight thousand Roman troops participated in the siege of Masada: the Tenth Legion (*Legio X Fretensis*) and a number of auxil-iary cohorts.[7] The Tenth Legion, now under Silva's command, had participated previously in the sieges at Gamla (or Gamala) (in the Golan), Jerusalem, and Machaerus. After the fall of Masada, the Tenth Legion was stationed in Jerusalem until circa 300, when the emperor Diocletian transferred it to Aila (modern Aqaba) on the Red Sea. Servants and slaves (including Jews), pack animals, and vendors accompanied the Roman troops at the siege of Masada.

The Roman Siege Camps

When the Romans arrived at the foot of Masada, they constructed a stone wall, 10–12 feet (ca. 3 meters) high and approximately 4,000 yards (4,500 meters) long, which completely encircled the base of the mountain. This circumvallation wall sealed off the fortress, preventing the besieged from escaping and making it impossible for others to join them. Gwyn Davies emphasizes "the clear symbolic message conveyed" by the construction of the siege works, both to the rebels holding out atop Masada and other peoples under Roman rule.[8] Guards posted at towers along the wall kept watch to ensure that no one scaled it. In addition to the circumvallation wall, the Romans established eight camps to house their troops, which archaeologists have labeled with the letters A–H (fig. 9). The camps surround the base of the mountain, guarding potential routes of escape. Josephus's description of the circumvallation wall and siege camps accords well with the archaeological remains:

> The Roman general advanced at the head of his forces against Eleazar and his band of Sicarii who held Masada, and promptly making himself master of the whole district, established garrisons at the most suitable points, threw up a wall all round the fortress, to make it difficult for any of the besieged to escape, and posted sentinels to guard it. (War 7.275)

The sequence of camps begins with A at the foot of the Snake Path and proceeds counterclockwise: Camps A–C on the eastern side of the mountain; D at the northern tip; E–F on the northwest side; G to the southwest; and H perched atop Mount Eleazar to the south of Masada. The camps are connected by the circumvallation wall and by a path called the "runner's path" which can still be hiked today. In an era before field telephones and walkie-talkies, the runner's path was the line of communication, used by runners who carried Silva's orders from camp to camp. The 1981 film *Gallipoli* directed by Peter Weir featured a young Mel Gibson in the role of an Australian runner in that famous World War I battle.

The layout of the siege camps at Masada reflects the efficient and standardized operating procedure of the Roman army. All of the camps are square or roughly square in shape, with the sides oriented to the four cardinal points. In the middle of each wall is a gate that led to two main roads running north-south and east-west, which intersected in the center of the camp. The units within each camp were laid out around these roads, with the most important units (such as the commander's living quarters and the camp headquarters) in the center and other units farther away. Camp B on the east and Camp F on the northwest are conspicuously larger than the others, as they housed the legionary troops, while the other camps were occupied by auxiliary soldiers.[9] Camp B served as the distribution point for supplies transported by boats from areas surrounding the Dead Sea, which were offloaded at a dock on the shore to the east of Masada. Camp F was positioned so Silva could oversee the construction of the assault ramp, as Josephus describes: "He himself [Silva] encamped at a spot which he selected as most convenient for siege operations, where the rocks of the fortress abutted on the adjacent mountain, although ill situated for commissariat purposes" (*War* 7.277).

A square walled area in the southwest corner of Camp F, called F2, postdates the fall of Masada. Camp F2 housed a small garrison that remained for a short period after the siege ended, until they ensured the area was completely subdued.

The 1995 Excavations in Camp F

Although Yigael Yadin was a specialist in ancient warfare and served as chief of staff of the IDF, his excavations focused on the remains on Masada's summit and largely ignored the Roman siege works. These remained virtually untouched until summer 1995, when I co-directed excavations in the siege works with three Israeli colleagues: Professor Gideon Foerster (at the Hebrew University of Jerusalem); Professor Haim Goldfus (now at Ben-Gurion University); and Mr. Benny Arubas (at the

Hebrew University). We focused on Camp F as it is the better-preserved of the two legionary camps (fig. 10). Our excavations provide valuable information about Roman siege warfare in general and the fall of Masada in particular.[10] The remains at Masada are arguably the best-preserved example of siege works anywhere in the Roman world, for two reasons: (1) they are constructed of stone, whereas in other parts of the Roman world siege works often were made of perishable materials such as wood and sod; and (2) because of their remote desert location, the Masada siege works have never been destroyed or built over.[11] The circumvallation wall and camps are clearly visible today, evidenced by heaps of stones that can be seen from the top of the mountain. Although the camps appear barren and sterile, our excavations revealed that the units within them are filled with broken pottery and other artifacts.

The circumvallation wall and the walls of the camps are constructed of dry field stones, that is, unhewn stones collected from the rocky surface of the ground, with no mud or mortar binding. The outer walls of each camp originally stood to a height of 10–12 feet (ca. 3 meters), while the walls of the units inside the camps were about 3–4 feet high (ca. 1 meter). The latter were not actually walls; rather, they were bases or foundations for leather tents, which the Roman army pitched while on campaign in the field. We excavated several units inside Camp F, which consist of one or more rooms, with the interiors usually encircled by a low bench of dirt and stones. The benches were used both for sleeping and as dining couches. The praetorium—the living quarters of the commander, Silva—is located in the center of Camp F, by the intersection of the two main roads. Although most of the stones of the praetorium were removed for use in the construction of Camp F2, the discovery of luxury goods including imported glass vessels from Italy and eggshell-thin painted Nabataean pottery bowls confirm that this was indeed the commander's living quarters. My personal favorite is a stump-based *amphoriskos*—a table jar—painted with ivy leaves, from which I like to imagine Silva's servant poured his wine (fig. 11).

Next to the praetorium is a stone platform, which was a tribunal from which Silva could review and address his troops, who mustered in the open space around it. Nearby is a rectangular pi-shaped structure, oriented so that its narrow end opens toward Masada. This structure was stripped to the foundations when the wall of Camp F2 was constructed over it. Nevertheless, the plan and location indicate that it was a *triclinium*— the officers' mess. Triclinium in Greek means "three couches," referring to the arrangement of dining couches around three sides of a formal dining room. As the officers in this triclinium dined, they gazed out at the mountain of Masada.

Just inside the wall of Camp F2 and partly covered by it is the *principia*—the camp headquarters. Although the principia yielded almost no finds, it was the only unit we excavated with plastered walls and floors. Nearby and also within the walls of F2, we excavated a row of identical one-room units called *contubernia*. A contubernium was the smallest subdivision of a legion, consisting of eight enlisted men who marched and camped together on campaign. Each of these one-roomed units housed a group of eight men—a contubernium (fig. 12). The interior of the room was lined with a rough stone-and-dirt bench used for sleeping and dining. The contubernia are small because the men ate and slept in shifts, similar to living quarters in a modern submarine. In front of each room is a small open porch or courtyard enclosed by a wall, with a small hearth in the corner where the men prepared their food. Roman soldiers were equipped with mess kits which they used on campaign, as depicted on Trajan's Column in Rome, where soldiers are setting out with their mess kits dangling from a pole slung over one shoulder.

The floors of the units we excavated in Camp F were covered with layers of broken pottery, mostly from storage jars. The rarity of cooking pots and dining dishes such as bowls and cups apparently is due to the use of mess kits by the enlisted men, whereas Silva and his officers were provided with fine ceramic and glass tableware. The storage jars, which have a bulky, bag-shaped body, are characteristic of Judea in the first century CE and presumably were produced for the Roman army by Jewish potters. The siege of Masada was a logistical challenge for the Romans due to the scarcity of food and water in the immediate vicinity. They had to import enough supplies every day to provision approximately eight thousand soldiers as well as pack animals, servants, and slaves. Food and water were hauled from great distances over land on pack animals or shipped on boats from points around the Dead Sea.[12] Josephus describes the provisioning of the Roman troops at Masada: "For not only were supplies conveyed from a distance, entailing hard labor for the Jews told off for this duty, but even water had to be brought into the camp, there being no spring in the neighborhood" (*War* 7.278).

As Josephus indicates, Jewish slaves hauled the food and water. The supplies were transported in baskets and animal skins, which are lighter, easier to carry, and less susceptible to breakage than ceramic jars. Upon arrival at Masada, the contents of these containers were emptied into ceramic jars for storage. After the siege ended, the storage jars were emptied and left behind.

Roman Military Equipment

Not surprisingly, we found few remains of military equipment in our excavations in Camp F, as the soldiers took their weapons with them when the siege ended. However, in and around the tent units were piles of large, egg-shaped pebbles, which had been collected from *wadis* (river beds/washes) in the vicinity. They were used as slingshot stones and were left behind because they had no inherent value. In contrast to Camp F, Yadin's excavations atop Masada yielded a large and diverse quantity of military equipment, which I co-published with Guy Stiebel.[13] Yadin's finds included hundreds of iron arrowheads, nearly all of which represent the standard Roman Imperial type: a head with three barbed wingtips to stick into the flesh, and a long tang that was inserted into a wooden or reed shaft (fig. 13). The arrows were fired in volleys by archers. Three bone ear laths from Yadin's excavations come from the reinforced ends of composite bows.[14] Yadin also discovered hundreds of small bronze scales, most of which are narrow and elongated, and have four holes at the top and a raised rib down the center (fig. 14). Originally the scales were sewn onto a cloth or leather backing so that they overlapped. In the first century CE, scale armor was typically worn by auxiliaries. One large group of scales was colored red, gold, and perhaps silver, and apparently belonged to a suit of parade armor.

Legionary soldiers wore segmented armor (*lorica segmentata*), which consisted of overlapping iron strips, a few fragments of which were found in Yadin's excavations. The armor covered only the upper part of the body and was worn over a short tunic that stopped just above the knees. On their heads, legionaries wore a bronze helmet with large cheek-pieces attached to the sides; we discovered one such cheek-piece in Camp F. The typical footgear worn by Roman soldiers consisted of heavy hobnailed leather sandals called *caligae*, examples of which were preserved at Masada thanks to the arid desert atmosphere. The emperor Gaius was nicknamed Caligula—"little boots"—after the hobnailed sandals worn by the soldiers who he befriended as a child. The lower part of a legionary's body was left unprotected by armor to allow for mobility.

Around their waists, legionaries wore a leather belt to which several items were attached. An apron consisting of narrow strips of leather with bronze studs dangled from the front of the belt, which protected the soldier's genitals (as nothing was worn under a tunic) and made a clanking noise intended to frighten the enemy in battle. A leather sheath holding a dagger was attached to the right side of the belt, and on the left side was a leather sheath with a gladius—the double-edged sword used by legionaries. The tip of the sword sheath was reinforced with a bronze casing called a scabbard chape. Yadin found a complete scabbard chape with delicate cut-out designs, through which the dark leather sheath would have been visible (fig. 15). This scabbard chape, which must have belonged to a legionary officer, has parallels in Italy dating to the mid-first century CE. In the left hand, legionaries held a large rectangular shield to protect the unarmored lower part of the body. In the right hand, they carried a tall, skinny javelin called a *pilum*, which was the characteristic offensive weapon of legionaries. In battle, the pilum was thrust or thrown to pin the opponent, who was then killed with the sword in hand-to-hand combat.

The Assault Ramp

The Romans undertook the siege of Masada by constructing their camps and the circumvallation wall, thereby sealing off and isolating the mountain. In some sieges, no additional measures were required to starve an enemy into surrender. This was not the case at Masada, where the besieged were provisioned with large quantities of food and water stored in Herod's palaces, whereas the Roman forces had to import supplies from long distances. Therefore, at Masada the Romans sought to bring the siege to a swift resolution. To accomplish this, they had to move their troops and siege machinery up the steep, rocky slopes of the mountain and break through Herod's fortification wall at the top. There were two paths to the top of Masada: the Snake Path on the east and another path on the west (today buried under the Roman ramp) (see chapter 4). Using these paths would have required the soldiers to climb up in single file while carrying their personal equipment as well as the battering ram, which had to be erected at the top to break through the Herodian casemate wall—all the while leaving the soldiers vulnerable to stones, boulders, and other projectiles thrown or fired by the defenders above. To solve this problem, Silva ordered his men to construct an assault ramp of dirt and stones, which ascended to the summit from a low white hill (called the *Leuke* by Josephus) at the foot of the western side of the mountain:

> The Roman general, having now completed his wall surrounding the whole exterior of the place, as we have already related, and taken the strictest precautions that none should escape, applied himself to the siege. He had discovered only one spot capable of supporting earthworks. For in rear of the tower which barred the road leading from the west to the palace and the ridge, was a projection of rock, of considerable breadth and jutting far out, but still three hundred cubits [1 cubit = ca. 1.5 feet or 0.5 meters] below the elevation of Masada; it was called Leuce. Silva, having accordingly ascended and occupied this eminence, ordered his troops to throw up an embankment. (Josephus, *War* 7.304–5)

Once completed, the ramp provided a gentle slope that the soldiers could ascend easily with several men across. At the top of the ramp, they erected a stone platform for the battering ram:[15]

> Working with a will and a multitude of hands, they raised a solid bank to the height of two hundred cubits. This, however, being still considered of insufficient stability and extent as an emplacement for the engines, on top of it was constructed a platform of great stones fitted closely together, fifty cubits broad and as many high. (Josephus, *War* 7.306–7)

During the siege operation, auxiliary troops provided cover fire with a barrage of arrows and ballista stones—large, round stones shot from torsion machines:

The engines in general were similarly constructed to those first devised by Vespasian and afterwards by Titus for their siege operations; in addition a sixty-cubit tower was constructed entirely cased in iron, from which the Romans by volleys of missiles from numerous quick-firers and ballistae quickly beat off the defenders on the ramparts and prevented them from showing themselves. (Josephus, *War* 7.308–9)

Yadin found iron arrowheads and ballista stones surrounding the area at the top of the ramp, confirming Josephus's description of a concentrated barrage of cover fire.[16] Andrew Holley, who published the ballista stones, notes that their relatively light weights (nearly all weighing less than 4 kg and most of these less than 1 kg) indicate they were fired from small-caliber engines and were aimed at human targets rather than being intended to make a breach in the casemate wall.[17] Most of the ballista stones were discovered along the northwest edge of the mountain, facing the assault ramp, with large deposits in two casemate rooms (L1039 and L1045). Holley has argued persuasively against Ehud Netzer's suggestion that these stones were associated with engines used by the Jewish rebels, as the Romans would not have established Camps E and F within range of artillery fire. Instead, the ballista stones in L1039 ("the Casemate of the Scrolls"—see chapter 8) and L1045 were fired into the fortress by Roman artillery mounted in the tower on the assault ramp, and were collected and dumped in these rooms after the siege ended.[18] The Casemate of the Scrolls also yielded rare fragments of Roman shields made of three layers of wood faced with glue-soaked fabric, which were covered with leather that still bears traces of red paint.[19]

In the above passage, Josephus describes the Romans firing volleys of ballista stones and "missiles" to provide cover during the siege operation. And indeed, numerous ballista stones and iron arrowheads of the characteristic Roman barbed, trilobite type with a tang (which originally was set into a wooden or reed shaft) were discovered in Yadin's excavations at Masada. Puzzlingly, however, there is not a single definite example of an iron projectile point (catapult bolt). Catapult bolts are heavier than arrowheads (which were shot from manual bows) and differ in having a solid head and a socket instead of a tang. In contrast, numerous iron projectile points were found at Gamla in contexts associated with the Roman siege of 67, where, according to Josephus, the Romans employed catapults (see chapter 7).

In light of the absence of iron projectile points at Masada, Guy Stiebel and I originally proposed that catapults were not employed during the siege, perhaps due to the steep angle of projection from the ramp to the fortification wall.[20] This would contradict Josephus's account and suggest that his description of the artillery barrage was formulaic. However, I now believe that the archaeological evidence can be reconciled with Josephus's testimony. As Gwyn Davies has observed, "It is inconceivable that the Romans didn't have bolt-firers at the siege [of Masada]. In fact, the bolt-firers would almost certainly have been mounted in the siege tower for the purposes of sweeping the parapets, even if they were not advanced up the ramp when the tower was being winched up or emplaced at the foot of the ramp."[21] Davies suggests that the bolts were collected and recycled by the Romans in cleanup operations after the siege, just as the ballista stones were gathered and dumped.

Although it may be difficult to believe that the Romans were so thorough that they retrieved every iron bolt head in their cleanup operations, an examination of the distribution of iron arrowheads at Masada supports this possibility. The overwhelming majority of arrowheads come from the lower terrace of the northern palace and the workshop in the western palace (for the latter, see chapter 8). These spots were buried in collapse from conflagrations, and for this reason presumably were not retrieved by the Romans. Other locations with small groups of arrowheads are on the western side of the mountain, around the area that would have been swept by cover fire from the direction of the ramp. However, aside from the arrowheads in the northern palace and the western palace, which were buried in collapse, the Romans seem to have retrieved most of the arrowheads as well as all the iron bolt heads. The small groups of remaining arrowheads seem to have been left where they were gathered, perhaps because their poor condition rendered them unusable. And unlike Masada, the Romans did not occupy Gamla after the siege. Presumably they retrieved some of the iron bolt heads at Gamla, but without a garrison left to occupy and clear the site, the rest of the bolts remained among the destruction debris.[22]

In addition to biblical and extra-biblical scrolls, the only examples of Latin papyri at Masada were discovered in the Casemate of the Scrolls.

The Latin papyri either date to around the time of the siege or are associated with a detachment of legionaries that was stationed atop the mountain for up to several decades after the siege ended.[23] One of the Latin papyri is inscribed with a line in hexametric verse from Virgil's epic poem, the *Aeneid* (4.9). Another Latin papyrus—the longest one discovered at Masada—is a military "pay record." This document records payments made by a legionary named C. Messius of Beirut, which were deducted from his salary for items such as barley and clothing. A third, poorly preserved Latin papyrus lists medical supplies for injured or ill Roman soldiers, specifically mentioning bandages and "eating oil."[24] In addition to the papyri, twenty-two *ostraca* (inscribed potsherds) inscribed in Latin with the names of Roman soldiers were found in the vicinity of the large bathhouse in the northern palace complex (see chapter 4). The names—including Aemilius, Fabius, and Terentius—belong to legionaries and are unusual in that they are written on the inside rather than the outside of the potsherd.[25]

During the 1995 excavations in the siege works, we cut a section through the ramp a little over halfway up, to determine how it was constructed. Today the ramp, which can still be climbed, appears to consist of fine, white chalky dust that poofs up in clouds underfoot, mixed with small to medium-sized stones. Our excavations revealed that the Romans constructed the ramp by taking pieces of wood—mostly tamarisk and date palm—and laying some of them flat and using others as vertical stakes to create a timber bracing filled with packed stones, rubble, and earth.[26] Today the tips of timbers are visible protruding near the bottom of the ramp. Geological analyses suggest that the ramp was built on a natural spur that ascended the western side of the mountain from the Leuke, although we did not reach the spur in our excavations.[27] Once the ramp was completed, the Romans erected a stone platform for the battering ram and began to break through Herod's fortification wall. A large breach in the casemate wall at the top of the ramp is still visible today.

The Last Stand

Josephus reports that once the Romans breached the wall, they found the rebels had constructed a second wall of wooden beams filled with earth, which not only withstood the battering ram but was compacted by its blows:

> The Sicarii, however, had already hastily built up another wall inside, which was not likely to meet with a similar fate from the engines; for it was pliable and calculated to break the force of the impact, having been constructed as follows. Great beams were laid lengthwise and contiguous and joined at the extremities; of these there were two parallel rows a wall's breadth apart, and the intermediate space was filled with earth. Further, to prevent the soil from dispersing as the mound rose, they clamped, by other transverse beams, those laid longitudinally. The work thus presented to the enemy the appearance of masonry, but the blows of the engine were weakened, battering upon a yielding material which, as it settled down under the concussion, they merely served to solidify. (*War* 7.311–14)

While preparing the final publication describing the architecture of Masada, Ehud Netzer noticed that only about 10 percent of the buildings on the mountain showed evidence of destruction by fire, and they were not contiguous. Netzer reasoned that had the buildings been set on fire, they all should have burned down. He proposed that the absence of burning in most of the buildings means their wooden ceiling beams were dismantled, presumably for the construction of the second wall as described by Josephus.[28] If Netzer's interpretation is correct, it would corroborate this part of Josephus's testimony about the fall of Masada.

Once the Romans noticed that the rebels had constructed a second wall of wood and earth, Silva ordered his soldiers to set it on fire. At first, a strong wind blew the flames toward the Romans, threatening to burn down their battering ram. However, the wind suddenly changed course and blew back toward the wall, causing it to go up in flames. At this point, Josephus says, Eleazar ben Yair convened the men and convinced them to take their own lives to escape capture, thereby depriving the Romans of their victory:

> Let our wives thus die undishonored, our children unacquainted with slavery; and when they are gone, let us render a generous service to each other, preserving our liberty as a noble winding-sheet. But first let us destroy our chattels and the fortress by fire . . . Our provisions

only let us spare; for they will testify, when we are dead, that it was not want which subdued us, but that, in keeping with our initial re-solve, we preferred death to slavery. (*War* 7.334–36)

FLAVIUS JOSEPHUS (37–CA. 100 CE)

Josephus concluded his account of *The Jewish War* not with the fall of Jerusalem and the destruction of the second temple in 70, but with the siege of Masada and mass suicide three years later—a story not reported by any other ancient author. In fact, much of our information about the history of Judea in the late Second Temple period and especially the First Revolt comes from Josephus's writings.[29] Josephus was an eyewitness to some of the events he describes—such as the siege of Jerusalem—and in other cases he drew on literary sources that have since been lost.[30] One of the great ironies of history is that whereas in Jewish tradition Josephus is remembered as a traitor, for Christians his testimony has great significance. Was Josephus a villain who betrayed the Jews or a hero whose works preserve a treasure trove of information about Judea in the late Second Temple period?

Josephus's Biography

Josephus was born Joseph son of Mattathias in Jerusalem in 37 CE, the same year Gaius Caligula became emperor. He was from a priestly fam-ily and claimed to be related to the Hasmoneans (see chapter 5) on his mother's side. All our biographical information about Josephus comes from his works, including his autobiography (called the *Life [Vita] of Flavius Josephus*, written as an appendix to *Antiquities*).[31]

Josephus presents himself as a precocious young man.[32] At the age of sixteen, he set out to learn firsthand about the three major sects of Judaism—Sadducees, Pharisees, and Essenes—and spent three years in the wilderness as the disciple of an ascetic named Bannus. At the age of nineteen he became a Pharisee (*Life* 9–12).[33] Josephus is the only ancient writer about the Essenes who claims firsthand knowledge of them (see chapter 5). He is also only one of two ancient Jews who self-identifies as a Pharisee; the other is Paul of Tarsus.[34] In 64 CE, at the age of twenty-six, Josephus traveled to Rome on an embassy to negotiate for the release

of priests who had been sent there by the procurator Felix to be tried by
Nero (*Life* 13).[35] Coincidentally, this was the year of the Great Fire in
Rome, when "Nero fiddled while Rome burned."

After the First Revolt erupted in 66 CE and the Jews organized a pro-
visional government, Josephus was put in charge of the district of Galilee. This was the region subdued first by the Roman army as the general
Vespasian made his way south to Judea from Antioch. Galilee fell quickly,
as the Jews were no match for the Roman forces, and some settlements
including the city of Sepphoris capitulated without a fight. The last fortress, Jotapata (Yodefat), fell following a siege that lasted forty-seven days
(see chapter 7). After the siege ended, Josephus and forty other survivors took refuge in a cistern. When they were discovered by the Romans,
Josephus's comrades made a suicide pact. Josephus did not want to
commit suicide but had to go along with the others. He convinced them
to draw lots, and then, as he says, "by fortune or by the providence of
God," he drew the last lot (*War* 3.391).[36] Instead of committing suicide
Josephus surrendered to the Romans, which is why later Jewish tradition
considers him a traitor.

When brought before Vespasian, Josephus predicted that one day the
general would become emperor: "You will be Caesar, Vespasian, you will
be emperor, you and your son [Titus] here" (*War* 3.401). This prediction
illustrates Josephus's awareness of events in Rome in 67 CE, where, following the great fire Nero was very unpopular, having appropriated a
huge piece of urban property for his "Golden House" (*Domus Aurea*) instead of rebuilding residents' homes. Josephus must have suspected
that Nero would not last much longer, and that a powerful general like
Vespasian would have ambitions to become emperor. Upon hearing
Josephus's prediction, Vespasian took him alive into captivity instead
of sending him to Nero for a trial in Rome. Events in Rome soon proved
Josephus right. In 68 CE, Nero committed suicide, and after a year of
civil war, Vespasian was proclaimed emperor. He then set Josephus free.

Josephus was present during Titus's siege of Jerusalem and witnessed
the city's destruction. He was hated by the Jews because he walked
around the walls on behalf of the Romans and encouraged the besieged
to surrender. After the fall of Jerusalem, Josephus settled in Rome. He
received Roman citizenship and became a client of the Flavians, whose
family name he adopted—becoming known as Titus Flavius Josephus

instead of Joseph son of Mattathias. Josephus was commissioned by his imperial patrons to write histories of the Jewish people and the First Revolt.[37] He lived in Rome until his death around 100 CE.

The Jewish War

Josephus's first work is his seven-volume account of *The Jewish War*, which was completed in the late 70s–early 80s—that is, about a decade after the First Revolt ended.[38] *War* is written in Greek, although in the preface Josephus refers to an earlier version in Aramaic.[39] The work follows a pattern of history-telling that originated with the Greeks, most famously with Thucydides's eight-book account of *The Peloponnesian War*.[40] As Tessa Rajak remarks, "For what is striking and even bold in Josephus is the very fact that he had introduced a distinctive Jewish interpretation into a political history which is fully Greek in form, juxtaposing the two approaches."[41]

Whereas Thucydides began by describing the war between Athens and Sparta as "the greatest disturbance in the history of the Hellenes, affecting also a large part of the non-Hellenic world" (1.1), Josephus claims that, "the war of the Jews against the Romans [was] the greatest not only of the wars of our own time, but so far as accounts have reached us, well nigh of all that ever broke out between cities or nations" (1.1).[42] Josephus followed Thucydides's example and introduces himself as an eyewitness to many of the events he describes, thereby presenting himself as an accurate and trustworthy source: "In these circumstances, I—Josephus, son of Mattathias, a Hebrew by race, a native of Jerusalem and a priest, who at the opening of the war myself fought against the Romans and in the sequel was perforce an onlooker—propose to provide the subjects of the Roman Empire with narrative of the facts" (1.1). Thucydides commenced his narrative by identifying the causes of the Peloponnesian War: "this is in order that there should be no doubt in anyone's mind about what led to this great war falling upon the Hellenes" (1.23). Similarly, Josephus begins his account with the Maccabean Revolt, which he credits with setting in motion the chain of events that led to the outbreak of the First Jewish Revolt against the Romans.[43] Kenneth Atkinson notes that Polybius's *Histories* and Julius Caesar's *Gallic*

War also influenced Josephus's *War*, as all these works aimed to defend Rome and the authors' homelands and personal reputations.[44]

War has multiple messages.[45] On the one hand, it is intended as a cautionary tale for subject peoples living under Roman rule not to consider the possibility of revolt. For example, Honora Chapman argues that Josephus's account of the mass suicide at Masada illustrates the futility of resisting Rome's imperial might.[46] On the other hand, for the benefit of a Roman audience, Josephus pins the blame for the First Revolt on extremists and criminals who do not represent Judaism or the Jews. In this regard, *War* is an apologetic intended to exonerate most of the Jews who participated in the revolt, especially the upper classes—including Josephus himself. As Atkinson observes, "Studying the *War* is complicated because Josephus was both its author and one of its major characters."[47]

Jewish Antiquities

Around 93–94 CE, Josephus completed a twenty-volume work called *Jewish Antiquities* (or *Antiquities of the Jews*; Greek *Archaeologia* [Archaeology]).[48] This is a much longer and more ambitious project than *War*. Written in Greek, *Antiquities* was intended to present to a Roman audience the entire scope of Jewish history beginning with creation and ending on the eve of the First Revolt. The first ten volumes are based on the books of the Hebrew Bible, while the second ten volumes cover the rest of Jewish history up to the revolt. There is much overlap in the material covered by *War* and *Antiquities* (including *Life*), but with significant differences and even some contradictory information.[49]

Written at a time when the First Revolt was less immediate and political fortunes had shifted dramatically in Rome and Judea, *Antiquities* has a different tone than *War*.[50] Instead of warning subject peoples against rebellion, *Antiquities* seeks to elevate the Jews and Judaism in the eyes of the Greco-Roman world—a goal reflecting Josephus's own changed circumstances and perspective.[51] By the time he wrote *Antiquities*, Josephus had been a Diaspora Jew for more than a decade. Many Jews in Rome lived in squalor with other eastern immigrant communities in Trastevere, on the west bank of the Tiber River. After 70 CE, these impoverished Jews, whose patron deity had been vanquished and temple

cult obliterated, became the butt of ridicule among the Roman population, as expressed in Juvenal's satires:

> No sooner has that fellow departed than a palsied Jewess, leaving her
> basket and her truss of hay, comes begging to her secret ear; she is an
> interpreter of the laws of Jerusalem, a high priestess of the tree, a trusty
> go-between of highest heaven. She, too, fills her palm, but more spar-
> ingly, for a Jew will tell you dreams of any kind you please for the mi-
> nutest of coins. (*Satires* VI, 542–47)[52]

The Romans respected ancient peoples and their gods. By recount-
ing the history of Jews based on sacred scripture, Josephus sought to
demonstrate the antiquity of the Jewish people, and by extension, the
continued power of the God of Israel and the need to observe biblical
law.[53] Josephus's last work, *Against Apion*, was written in response to vi-
cious attacks on Judaism by a well-known Jew-hater from Egypt.[54] This
same Apion led the gentile delegation to Gaius Caligula in 40 CE as a
counter to the Jewish delegation headed by Philo (see chapter 6).

Josephus's Biases and Apologetic Tendencies

Josephus's works are complex for various reasons, including (1) much of
the information is drawn from lost or unknown sources; (2) the works
were aimed at different audiences and therefore were intended to convey different messages; (3) Josephus wrote with biases and apologetic tendencies aimed at exonerating his Roman patrons from responsibility
for the outcome of the revolt, and to justify and glorify his own behavior.[55] In other words, much of Josephus's writings constitute an apology
in the classical sense, meaning a defense. For example, Josephus shifts
the blame for the revolt and its consequences away from the Jewish aristocracy, including himself, by pinning it on extremists and fanatics. Josephus's apologetic for the Romans is equally clear. Vespasian and Titus are
portrayed as having given the Jews every opportunity to surrender. According to Josephus, Titus did his best to save the temple and even wept
when he saw its destruction, whereas the Roman historian Tacitus apparently reported that Titus ordered the temple's destruction (see chapter 7).

Recently scholars have employed postcolonial theory (which ana-
lyzes the negotiation of relationships between imperial powers and

conquered peoples) to understand how Josephus manipulated and subverted Greco-Roman cultural values and norms.[56] Scholars have also become increasingly skeptical of Josephus's credibility and therefore less confident of our ability to reconstruct history based on his accounts. Already in 1979 Shaye Cohen stated, "By now it should be clear how little we know of the events of 66–90. Because Josephus is our only extensive source and because he is so unreliable our knowledge is very defective."[57]

The Afterlife of Josephus's Works

Why have Josephus's works survived when so many other ancient writings have not? The reason is simple: because Christians preserved them. For Christians, Josephus was an important witness to events during and after Jesus's lifetime. Christian authors such as Eusebius, who was bishop of Caesarea in the early fourth century, used Josephus's writings to blame the Jews for Jesus's death, a crime for which (in their view) God had punished the Jews by allowing the destruction of the Jerusalem temple.[58] One passage in *Antiquities* (18.63–64) even refers to Jesus, although scholars disagree on whether it was written by Josephus or inserted by Christian copyists. If the passage is original, parts show signs of later reworking and alteration:

> About this time there lived Jesus, a wise man, if indeed one ought to call him a man. For he was one who wrought surprising feats and was a teacher of such people as accept the truth gladly. He won over many Jews and many of the Greeks. He was the Messiah (*Christos*). When Pilate, upon hearing him accused by men of the highest standing amongst us, had condemned him to be crucified, those who had in the first place come to love him did not give up their affection for him. On the third day he appeared to them restored to life, for the prophets of God had prophesied these and countless other marvellous things about him. And the tribe of the Christians, so called after him, has still to this day not disappeared.[59]

Other passages that are believed to have been written by Josephus but later reworked refer to John the Baptist (*Ant.* 18.116–19) and James, the brother of Jesus (*Ant.* 20.200).

Josephus is the last ancient Jewish author to write about the history of the Jews whose writings have survived.[60] A vast corpus of Jewish literature was produced after 70 by the rabbis (sages), which contains their rulings on biblical law and other matters related to religious life. However, they were not interested in the writings of Jewish authors such as Josephus and Philo, as these have no relevance to the rabbinic approach to Torah interpretation through oral law. Moreover, the rabbis viewed the Jewish rebels as crazed fanatics who brought disaster on Israel. Whereas for Christians Josephus's writings provide important testimony about events that occurred during Jesus's lifetime and after his death, for Jews they memorialize the trauma of the First Revolt. Jews reacted to the Christian appropriation of Josephus's works to express an anti-Jewish message by turning their backs on Josephus.[61]

Because of *War*, we are better informed about the First Revolt than any other native rebellion against Rome. The revolt has retained an importance far beyond the Jewish tradition because the Gospels report that Jesus foretold the destruction of the second temple: "As Jesus came out of the temple and was going away, his disciples came to point out to him the buildings of the temple. Then he asked them, 'You see all these, do you not? Truly I tell you, not one stone will be left here upon another; all will be thrown down'" (Mt 24:1–2; also see Mk 13:1–2; Lk 21:5–6).

Christian interest in preserving Josephus's writings was based on supercessionism and triumphalism: Christianity's victory over Judaism is confirmed by Josephus's eyewitness account of the temple's destruction as predicted by Jesus and is God's punishment of the Jewish people for their culpability in Jesus's death.

Postscript: Josephus at Masada

The name "Josephus" was stamped onto the wall of a casemate room on the southeastern side of Masada. Since Flavius Josephus was not present at the siege of Masada and probably never visited the mountain, the graffito must refer to another individual with this name. The casemate room is a tower that was remodeled during the rebel occupation and contained numerous installations, including a cooking stove with two "burners," two silos, a small baking oven (*tabun*), and a niche in the wall for an oil lamp. The wall inside one of the silos was stamped with seal impressions with the name Josephus in Latin (*Iosepu[s]*). The seal impressions belong to bread stamps, suggesting that Josephus was a baker. Because the impressions were made when the plaster on the wall was still wet, they must date to the time of the rebel occupation of Masada. Hannah Cotton and Joseph Geiger note that this is the only Jewish inscription in Latin from ancient Palestine and describe it as a "highly puzzling" find.[62]

CHAPTER 2

THE SEARCH FOR MASADA

Although today visitors to Masada do not question its identification, for centuries the site's location was unknown, lost in the mists of time. Masada's (re)discovery in the modern era was the by-product of a wave of visits to the Holy Land by Western explorers in the nineteenth century, many of whom sought to validate biblical stories by identifying the remains of sites associated with the Bible. Despite their religious motivations and orientalist tendencies as well as the difficult travel conditions, these early explorers compiled a wealth of data, much of it still valuable today. Because of the swampy conditions in much of the country at the time, many of them became ill with malaria, to which some succumbed. This chapter highlights the contributions and sacrifices made by these early explorers and describes the continued exploration of Masada to the present day.[1]

THE EXPLORATION OF MASADA AND THE DEAD SEA REGION: THE NINETEENTH CENTURY

Edward Robinson and Eli Smith

Two Americans, Edward Robinson and Eli Smith, were the first early explorers to identify Masada, although they never actually visited it. Edward Robinson was the son of a Congregationalist minister from Connecticut, who became a brilliant biblical scholar. He taught at Andover Theological Seminary before being appointed the first professor of biblical literature at Union Theological Seminary. Robinson was also a conservative Christian who defended the literal accuracy of the Bible. As part of his quest to better understand and defend the Bible, Robinson arrived in Palestine in 1837 with fellow Andover graduate Eli Smith. Smith had been sent to the Middle East to master Arabic as part of Protestant missionary plans to translate the Bible. Following in the footsteps of the Israelite tribes who fled Egypt by way of the Sinai (or so they believed), Robinson and Smith made their way to Jerusalem. From there they made forays around the rest of the country, including to the Dead Sea. On May 11, 1838, Robinson and Smith visited Ein Gedi. Gazing south through a telescope, they identified a prominent mountain in the distance (then called by its Arabic name Sebbeh) as Masada. Four years later, in 1842, an American missionary named Samuel W. Wolcott visited Masada with William J. Tipping, a British painter. Wolcott wrote a detailed description of the remains on the mountain, accompanied by Tipping's engravings.[2]

Christopher Costigan

Today most visitors to Masada ascend via cable car, arriving by way of a modern highway in the air-conditioned comfort of buses and cars, supplied with plenty of bottled water, and enjoying the refreshments offered in the restaurants and shops at the base of the mountain. Under these circumstances, it is difficult to appreciate the hardships that early explorers to the Dead Sea endured, as illustrated by the fate that two of them suffered. Just two years before Robinson and Smith identified Masada during their visit to Ein Gedi, an Irishman named Christopher Costigan decided to survey the Dead Sea by boat.[3] Upon arrival in Beirut, he purchased a boat and hired one Maltese sailor as crew. From Acre (Akko) on the coast, Costigan had the boat transported on camels to the Sea of Galilee. After unsuccessful attempts to sail down the Jordan River (where the water was at a low level because it was July), Costigan had the boat taken apart and carried by camels to Jericho. He and his crewman set sail on the Dead Sea on August 26, 1835—at the hottest and driest time of year! Furthermore, the boat had no shade aside from that cast by the sail.

Two to three years later, an American explorer named John Lloyd Stephens (the first American to visit Petra, in 1836), tracked down the Maltese crewman in Beirut and interviewed him. Stephens reports, "He was a little dried-up Maltese sailor. He said that he had rowed about the sea without knowing why, except that he was paid for it, for he did not seem to think that he had done anything extraordinary . . . He told me that they had moved in a zigzag direction, crossing and recrossing the lake several times."[4] From the eastern shore, Costigan and his crewman made their way south, landing at the northern tip of the Lisan peninsula—a spot that came to be called "Cape Costigan." Costigan also explored Ein Boqeq, which he thought was ancient Gomorrah.

On the sixth day at sea, their water ran out and Costigan was too exhausted to continue rowing. The following day they reportedly drank sea water. On the eighth day the crewman used sea water to make coffee, and they managed to reach land near Jericho. The crewman set out to seek assistance for Costigan, who was ill with a fever, apparently from a combination of dehydration, sunstroke, the effects of ingesting the sea water, and perhaps malaria. Félicien de Saulcy, a French explorer who visited the Dead Sea in 1851 (see below), described as follows his experience trying to drink the water: "At first it seems to have the taste of ordinary water, but in less than a second it acts with such nauseous effect on the lips, the tongue, and the palate, that your stomach instantly rejects it with insufferable disgust. It seems to be a compound of salt, coloquintida, and oil, with the additional property of inflicting an acute sensation of burning. In vain you clear your mouth of this horrible liquid: it acts so violently on the mucous system that the taste remains for many minutes, causing at the same time a painful contraction of the throat."[5] The high magnesium and calcium levels in the Dead Sea's water are toxic, causing paralysis of the muscles, kidney failure, and damage to the central nervous system and respiratory system.[6]

The daughter of an Anglican missionary named John Nicholayson, who arranged to have Costigan transported from Jericho to Jerusalem, reports that her father described Costigan's condition upon disembarking from the boat: "Overcome with heat and thirst and hunger, and tormented with the effects of the dreadfully salty and corrosive water of the Dead Sea, which made their skin blister all over—they having imprudently poured water upon their clothes, to procure a little cooling, which only served to make the fever rage within."[7]

Costigan spent a couple of days lying in a fevered state in a hut in Jericho, as Nicholayson's daughter described: "They found Mr. Costigan lying out under the open heaven, preferring this to the miserable hovel in which he found shelter during the heat of the day. He had had a very severe paroxysm of fever in the evening and during the night, and it had just left him in a state of extreme exhaustion. Soon after dawn the heat became so excessive that they were obliged to take shelter in the hovel." In the meantime, Nicholayson had arrived from Jerusalem and was trying to find a way to transport Costigan, who was too ill to ride a horse on his own. Eventually, Costigan was laid on top of saddle bags filled with straw and placed on horseback for the ride to Jerusalem. They reached Jerusalem on September 5, but Costigan died two days later, at the age of twenty-five. Ernest William Gurney Masterman, who published an article in 1911 about early explorers to the Dead Sea, says, "The gravestone of Mr. Costigan is still to be seen in the Franciscan Cemetery [the Catholic or Latin cemetery on Mount Zion in Jerusalem], but when first rediscovered it was lying upside down. It no longer marks the site of the grave, which is forgotten."[8]

Masterman himself was an early explorer. Sponsored by the Palestine Exploration Fund, from 1900 to 1913 he documented fluctuations in the Dead Sea's level using a large conglomerate boulder near Ein Feshkha as a point of reference. The boulder, incised with the letters PEF under a horizontal line, is still visible today beside Highway 90.[9]

Costigan's tombstone was lost again after its rediscovery by Masterman. On the centennial of Costigan's expedition to the Dead Sea in 1935, the Israeli geographer Zeev Vilnay tried to relocate the tombstone, but without success. Following Jerusalem's partition in 1948, the cemetery lay in a no-man's land between Israeli- and Jordanian-held territory, studded with land mines. After Israel took East Jerusalem in 1967 in the Six-Day War, the mines were cleared and Franciscan monks cleaned up the cemetery, re-exposing Costigan's tombstone. Since the site of the grave could not be located, the tombstone was placed in the cemetery's wall.[10]

William Molyneux

In 1847, a British Navy lieutenant named William Molyneux attempted another survey of the Dead Sea.[11] Molyneux was stationed on a frigate called the *Spartan*, which was docked at Beirut, and got permission to take the ship's dinghy and three seamen for an expedition. From Acre the dingy was transported by camels to Tiberias, where it set sail down the Jordan River on August 23—at the same hot and dry time of year as Costigan's expedition! Due to the low water level, the dingy had to be carried overland at some spots, but somehow Molyneux managed to navigate much of the river. Along the way, the group was ambushed by bandits and the three seamen disappeared. After unsuccessful attempts to locate his companions, Molyneux proceeded with his mission, hiring a few locals with the assistance of James Finn, the British consul in Jerusalem. Finn accompanied Molyneux to Jericho and returned to Jerusalem after seeing him set sail on September 3: "I had the unprecedented honour of taking the stroke oar in launching a British man-of-war's dingey [sic] upon [the Dead Sea]."[12] However, Molyneux's expedition to the Dead Sea lasted only two days, as Finn recounts: "Molyneux had been two nights and a day and a half upon the water, sometimes in rough weather, and thermometer sometimes 130 degrees Fahrenheit, in an atmosphere of steam, producing drowsiness and depression of spirits. The party had become much browner since I had left them on Friday night, and were overwhelmed with fatigue."[13]

During those two days, Molyneux recorded the sea's depth for the first time. He and his party made it to Jaffa, but Molyneux developed a fever (perhaps from malaria) and died on October 30 while en route to Beirut. In the meantime, the three missing British crewmen turned up in Tiberias, as Finn says, "having made their way thither as being the last town they had left. They had wandered about for a day in search of their officer, and on the second day afterwards arrived utterly naked, two of the three carrying the wounded man. They had fed on berries, etc., as well as they could, had drank nothing from fear of approaching the river [due to bandits], and had travelled mostly by the late moonlight of nights."[14]

In a footnote to his account of this episode, Finn reports that he found the following entry in a visitor's book in Tiberias:

September the 3.

We three Seamen belongen to her M. S. Spartan was received with kindeness at this house, we ware watout food or Ramant 3 dayes before we came hear.

And the Landlord supplyd us with Bouth, tharfore we recommend this house to travelears.

(Signed) Ian Grant
John Lescomb
George Winter.[15]

The southern tip of the Lisan peninsula is now called Cape Molyneux.

William Francis Lynch

In 1848, one year after Molyneux's visit, a forty-six-year-old navy lieutenant from Virginia named William Francis Lynch mounted an expedition to the Dead Sea.[16] The expedition was sponsored by the US Department of War, which provided the store ship *Supply* to transport
Lynch, five staff members, ten seamen, and two specially constructed
boats (one from copper and the other from galvanized iron) to Acre.
Upon arrival, Lynch wisely hired the most powerful Bedouin chief in
the region to protect the party. Following in Costigan's and Molyneux's
footsteps, the boats were carried overland by camels and launched on
the Sea of Galilee for a circuitous but successful trip down the Jordan
River. At Ein Gedi the party pitched a base camp, dubbed "Camp
Washington."

Lynch's expedition spent seventeen days on the Dead Sea—from April
19 to May 9—more than twice as long as Molyneux. Although it was not
yet summer, the heat was torrid—a common phenomenon in May, which
is a transitional month between the cool, rainy season and the hot,
dry season, characterized by extreme temperature fluctuations and
heat waves. Lynch described as follows the conditions on Wednesday,
April 26:

> At 3:50, a hot, blistering hurricane (Arabic *khamseen*; Hebrew *sharav*)
> struck us from the south-east, and for some moments we feared being
> driven out to sea. The thermometer rose immediately to 102°. The men,
> closing their eyes to shield them from the fiery blast, were obliged to
> pull with all their might to stem the rising waves, and at 4:30, physi-
> cally exhausted, but with grateful hearts, we gained the shore. My own

eye-lids were blistered by the hot wind, being unable to protect them, from the necessity of steering the boat. . . . One mounted spectacles to protect his eyes, but the metal became so heated that he was obliged to remove them. Our arms and the buttons on our coats became almost burning to the touch . . . At 8 pm, the thermometer was 106° five feet from the ground. At one foot from the latter it was 104°.[17]

Despite these conditions, Lynch's expedition managed to circumnavigate the Dead Sea, amassing a great deal of scientific information. They took salt specimens from Mount Sodom, visited Ein Boqeq and Machaerus, and discovered that the Dead Sea has two basins. On Saturday, April 29, Lynch sent one of his junior officers, Lieutenant John Dale, with other members of the expedition from Ein Gedi to explore Masada. The party traveled on horseback, accompanied by a camel with water bags, and ascended the cliff to the north of the mountain and then up the Roman ramp. On the east side, "the officers amused themselves by displacing some of the stones and sending them over the cliff, and watching them as they whirled and bounded to the base, upwards of 1200 feet down, with more fearful velocity than the stones from the Roman ballistae when Silva pressed the siege."[18]

When Lynch's expedition departed the Dead Sea on May 9, they left a float with an American flag moored in its center and made their way overland to Jerusalem. From there, Lynch sent Dale and a small party to the swampy area north of the Sea of Galilee, to explore the sources of the Jordan River. Lynch rejoined them in Nazareth, only to find that the men had become ill with malaria. Although they managed to reach Beirut and received medical treatment, Dale died on July 24.

Louis-Félicien Caignart de Saulcy

In the winter of 1850–1851, a Flemish explorer named Louis-Félicien Caignart de Saulcy led a small expedition to the Dead Sea.[19] Despite being well-educated and proficient in Arabic, Greek, Latin, and some Hebrew, de Saulcy was an uncritical scholar. The expedition appears to have been motivated primarily by his desire to find the biblical five cities of the plain: Sodom, Gomorrah, Admah, Zeboim, and Bela. During the twenty-one-day journey around the Dead Sea, de Saulcy disputed many of Lynch's findings (which were of a much higher scientific standard), confidently identifying ruins he visited with biblical sites, often based only on his own analysis of the Arabic place names. For example, de Saulcy described a series of ruins "called by the Arabs Kharbet-il-Yahoud, Kharbet-Fesckhah, and Kharbet-Goumran (or Oumran), which form a continuous mass, extending without interruption over a space of more than six thousand yards." He identified these sites collectively as biblical Gomorrah, supposing that "Goumran" preserved the name "Gomorrah."[20] Instead, de Saulcy's Kharbet-Fesckhah and Kharbet-Goumran are actually Qumran (but certainly *not* Gomorrah), and Kharbet il-Yahoud appears to be Ein Feshkha. These claims were rejected and even ridiculed by most of his contemporaries.

De Saulcy also visited Masada, climbing it from the north and up the Roman ramp, like Lynch's expedition. Although he spent only two hours on the mountain, he devoted thirty pages in his published account to Masada, much of it summarizing Josephus's account.[21] De Saulcy cleared the mosaic floor in the Byzantine chapel atop Masada, which he thought was a palace, taking with him some of the tesserae. He also provided the first (albeit inaccurate) plan of the Roman siege works at Masada.[22]

Henry Baker Tristram

Henry Baker Tristram was a British clergyman, biblical scholar, and naturalist who visited Palestine in 1863–1864 and 1871.[23] He was also an avid ornithologist; the large, black crow-like birds with bright orange patches on their wings and a distinctive whistle that are common at Masada are named for him—Tristram's grackle (or starling). The preface to Tristram's book reflects his approach to religion and nature: "Though Palestine boasts in its productions neither the tropical splendor of India, nor the gorgeous luxuriance of Southern America, yet from *its* fowls of the air are drawn for us our lessons of faith and trust, from the flowers of *its* fields our lessons of humility."[24] Tristram was attracted to the Dead Sea region and Transjordan because they were less well-known. His visit to Masada took place in late January 1864, when his Arab guides assumed (not unreasonably) that there would be pools of water remaining from flash floods in the nearby canyon (Wadi Seiyal/Nahal Ze'elim). However, the pools were dry, and having brought only two goatskins of water, Tristram and his party had to cut short their visit to Masada from two days to only one. Like their predecessors, they ascended by way of the cliff to the north and then up the Roman ramp on the west. Tristram does not add much new information about Masada. Gazing at the Roman siege works, he remarked, "All round at our feet we could trace the wall of circumvallation by which the Romans hopelessly enclosed the devoted garrison."[25]

The Survey of Western Palestine

From 1871 to 1877, the London-based Palestine Exploration Fund sponsored a mapping project of western Palestine, including archaeology, anthropology ("manners and customs"), topography, geology, botany, and zoology—in other words, the documentation of every natural and historical feature in the region.[26] This project, called the Survey of Western Palestine (SWP), was carried out by a team of Royal Engineers, led at various times by Captain Charles William Wilson; Lieutenant Claude Reignier Conder; Charles Francis Tyrwhitt Drake (a civilian archaeologist); Lieutenant Horatio Herbert Kitchener (replacing Tyrwhitt Drake, who died of malarial fever in 1874 at the age of 28); and Captain Charles Warren. The result is a twelve-volume series of accurate topographic maps on a scale of eight miles to three inches, marked with approximately 10,000 place names and accompanied by drawings of antiquities and plans of ruined sites (a thirteenth volume on the survey of eastern Palestine was published later).

Whereas most of the survey maps ("sheets") cover varying amounts of territory containing numerous sites, Masada comprises its own sheet (XXVI), reflecting its importance. Conder, who visited on March 5, 1875, produced an accurate map of the mountain accompanied by succinct descriptions of the remains. Like the explorers before him, Conder climbed up the cliff to the north of Masada and ascended via the Roman ramp. A few years earlier, in 1867, Warren had been the first to ascend the mountain on the east by way of the Snake Path, which at the time was nearly impassable.[27]

The introduction to the first volume of the survey maps describes the motivation for the project—which was approved by the Palestine

Exploration Fund in 1865—as the investigation of the science and sacred history of Palestine. There was also an underlying political motivation, specifically, British interest in the Suez Canal, which was being dug at that time under an agreement between the French authorities and the Ottoman governor of Egypt.[28] The canal was opened in 1869. Six years later, Great Britain became the largest shareholder in the Suez Canal Company (which held the right to operate the canal), and seven years after that (in 1882), the British seized control of Egypt.

In his book on the early exploration of the Holy Land, Neil Asher Silberman points out that one long-term consequence of the SWP was the definition of the future geographical borders of Palestine.[29] Before that time, Palestine had not been a province or district, but was simply the southern part of the Ottoman province of Syria. After the Ottoman Empire collapsed in the wake of World War I, the former province of Syria was divided among the European colonial powers. The League of Nations granted the British jurisdiction over the territory from the Mediterranean coast to Upper Galilee on the north and the Jordan River on the east. This area—the British Mandate of Palestine—corresponded precisely with the territory covered by the SWP. The British placed Transjordan, to the east of the Jordan River, under the rule of the Hashemite family.

Alfred von Domaszewski

Alfred von Domaszewski was an Austrian who was appointed professor of ancient history at the University of Heidelberg. In 1895, 1897, and 1898, he and his colleague Rudolf Ernst Brünnow (professor of Semitic philology and languages at the University of Heidelberg) surveyed the Roman province of Arabia. Although most of their fieldwork focused on the region to the east of the Jordan River, they also explored the western shore of the Dead Sea, including a visit to Masada on February 18–20, 1897.[30] Von Domaszewski and Brünnow published their findings in three large volumes, richly illustrated with plans, drawings, and photographs. Because von Domaszewski was interested in the Roman military frontier (*limes* [pronounced LEE-mays]), he devoted most of his attention to the siege works at Masada. Although earlier explorers had described the siege works from the top of the mountain, von Domasze-wski was the first to survey and document the remains on the ground.[31] His publication also reproduces in full previous descriptions of Masada.

The Exploration of Masada: From the Twentieth Century to the Present

Adolf Schulten

Prior to Yigael Yadin's expedition in the 1960s, the most thorough exploration of Masada was conducted by Adolf Schulten, a German historian and archaeologist. In March 1932, Schulten spent one month camped at Masada (but visited the top on only two mornings), publishing the results in a monograph a year later.[32] Like von Domaszewski, Schulten was particularly interested in the siege works at Masada, as he had previously excavated the Roman military camps at Numantia in Spain. Approximately half of Schulten's book on Masada is devoted to the siege works, especially the eight Roman camps, accompanied by detailed plans. However, as Yadin notes, Schulten made a few errors, including rejecting Warren's discovery of the Snake Path, locating it instead on the north and identifying Herod's northern palace as a fortification associated with that path.[33]

Post-1948: The Israeli Exploration of Masada

Beginning in the 1940s, members of Israeli youth movements began to visit Masada in large numbers, attracted by the challenge of camping in the desert and climbing the mountain's cliffs. One of these visitors was Shmaryahu Gutman (sometimes rendered Shmarya and Guttman or Gutmann) of Kibbutz Na'an, who located and restored the entire course of the Snake Path, as well as restoring its gate and Roman siege camp A. Gutman played a key role in the Israel Exploration Society's Survey of Masada and was a supervisor on Yadin's excavations (see chapter 9). About a decade after Yadin's excavations at Masada, Gutman began his own excavations at Gamla in the Golan, a site that is sometimes compared to Masada because of the tragic fate of its Jewish inhabitants at the time of the First Revolt. The growing interest in Masada prompted the Israel Exploration Society to organize an expedition, which was led by a team of archaeologists and other specialists. Although they were in the field for only ten days each in 1955 and 1956, the expedition produced detailed plans of the remains on top of the mountain and excavated the middle (circular) terrace of Herod's northern palace.[34]

The results of the Israel Exploration Society's survey laid the foundations for large-scale excavations a decade later, under Yadin's direction. The excavations were conducted during two seasons for a total of eleven months, from October 1963 to May 1964 and from November 1964 to April 1965. The staff included veterans of the previous survey as well as Israeli graduate students who later became distinguished archaeologists and faculty members at the Hebrew University of Jerusalem.[35] At the time of Yadin's excavations, there was no cable car to the top of Masada, and the road from Arad to the western side of Masada (the foot of the ramp) did not exist. Yadin rightly rejected establishing the expedition's camp on the summit because of the damage it would cause to the remains as well as the logistical difficulties of provisioning. He also decided against staying at the eastern foot of the mountain, despite the presence of a youth hostel there and its accessibility by road from the south (the area of Sodom), due to the difficulty of ascending and descending each day by way of the Snake Path. Instead, Yadin established the expedition's camp on the western side of the mountain, at the foot of the Roman ramp and adjacent to Camp F, where the Romans had an engineering yard for assembling siege machinery. Here, participants on the excavations, which included large numbers of volunteers from abroad, lived in tents. Heavy equipment, pottery, and other finds were transported to and from the top of the mountain by a cable ferry above the ramp, which is still used.[36] Nearly all the remains seen today by visitors to Masada were uncovered by Yadin's expedition, and subsequently were restored and maintained by the Israel Nature and Parks Authority.

Immediately after the excavations, Yadin published a popular book on Masada and a preliminary scientific report. However, when Yadin died suddenly in 1984, he had not yet produced the final report. Following Yadin's death, his colleagues Gideon Foerster and Ehud Netzer of the Institute of Archaeology at the Hebrew University were appointed to oversee the publication of this material. Since then, eight volumes of the final reports on Yadin's excavations at Masada have appeared in print.[37]

Between 1995 and 2000, Netzer and his student Guy Stiebel conducted limited excavations on Masada's summit, in connection with the development of the site for tourism. One of their most sensational finds was an amphora (jar) fragment inscribed "Herod king of Judea."[38] Also in 1995, a team of archaeologists from the Hebrew University of Jerusalem (Gideon Foerster, Benny Arubas, and Haim Goldfus, together with Jodi Magness who was then at Tufts University) co-directed excavations in Camp F and on the assault ramp.[39] In 2017, excavations atop Masada resumed under the direction of Stiebel, who is now on the faculty at Tel Aviv University.[40]

CHAPTER 3

MASADA IN CONTEXT

In this chapter we explore Masada's setting within the Dead Sea region—a land of harsh contrasts and rugged beauty. We begin with Masada's natural setting and then survey the history of settlement around the Dead Sea.

MASADA'S NATURAL SETTING

The Judean Desert

Masada's natural setting forms a fitting backdrop to the drama of the mass suicide reported by Josephus.[1] The mountain's steep cliffs rise approximately 400 meters (1,300 feet) above the Dead Sea (figs. 1–2). The Dead Sea is the lowest point on earth because it lies at the base of the Great Rift Valley (or Afro-Syrian Rift)—a 6,400-kilometer (4,000-mile)-long rift running from southern Turkey to eastern Africa. Driving to the Dead Sea from Jerusalem's mountainous location causes the sensation of ears popping due to the rapid descent of approximately 1,200 meters (4,000 feet) in less than half an hour. The Great Rift Valley is a product of the separation of the Mediterranean and Arabian continental plates (continental drift), which has opened a huge gap where the continents have pulled apart.[2] The movement of the continental plates is vertical as well as lateral, with the Arabian side shifting northward and the Mediterranean side southward. At the northern end, the Arabian plate has pushed into the preexisting landmass, lifting it and creating Mount Hermon in Syria and northern Israel. Because continental drift is an ongoing process, earthquakes occur frequently along the valley. Highway 90 in Israel follows the Great Rift Valley from the Sea of Galilee in the north through the Jordan Valley, along the western shore of the Dead Sea, through the Arabah Valley, and terminating at Eilat on the Red Sea. Most visitors to Masada drive along this highway to the mountain's east side, where the Snake Path begins and the cable car ascends.

Few landscapes in the world match the spectacular beauty of the Dead Sea region, especially when the late afternoon sun turns the sea a dark blue color and the mountains on its east side (in Jordan) deep orange. Here, the sides of the Great Rift Valley are sheer, jagged cliffs towering 400 meters (1,300 feet) or more above the sea. The rocky escarpment along the western side of the Dead Sea is the product of the Tethys Sea, an ancestor of the Mediterranean Sea that covered the entire region approximately 100 million years ago. After the Tethys Sea receded, the sediments that had accumulated on its floor hardened into layers of limestone, dolomite, and chalk (which is interspersed with lenses of flint or chert). About three million years ago, the Great Rift Valley began to form, cutting through these layers of rock and creating the escarpment along the western side of the Dead Sea. The level of the Dead Sea has fluctuated over time; approximately 25,000 years ago it was only about 180 meters below sea level, compared to its current level of approximately −430 meters. During that period, alluvial sediments accumulated at the bottom of the sea. When the sea level dropped, these sediments were exposed along its sides. Today the area around the Dead Sea is ringed with the eroded remnants of these sediments, which consist of soft chalky white and clay-like grey deposits called Lisan marls, the white color of which contrasts with the underlying brown limestone and dolomite.[3] At the foot of Masada, the marl deposits have been carved by gullies into badlands. Many ancient sites in the Jordan Valley and along the Dead Sea, including Qumran (where the Dead Sea Scrolls were found), sit on terraces of Lisan Marl. Some of the scroll caves at Qumran are man-made caves cut into the marl, while others are natural caves in the limestone and dolomite cliffs.

The Dead Sea lies at the eastern edge of the Judean Desert. Unlike the Negev and Sinai deserts farther south, which are part of an arid zone ringing the globe at this latitude (including the Sahara), the Judean

Desert is created by local conditions.[4] It is a desert "in the shadow of rain," resulting from the Judean Mountains to the west blocking rainfall. The Judean Mountains are a ridge running from north to south through the center of Israel. Jerusalem sits atop this ridge, at approximately 800 meters (2,600 feet) above sea level, while to its south the mountains rise to approximately 1,000 meters (3,300 feet) above sea level. Moving west from Jerusalem, the mountains drop off to foothills and then lowlands (the Shephelah), before reaching the plain along the Mediterranean coast. Precipitation rising eastward (inland) from the Mediterranean Sea condenses and falls along the western side of the Judean Mountains, but evaporates to the east as the ground level descends to the Dead Sea, creating a desert in the shadow of rain. The eastern side of the Dead Sea (in Jordan) is also a desert but has more freshwater springs because of precipitation condensing and falling on top of the mountains on that side (the mountains of Moab and Edom, which are higher in elevation than the Judean Mountains).

Rain falls on the western side of the watershed of the Judean Mountains, leaving the eastern side arid (the Judean Desert). Some of the rain penetrates through cracks in the bedrock, feeding aquifers (underground water tables) that flow down to the east. Perennial freshwater springs are located at points where the escarpment along the Dead Sea has exposed the aquifers, creating desert oases such as those at Jericho and Ein Gedi, both north of Masada (*ein/en/ayn/ain* means "spring [of water]" in Hebrew and Arabic). Another group of small springs is located south of Masada at Ein Boqeq. Cracks in and along the Dead Sea bed, caused by continuing tectonic activity in the Great Rift Valley, allow water from other underground sources to rise and form marshy, brackish water springs, as for example at Ein Feshkha (Einot Zukim), Ein el-Ghuweir, and Ein Tureiba to the south of Qumran. Just south of Ein Gedi, hot sulphur springs are created by water rising from sources deep underground, which mixes with minerals before reaching the surface.[5]

The rocky escarpment along the Dead Sea is scored by dozens of canyons, nearly all of which are dry riverbeds or washes (Arabic *wadi*; Hebrew *nahal*) created by water erosion. Rainwater falling on the Judean Mountains that is not absorbed into the ground flows down to the Dead Sea, collecting in rivulets and eroding them over time. This happens only when enough rain falls in a short period to saturate the ground, resulting in water flowing in torrents through the washes to the Dead Sea. These torrents or flash floods are rare events, limited to the rainy season (October–May). The annual mean rainfall around the Dead Sea is less than 50 millimeters (2 inches), with little or no rain falling during the summer months, when temperatures average 90–100° Fahrenheit.[6]

With such a harsh landscape and so little rainfall, it is not surprising that the Dead Sea region is desolate. Outside of the oases, most of the plant life is concentrated in the beds and alluvial fans of the canyons. The trees, such as acacia, are typical of savannahs or deserts—with tiny leaves to conserve moisture and large numbers of thorns to protect against grazing animals—but most of the plants are much smaller, and many bloom only during the rainy season (mainly January–March).[7] There is a surprising amount of wildlife, including snakes and lizards, scorpions and beetles, desert snails, desert mice, foxes, jackals, hyenas, songbirds and raptors, and even a few leopards. Hyrax (which look like large rats but are actually the smallest members of the pachyderm family) and ibex (a kind of wild mountain goat) are common in rocky areas around the oases, especially during the summer months when water sources and vegetation elsewhere dry up. Occasionally gazelles can be glimpsed on the plateaus.[8]

Masada is a limestone and dolomite mountain overlooking the southwestern shore of the Dead Sea. In geological terms it is a horst, that is, a raised rocky outcrop separated from the surrounding cliffs by deep ravines. The mountain's flat top gives it the shape of a mesa—a tabletop mountain. From above, the mountain appears diamond-shaped, measuring about 580 meters (1,900 feet) long from north to south (about the length of five football fields), and about 200 meters (650 feet) from east to west at its widest point. Bounded on all sides by sheer cliffs, Masada's name (Hebrew *Mezada*) derives from the biblical Hebrew word for fortress, especially a mountain fortress (*mezad*), aptly reflecting its appearance.

The Dead Sea

In addition to being the lowest point on earth, the Dead Sea is one of the world's saltiest bodies of water. Approximately one-third of its content is minerals, compared with 3 percent in most oceans, 4 percent in most seas, and 1 percent in brackish springs such as Ein Feshkha.[9] Although no living creatures can survive in the Dead Sea, some microorganisms are found there. The density of minerals in the Dead Sea is higher than the density of our body mass, supporting us in the water and causing us to float. When the Roman general Vespasian subdued Jericho during the First Revolt in June 68 CE, he ordered bound Jewish prisoners thrown into the sea, as he had been told they could not sink:

> Its waters are, as I said, bitter and unproductive, but owing to their buoyancy send up to the surface the very heaviest of objects cast into them, and it is difficult, even of set purpose, to sink to the bottom. Thus, when Vespasian came to explore the lake, he ordered certain persons who were unable to swim to be flung into the deep water with their hands tied behind them; with the result that all rose to the surface and floated, as if impelled upward by a current of air. (Josephus, *War* 4.476–77)

The Romans called the Dead Sea "the Asphalt Lake" (Lake Asphaltitis), referring to the lumps of bitumen that originate beneath the sea's floor and float to its surface, washing up along the shores.[10]

The Dead Sea's high mineral content and the hot springs along its shores are believed to have therapeutic properties, especially for certain skin diseases such as psoriasis and eczema as well as pain due to ailments such as arthritis. These purported healing properties attract visitors from around the world, who flock to spas on the shore of the Dead Sea, seeking cures by bathing in its water and applying mineral-rich mud. In addition, because the Dead Sea lies below sea level, fewer ultraviolet rays penetrate the atmosphere, making the sun's effects less damaging to the skin.[11] In the 1970s, Israel decided to preserve the natural beauty of the Dead Sea by concentrating hotels and spas in one location, at Ein Boqeq to the south of Masada. Today, Ein Boqeq is a bustling tourist hub with twenty-one hotels and numerous restaurants. The rest of the western shore of the Dead Sea remains undeveloped, except for a few scattered settlements and hostels: a hostel at the foot of Masada; a kibbutz, youth hostel, and field school at Ein Gedi; a kibbutz at Mitzpe Shalem (midway along the western shore); and a kibbutz at Kalia by Qumran. Despite the Dead Sea's claimed therapeutic properties, bathers must take care not to allow water to come into contact with the eyes, ears, nose, or mouth. The water is warm and feels oily, stinging fresh cuts and open wounds. Once out of the sea, bathers must rinse off immediately in fresh water to avoid discomfort.

At the southern end of the Dead Sea is a large factory called the Dead Sea Works, which extracts potash, bromide, and other minerals from the mud.[12] The first factory was established at Kalia in 1930 (as the Palestine Potash Company), but the enterprise moved south after the British Mandate ended and the northwestern shore of the Dead Sea, including Kalia, came under Jordanian rule.[13] A glance at a map of the Dead Sea shows that it consists of two parts: a large northern basin and a smaller southern basin, which are separated by a promontory on the east called the Lisan (Arabic for "tongue") peninsula. The northern basin is much deeper than the southern basin (about 300 meters or 1,000 feet deep), and, in fact, due to a steady drop in the Dead Sea's level, the southern basin has dried up altogether. Nowadays there is water in the southern basin only because the Dead Sea Works dug a channel around the Lisan peninsula to feed large evaporation pools in the southern basin. Masada overlooks the Lisan peninsula, which is clearly visible to visitors from the top of the mountain.

The Dead Sea Works are located at Sodom, at the southern end of the Dead Sea. Despite the name, and contrary to occasional highly publicized claims, no archaeological remains of Sodom or Gomorrah have ever been found—at least, none that can be identified with any credibility. In fact, many scholars doubt these cities ever existed. Nearby is a fascinating natural formation called Mount Sodom.[14] Mount Sodom is a salt dome, that is, a mountain made entirely of salt, measuring approximately 6 miles (10 kilometers) long, 1.2 miles (2 kilometers) wide, and 650 feet (200 meters) high. The salt was deposited during the Pliocene and Pleistocene eras (ca. 5 million to 12,000 years BP [Before Present]), when the Dead Sea was even saltier than today. At that time, salt accumulated at the bottom of the sea to a depth of three kilometers (2 miles). After the composition of the water in the sea changed, other minerals and sediments accumulated on top of the salt. Although it is solid, salt becomes soft (liquefied) under pressure. Because liquids take up more space than solids, the salt has expanded, pushing up through a weak point in the ground's crust at Mount Sodom. Visitors driving alongside the mountain on Highway 90 can see the salt layers rising vertically from underground, a process that continues at the rate of 3–4 millimeters (0.009–0.013 inches) per year. The thin coating of dirt comes from the impurities that remain after rain dissolves the salt. One of the pillars of salt that has separated from the side of the mountain is popularly identified as "Lot's Wife" due to its vague resemblance to a human profile when viewed from below.

The Dead Sea's main source is the Jordan River, which enters at the northern end. Smaller quantities of water come from springs around the Dead Sea and occasional flash floods. The reason for the Dead Sea's high mineral content is simple: it has no outlet. The water that enters the Dead Sea has nowhere to go but into the air, through a high rate of evaporation due to the desert heat. During the summer months the evaporation forms a haze hovering over the sea and raises the humidity. The minerals washed into the sea are left behind when the water evaporates, becoming increasingly concentrated over time. The reason for the receding level of the Dead Sea is equally easy to explain. Both Israel and Jordan use the water in the Jordan River, leaving only about 5 percent of it to flow into the Dead Sea. As a result, in recent decades there has been a dramatic drop in the Dead Sea's level, creating an ongoing—and entirely human-made—environmental crisis. The sea is now receding at a rate of about 1 meter (3 feet) per year, for a total of 40 meters since the 1950s (when the amount of water entering the sea equaled the evaporation rate). Since then, the Dead Sea has lost more than one-third of its surface area, measuring only about 50 kilometers (30 miles) long today compared to approximately 80 kilometers (50 miles) in 1950.[15]

One consequence of the decline in the Dead Sea's level is the formation of sinkholes along its shores. As the sea recedes, water from underground sources rises to the surface, dissolving layers of salt along the way which collapse and create giant sinkholes. The Dead Sea shore is now pockmarked with more than 4,000 sinkholes, most of which have appeared since the 1970s. Because of the danger posed by the sinkholes, much of the Dead Sea shoreline has been closed to visitors, including the public beach, restaurant, and gas station at Ein Gedi, as described in this Wikitravel entry:

Ein Gedi Oasis and Kibbutz: Ein Gedi was a real oasis with lush vegetation, nestled between two streams, amidst the arid landscape. Today, it is abandoned due to sinkholes. The palm trees are dead and there are abandoned buildings everywhere. There is no longer a public beach here.[16]

For decades Israel and Jordan have sought a solution to this problem, the most popular of which is to dig a canal either from the Mediterranean Sea to the Dead Sea (the "Med-Dead" canal), or from the Red Sea to the Dead Sea (the "Red-Dead" canal).[17] The idea is that not only would this replenish the Dead Sea, but the drop in elevation from the Mediterranean Sea or Red Sea to the Dead Sea could be utilized to generate power. As attractive as this solution seems, there are numerous obstacles. Due to the geology of the region, there is no feasible route for a Med-Dead canal. The best route from the Red Sea lies on the Jordanian side of the border, which means that Jordan and Israel must negotiate an agreement. In 2015, the *Jerusalem Post* reported significant progress toward just such an agreement.[18] The proposed project involves constructing a large desalinization plant in Aqaba, with the residual hypersaline water (called brine) pumped 200 kilometers northward through a canal into the Dead Sea. Israel will be able to purchase desalinated water from the Aqaba plant, and, in return, Jordan will be allowed to increase the amount of water it purchases from Israel's main source, the Sea of Galilee. Opponents to this project include Israeli and Jordanian environmentalists who fear that the Dead Sea will be irreparably damaged by the addition of brine. Palestinians are opposed because they were not included in these negotiations, arguing that as it is part of the West Bank, the northwestern shore of the Dead Sea is Palestinian territory, and they should have a voice in any future allocation of water rights.

Masada's Historical Setting

Although the harsh climate, desolate landscape, and rocky terrain around the Dead Sea have not attracted much human settlement over the ages, Masada did not exist in a vacuum. Long-term permanent settlements (towns and villages) sprang up by oases with perennial freshwater springs at Jericho and Ein Gedi. Shorter term settlements such as

Qumran, Masada, Ein Feshkha, and Ein Boqeq (lasting less than a century or two) were established as a result of specific political or social circumstances. For example, Masada was a royal palace-fortress and desert refuge that protected the frontier of the kingdoms of the Hasmoneans and Herod. Qumran was settled by members of a Jewish sect who sought isolation in the wilderness. Indeed, the Dead Sea region's hostile environment generally attracted people looking for a temporary refuge rather than a permanent home. The proximity to Jerusalem on the one hand, and the thousands of natural caves pockmarking the limestone and dolomite cliffs on the other, have always made the Judean Desert—and especially the rocky escarpment along the Dead Sea—an ideal place to hide or live in isolation. According to the Hebrew Bible (Old Testament), when Saul sought to kill David out of jealousy, David fled to Ein Gedi:

> When Saul returned from following the Philistines, he was told, "David is in the wilderness of En-Gedi." Then Saul took three thousand chosen men out of all Israel, and went to look for David and his men in the direction of the Rocks of the Wild Goats [Ibex]. He came to the sheepfolds beside the road, where there was a cave; and Saul went in to relieve himself [Hebrew: to cover his feet]. Now David and his men were sitting in the innermost parts of the cave. (1 Sam 24:1–3)[19]

It is impossible to identify the cave in which David supposedly took refuge (assuming this episode is historical, which is debatable). However, many caves around the Dead Sea were occupied for brief periods, especially in the Chalcolithic period/Copper Age (fourth millennium BCE); the late Iron Age (eighth–seventh centuries BCE); the First and Second Jewish Revolts against the Romans (66–70 and 132–135 CE); and the Byzantine period (fifth–sixth centuries CE). In addition, a number of sites were established around the Dead Sea in the late Second Temple period (ca. 100 BCE to 70 CE). The following is a brief survey of some of these sites.[20]

The Chalcolithic Period

THE CAVE OF THE TREASURE

After the British Mandate ended and Palestine was partitioned, the northwestern shore of the Dead Sea (north of Ein Gedi) came under Jordanian rule, while the western shore from Ein Gedi southward was part of Israel (as a result of the Six-Day War in 1967, Israel took the north-western shore, which is part of the territory called the West Bank). After the first Dead Sea Scrolls were discovered at Qumran in 1946–1947, Bedouins (desert nomads) moved south into Israeli territory looking for more scrolls. In response, in 1960–1962, Israeli archaeologists mounted a campaign to explore the area. Different archaeologists were assigned the task of surveying different canyons. Although many caves in these canyons yielded archaeological finds, the most spectacular remains were discovered in Nahal Mishmar and Nahal Hever (see below), both located between Ein Gedi and Masada.[21]

Nahal Mishmar was explored by the Israeli archaeologist Pesach Bar-Adon, a colorful character who spent part of his life living among Bedouins. In a cave high in the cliff face of Nahal Mishmar, Bar-Adon found a cache of 429 vessels (six of hematite, six of ivory, and the rest of copper), wrapped in a straw mat—the reason this is called "the Cave of the Treasure." The vessels include copper chisels and axes, mace heads and crowns, scepters, standards, and many objects of unknown function, including perforated hippopotamus tusks. Among the other finds from the cave are pottery and stone vessels and tools, textiles (mostly flax and some wool), straw and leather objects including a pair of sandals, and a weaving loom. The cave floor was covered with a thick layer of occupation debris including ash from fireplaces and hearths with remains of food (animal bones, wheat, barley, lentils, onions, garlic, olives, dates, and acorns). Human burials were also found in this cave and in two caves nearby. As spectacular as these finds are, they are all the more astonishing because of their prehistoric origin, dating to the Chalcolithic period or Copper Age (fourth millennium BCE). Although we have more information now about the Chalcolithic period than at the time of Bar-Adon's discovery, the finds from the Cave of the Treasure are still unique. The cache remains unparalleled in terms of its quality, quantity, and diversity, and the function and purpose of these vessels are unknown. Where did they come from, and why were they hidden inside the cave? Bar-Adon speculated that the vessels were "ritual equipment" used in the Chalcolithic temple at Ein Gedi nearby, or at another (unidentified) cultic site.[22]

THE CHALCOLITHIC TEMPLE AT EIN GEDI

In 1956–1957, excavations by an Israeli scholar named Joseph Naveh on a mountainside overlooking the Ein Gedi oasis brought to light a rare Chalcolithic temple. The complex consists of a large open enclosure with a 3-meter (10-foot)-wide circular stone structure in the center. The main entrance to the enclosure is through a gatehouse, across from which is an elongated, narrow room, and a smaller room off to one side. Abutting the wall opposite the entrance to the large room is a horseshoe-shaped niche that may have been an altar. Stone benches line the walls of the large room, and pits dug into its floor were filled with burned bones, horns, pottery, and ashes—apparently the remains of sacrificial offerings. The excavator proposed that this temple served as a central sanctuary for the population of the region in the Chalcolithic period.[23]

The Iron Age

QUMRAN

Qumran is a small ruin located on a natural marl terrace by the northwestern shore of the Dead Sea, 13 kilometers (8 miles) south of Jericho. Although best-known as the site associated with the Dead Sea Scrolls (see below), Qumran was first settled in the late Iron Age (eighth–seventh centuries BCE), when it was part of the biblical kingdom of Judah. The excavator, Roland de Vaux, reconstructed the Iron Age settlement as a rectangular building with a row of rooms along the east side of an open courtyard. An enclosure attached to the western side of the building contained a large, round cistern that was filled by surface runoff. A long wall enclosed the marl terrace or esplanade to the south of the building. De Vaux noted similarities between the layout of this settlement and Israelite (Iron Age) strongholds in the Buqeia (a valley above Qumran) and Negev, which suggest that Qumran was established to protect the kingdom's eastern frontier. According to de Vaux, the settlement was destroyed around the time of the fall of the kingdom of Judah (586 BCE).[24]

The Late Second Temple Period (ca. 100 BCE–70 CE)

KHIRBET MAZIN (OR QASR EL-YAHUD OR KHIRBET EL-YAHOUD)

Khirbet Mazin is located on the Dead Sea shore, about one-half a kilometer (ca. 1,650 feet) north of the point where the Kidron Valley—which originates in Jerusalem—flows into the Dead Sea. Originally excavated in the early 1960s by a Belgian expedition, the site was re-excavated a decade later by Bar-Adon. Although there are Iron Age remains, the main occupation dates to the Hasmonean period (late second century and first half of the first century BCE). The Hasmoneans were descendants of the Maccabees, the family who led the Jews to independence from Alexander's Greek successors and established a kingdom in Judea. In 63 BCE, the Hasmonean kingdom was annexed by Pompey and Judea came under Roman rule.

The Hasmonean period remains at Khirbet Mazin consist of a single structure enclosed by thick stone walls, with a large courtyard measuring roughly 30 × 10 meters (100 × 35 feet) and a massive, two- to three-story high tower attached to its northeast corner. The tower was divided by walls into rooms used for living and storage. The entrance to the complex was by way of a 5-meter (15-foot)-wide gate on the east. A sloping 6-meter (20-foot)-wide ramp descends from the gate eastward toward the Dead Sea. The sides of the ramp are supported by stone walls, with a curved wall attached to the north side that might have served as a breakwater. The floors of the courtyard and ramp are lower than the surrounding ground level. These features indicate that the ramp functioned as a slipway and the courtyard as a dry dock for boats. The Israeli archaeologist Ehud Netzer suggested that the site was a fortified Hasmonean anchorage for royal boats. As many as four boats could have fit inside the walled courtyard, protected by a detachment of soldiers stationed in the tower. There is plenty of evidence for ancient maritime traffic and trade along the shores of the Dead Sea, which was easier and more efficient than traveling overland between these points.[25]

QUMRAN

Qumran is the site associated with the Dead Sea Scrolls, which were found in the surrounding caves. The first scrolls were discovered and removed by Bedouins in 1946–1947 from a cave (Cave 1) in the limestone cliffs behind Qumran. These seven scrolls were sold on the antiquities market and acquired by the State of Israel. From 1951 to 1956, de Vaux, a French biblical scholar and archaeologist affiliated with the École Biblique et Archéologique Française in Jerusalem, excavated the site of Qumran and searched the nearby caves for additional scrolls. Eventually, the remains of approximately one thousand different scrolls were discovered in eleven caves around Qumran (Caves 1–11). Approximately six hundred of the scrolls come from Cave 4, which is located in the marl terrace on which Qumran sits (fig. 16). Most of the scrolls are not complete but instead are small fragments surviving from what originally were complete scrolls.

De Vaux's excavations at Qumran brought to light a small settlement with rooms used for communal purposes (such as communal dining rooms and a scriptorium or writing room) and as workshops (including a potters' workshop). An aqueduct (channel) brought flash flood water from the nearby riverbed (Wadi Qumran) and filled plastered pools around the settlement. Some of the pools were used as cisterns for storing drinking water, while others functioned as Jewish ritual baths (Hebrew *miqveh*; pl. *miqva'ot*), as indicated by the broad sets of steps running along the width of the pools, from top to bottom, to facilitate immersion in the water (fig. 17). A large cemetery on the plateau to the east of the settlement contains approximately 1,100 graves, most of them lined up in neat rows oriented north-south, and with nearly all of the remains belonging to adult males.

Many scholars (including myself) identify the Qumran community and the wider movement of which it was a part with the Essenes, a Jewish sect of the late Second Temple period. We learn about the Essenes from contemporary outside authors—that is, authors who lived in the late first century BCE and first century CE, the most important of whom are Josephus, Philo Judaeus (a Jewish philosopher who lived in Alexandria), and Pliny the Elder (the Roman author who died during the eruption of Mount Vesuvius in 79 CE). Pliny even situates the Essenes on the northwestern shore of the Dead Sea—that is, in the same area where Qumran is located. The sectarian settlement at Qumran was established around 100 BCE and was destroyed in 68 CE during the First Revolt.[26]

EIN FESHKHA AND EIN EL-GHUWEIR

Along the western Dead Sea shore a couple of miles to the south of Qumran is a series of brackish springs called (from north to south) Ein Feshkha, Ein el-Ghuweir, and Ein et-Tureiba, which attracted permanent settlement during brief periods. De Vaux's 1956 excavations at Ein Feshkha brought to light a main building, an industrial area, and an enclosure. The rectangular, two-story-high main building apparently was a farmhouse. Scholars have speculated that the pools or basins and channels in the industrial area were used for the production of parchment (processed animal hides); for raising fish; for soaking flax; or as date presses.[27] Ein el-Ghuweir was excavated by Bar-Adon, who found a structure consisting of a large rectangular courtyard (which he described as a hall), with a long, narrow, pillared porch or room that contained ovens and granaries along one side. Although finds from Ein Feshkha and Ein el-Ghuweir indicate the inhabitants were Jewish, there is no clear evidence supporting the excavators' claims that they were members of the Qumran sect/Essenes.[28]

HYRCANIA (KHIRBET EL-MIRD)

The Hasmonean kings built a series of fortified palaces along Judea's eastern frontier—a system that was utilized and expanded by King Herod the Great. One of the Hasmonean fortified palaces is Hyrcania, which was built atop an isolated hilltop overlooking the Buqeiʿa, a valley above the escarpment west of Qumran. Hyrcania has never been excavated, although archaeologists have surveyed its ruins. The hilltop structure, which is supported on underground vaults used as cisterns, appears to consist of a central courtyard surrounded by rooms. In the Byzantine period (fifth–sixth centuries), monks reused the structure and installed a chapel. Numerous cisterns are cut into the slopes and the top of the hill, and two large, open water reservoirs lie at the foot of the western slope, on one side of a bridge with an aqueduct that provided access to the summit.[29]

CALLIRRHOE (AIN EZ-ZARA)

The perennial springs on the eastern side of the Dead Sea are more numerous, more copious, and have sweeter water than those on the western side. A large number of freshwater springs and hot mineral springs are located at Hammamat Ma'in—a popular resort in a narrow canyon called Wadi Zarqa Ma'in, about 4 kilometers (2.5 miles) inland and roughly across the sea from Ein el-Ghuweir. Although these springs were utilized in antiquity, the main archaeological remains are at ancient Callirrhoe (modern Ain ez-Zara), at the point where the Zarqa Ma'in riverbed reaches the Dead Sea shore. Since the 1980s, these remains have been investigated and partially excavated by German archaeological expeditions. In the first century BCE and first century CE, Callirrhoe was an oasis with a complex of thermal baths, villas, and farmhouses, accessed by a small harbor or anchorage. After a gap of about three hundred years, the site was reoccupied in the Late Roman period (mid-fourth to fifth century). Callirrhoe is best known as the spot where Herod sought relief from the agony of his terminal illness shortly before he died, as Josephus says: "Thus he crossed the Jordan to take the warm baths at Callirrhoe, the waters of which descend into the Lake Asphaltitis and from their sweetness are also used for drink" (*War* 1.607; also see *Ant.* 17.171).[30]

MACHAERUS

Machaerus sits atop a mountain on the south bank of Wadi Zarqa Ma'in, inland (east) of Callirrhoe (fig. 3).[31] It is one of the fortified desert palaces built by the Hasmoneans and rebuilt by Herod on the eastern frontier of their kingdoms, and the only one located east of the Jordan River and Dead Sea. This region, called Peraea, was conquered and "Judaized" by the Hasmoneans (meaning the Hasmoneans forcibly converted the native population to Judaism). Machaerus was situated to protect Peraea's southern border against the Nabataean kingdom, which encompassed much of southern Jordan, the Negev, and the Sinai (with the capital at Petra in modern Jordan) (see chapter 5).

From 1978 to 1981, Virgilio Corbo and Stanislao Loffreda of the Studium Biblicum Franciscanum excavated the fortified palace atop the mountain, bringing to light remains dating to the Hasmonean and Herodian periods and the time of the First Jewish Revolt. Since 2009, Győző Vörös of the Hungarian Academy of Arts has been directing excavations at Machaerus. The excavations revealed that the rooms of Herod's palace were laid out on either side of a north-south corridor, recalling the symmetrical layout of his palace on top of Herodium. The eastern wing has a central courtyard with long, narrow storerooms on the north side and a bathhouse on the south side. The western wing is dominated by a large peristyle courtyard on the north side and a possible double triclinium (dining room/reception hall) on the south side.[32] There is a large cistern on top of the mountain, and an aqueduct supplied other cisterns hewn into the northern slope. Also similar to Herodium, Machaerus had a lower city that served as a regional administrative center, which was located on its steep northern slope.

After the destruction of Jerusalem and the Second Temple in 70, Jewish rebels continued to occupy Herodium, Machaerus, and Masada. Machaerus was the penultimate fortress to fall to the Romans, after a siege. As at Masada, the remains of the Roman siege works are still visible, encircling the base of the mountain.[33]

EIN BOQEQ

Overlooking the southwestern shore of the Dead Sea is a small oasis fed by brackish springs which attracted permanent settlement during the first and sixth centuries CE. The remains were excavated in the 1960s and 1970s by an Israeli expedition led by Mordechai Gichon. They include a 20-meter (65-foot)-square building dating to the first century, which the excavators identified as an *officina* (factory) for the production of unguents and perfumes, because the rooms included numerous installations (such as pits, basins, and ovens). Presumably these products were manufactured from plants such as opobalsam which were cultivated at the oasis. In the Byzantine period (sixth century), a small fort (also measuring about 20 meters square) was built on the slope overlooking the shoreline.[34]

Today the springs at Ein Boqeq are under environmental threat. Not only has the oasis been developed intensively for tourism, but industrial waste from chemical factories located on a plateau to the west has seeped into the groundwater that feeds the springs. As a result, the spring water has become increasingly saline, damaging plant and animal species. In 2014, Israeli authorities began to pump in fresh water to restore the spring, but it will take decades until this process is completed.[35]

The Second Jewish Revolt against the Romans
(Bar Kokhba Revolt) (132–135 CE)

NAHAL HEVER

In 132 CE, the Jews of Judea rose up in revolt against the Romans a second time, after learning that the Emperor Hadrian planned to dedicate a rebuilt Jerusalem temple to the Roman god Capitoline Jupiter. The leader of the revolt was a messianic figure nicknamed Bar Kokhba (Aramaic for "son of a star"). The Jewish rebels conducted a highly effective campaign of guerilla warfare, hiding in underground caves and tunnels during the day and emerging after dark to ambush the Roman troops. As a result, an entire Roman legion was obliterated, and Hadrian ended up sending a third of the Roman army to subdue Judea. Eventually, however, the tide turned against the Jews, and in 135, Bar Kokhba perished in a last stand at the stronghold of Bethar near Bethlehem.

The 1960–1962 Israeli expedition to the Dead Sea identified a number of caves in which Jews took refuge at the time of the Bar Kokhba Revolt. For example, in a cliff high above Ein Gedi, the Israeli archaeologist Nahman Avigad found the "Cave of the Pool," so-called because a plastered pool for storing water was installed at the cave's entrance. Thanks to the water supply (and remains of food which Avigad also found), the Jews hiding in this cave apparently left it alive.[36]

The most spectacular discoveries associated with the Bar Kokhba Revolt were made by Yigael Yadin, who excavated Masada a couple of years later. Yadin had been assigned the north bank of Nahal Hever, a large canyon located a short distance south of Ein Gedi and just north of Nahal Mishmar. High up in the cliff, he discovered a cave that yielded a wealth of ancient finds including documents, for which reason it became known as the "Cave of Letters." A cave in the opposite (south) cliff, which was explored by another Israeli archaeologist named Yohanan Aharoni, is called the "Cave of Horror" because of the numerous human skeletons discovered in it. Human remains were also discovered in the Cave of Letters. The skeletons belong to Jewish families—men, women, children, and infants—from the nearby village of Ein Gedi, who fled from the Romans during the revolt and sought refuge in these caves. However, the caves were discovered by Roman troops, who camped on the cliffs above. Unable to leave to obtain food and water, the refugees perished of hunger and thirst inside the caves. Excavating the caves was challenging as they are located in the sheer cliff faces, making access very difficult.

When the Jewish refugees left their homes in Ein Gedi, they locked the doors to their homes and took with them their most valuable belongings. We know this because their house keys and other possessions remained inside the caves, some hidden in cracks and crevices. Most of the finds come from the Cave of Letters. For example, Yadin found a hoard of bronze vessels wrapped in a woven basket, its handles still tied together. In addition to jugs, the hoard includes incense shovels and paterae (libation bowls) decorated with Greek mythological figures, which were deliberately defaced by having their features rubbed smooth. Yadin surmised that this cache originally belonged to a Roman officer and was taken as booty after his unit was ambushed by rebels. Because the Jews considered the pagan images decorating the vessels offensive, they defaced them. Other objects found in the Cave of Letters include a set of wooden bowls and kitchen knives (still with their wooden handles); a valuable cut glass plate; leather sandals; and clothing (mostly woolen tunics and mantles, some brightly colored). The arid climate preserved these organic materials, which are rarely found in archaeological excavations in Israel.

The dry conditions also preserved ancient documents, including three archives (bundles) in the Cave of Letters. One of the archives belonged to a fascinating woman named Babatha, who originally came from Nabataea and was married twice. Her second husband was from Ein Gedi, which is how she ended up in the Cave of Letters. Although she was illiterate, Babatha kept her personal documents, including her marriage contract and financial records relating to property holdings, well-organized and neatly wrapped in a leather purse. Another group of documents found inside a water skin includes letters sent by Bar Kokhba to his commanders at Ein Gedi—the first time in history we heard Bar Kokhba speaking for himself. In fact, these letters reveal that Bar Kokhba's real name was Simeon Ben Kosiba. Bar Kokhba was a nickname alluding to the messianic hopes of his followers. In later Jewish tradition he was nicknamed Bar Koziba—the son of a liar/deceiver—as obviously he was a false messiah due to the failure of the revolt.[37]

The discoveries in Nahal Hever and other caves around the Judean Desert shed important light on the Bar Kokhba Revolt, about which we possess little other information. Josephus, who describes the First Revolt in great detail, died around 100 CE—more than three decades before the Second Revolt. There is no ancient author like Josephus who recorded for us the events of the Bar Kokhba Revolt. We possess only brief, scattered references in Roman writers (such as Cassius Dio), rabbinic literature, and the church fathers. Archaeology provides valuable information, supplementing the meager historical picture.

The Byzantine Period (Fourth–Sixth Centuries CE)

Beginning in the fourth century, when Constantine legalized Christianity and Theodosius made it the official state religion of the Roman Empire, Palestine was catapulted into a position of prominence. Over the next couple of centuries, hundreds of churches and monasteries were built throughout the country, and pilgrims eager to visit holy sites associated with Jesus and the Bible poured in from around the Mediterranean. Desert monasticism, which originated in Egypt, spread quickly as holy men pursued an ascetic lifestyle, far removed from physical pleasures and temptations. Some of these men lived alone in the wilderness as hermits, but many joined monastic communities (organized as *laurae* and *coenobia*).

Thanks to its proximity to Jerusalem and biblical sites on the one hand, and the harsh conditions and numerous caves on the other, the Judean Desert attracted an unusually large number of monks and hermits. At the height of the Byzantine period (sixth century), there were approximately sixty-five monasteries with hundreds of members in the Judean Desert (not including the plain around Jericho, which had many more monasteries). These include Masada (where there was a monastery called Marda), and Hyrcania (home to a monastery called Castellion). At other sites such as Ein Feshkha, there is evidence of occupation by small groups of Byzantine monks or hermits. In the centuries following the Sasanid Persian invasion of Palestine in 614 (which devastated a large number of churches and monasteries), and the Muslim conquest a couple of decades later with the subsequent spread of Islam, most of the monasteries declined and were gradually abandoned. Today only a handful are still active, including the monastery of Choziba (or St. George) in Wadi Qelt near Jericho, and Mar Saba in the Kidron Valley. In 1966, the British writer Derwas James Chitty published a book about the Byzantine monasteries of the Judean Desert monasteries called *The Desert a City*—an apt reference to a time when the population of this desolate region reached its greatest height.[38]

CHAPTER 4

MASADA AND HEROD'S OTHER BUILDING PROJECTS

Although Herod the Great's infamy has endured thanks to the story of the massacre of the innocents (Matthew 2:16–18), in archaeological circles he is known as the single greatest builder in the history of the Holy Land. More than any other individual, Herod's building projects and monuments left a lasting imprint on the country's landscape.[1] Many of these, including Jerusalem's Temple Mount, Herodium (his final resting place), and the port city of Caesarea Maritima, are still visible today. These building projects were paid for out of a combination of Herod's considerable personal wealth (much of which came from extensive land holdings) and taxes. Herod's building program stimulated the local economy by creating jobs for skilled workers and laborers, increasing the import and export of goods (through the port of Caesarea), and attracting throngs of pilgrims to the rebuilt Jerusalem temple.[2] The following is a brief survey of Herod's major building projects and monuments, beginning with Masada.

MASADA

Masada's steep cliffs make the 350-meter (ca. 1,200-foot) climb to the top difficult and even treacherous (figs. 1–2).[3] There have always been two main routes of access: the narrow, winding Snake Path on the east slope (seen from above by visitors riding in the cable car today) and a more easily accessible route on the west side that is largely buried under the Roman siege ramp. Josephus describes climbing Masada's rugged cliffs via the Snake Path as a terrifying experience:

> A rock of no slight circumference and lofty from end to end is abruptly terminated on every side by deep ravines, the precipices rising sheer from an invisible base and being inaccessible to the foot of any living creature, save in two places where the rock permits of no easy ascent. Of these tracks one leads from the Lake Asphaltitis, on the east, the other, by which the approach is easier, from the west. The former they call the snake, seeing a resemblance to that reptile in its narrowness and continual windings; for its course is broken in skirting the jutting crags and, returning frequently upon itself and gradually lengthening out again, it makes painful headway. One traversing this route must firmly plant each foot alternatively. Destruction faces him; for on either side yawn chasms so terrific as to daunt the hardiest. (*War* 7.280–83)

Although Josephus tells us that Masada was first fortified by a Hasmonean king named Jonathan (referring either to Judah Maccabee's brother or Alexander Jannaeus; see chapter 5), archaeologists have not conclusively identified any buildings that antedate Herod's reign. Apparently, when Herod constructed his palaces atop Masada, he obliterated all earlier architectural remains. The following discussion presents Herod's buildings at Masada as a whole, although different construction phases can be distinguished over the course of his reign (figs. 18, 19).[4]

Herod fortified the top of the mountain with an approximately 1,300-meter (4,250-foot)-long casemate wall and twenty-seven towers encircling the edge of the cliff.[5] The casemate wall consists of two parallel walls divided into a row of approximately seventy rooms, which were used for garrisoning soldiers and other personnel, and storing supplies and military equipment. Gates furnished with guardrooms provided access through the wall at the top of the Snake Path and the western route.

Herod's main buildings inside the fortifications consisted of two palace complexes, one on the north and one on the west. Both complexes included palace rooms (living rooms, dining rooms, etc.), administrative offices, servants' quarters, workshops, bathhouses, and storage rooms. Herod apparently intended the two palaces to serve different functions: the western palace included Herod's throne room and was used for official ceremonies, whereas the northern palace contained Herod's private living quarters. In addition to the two palace complexes, there are smaller palace buildings scattered around the top of Masada, which apparently housed local commanders or officials, members of Herod's family, and perhaps visiting dignitaries. These include a small palace to the north of the Snake Path gate and three small palaces to the southeast of the western palace (designated by the excavators as Buildings 8, 11, 12, 13). Unlike the other structures, one large building (9) between the northern palace and the western palace consists of nine identical dwelling units arranged around a central courtyard (three on each side), a layout that suggests it served as a hostel for visitors. All of Herod's buildings at Masada were constructed of cut stone blocks consisting mostly of dolomite (a hard limestone) that was quarried on top of the mountain, bonded with mud or plaster mortar. Originally the walls of the buildings were covered inside and out with plaster or mud. Most of the rooms had flat ceilings or roofs with layers of reeds and mud or plaster laid over wooden beams, and most had beaten earth or plastered floors.

The Northern Palace Complex: The Palace

The rooms of the northern palace are situated spectacularly on three terraces supported by retaining walls that spill over the edge of the cliff (fig. 20). A massive, white-plastered stone wall that broadened at the base separated the northern palace from the rest of the mountain (fig. 21). The only access to the rooms of the northern palace was around the eastern end of the wall, through a courtyard that led to a guardroom, effectively creating a fortress within a fortress. Graffiti depicting a garden enclosure and ships—perhaps etched by bored guards—were scratched onto the plastered walls around benches adjacent to the doorways in the courtyard and guardroom, and on the walls of a storeroom just to the south.[6] The guardroom opened on to the upper terrace of the northern palace, which contained a relatively modest suite of bedrooms paved with simple black and white mosaics of geometric designs resembling a honeycomb pattern. A semicircular porch (originally roofed) in front of the bedrooms provides a breathtaking view of the rugged desert landscape and the Dead Sea, including the oasis at Ein Gedi, which is visible as a dark patch in the haze at the foot of the mountains some 17 kilometers (11 miles) to the north. The area between the base of Masada and the Dead Sea shore is filled with badlands created by the erosion of soft marl (chalk) deposits.

In Herod's time, the three terraces of the northern palace were connected by enclosed staircases, with steps that wound around a square stone pier (pillar). Today visitors to Masada climb down a modern wooden staircase that runs alongside the mountain. The middle terrace of the northern palace was constructed of two circular concentric walls, the inner one partly hewn out of the bedrock of the cliff and partly built of stone, and the outer one built of stone. The walls extended the terrace beyond the edge of the cliff and were covered by a floor. Columns around the edge of the terrace supported a roof surrounding the circular structure, creating a covered patio with a spectacular panoramic view. The function of the circular structure (called a *tholos* in Greek) is unknown. A row of vertical niches in the terrace's back wall (the bedrock side) have grooves in the sides to hold wooden shelves, perhaps for storing scrolls (indicating it was a library) or food and drink (for use as a dining room/reception area).[7]

The lower terrace of the northern palace was used as a dining room and reception hall (triclinium). The terrace is rectangular in plan and had an outer peristyle surrounding an inner rectangle created by a low wall with columns at intervals, mirroring the outer peristyle. From the center of the inner rectangle, the desert landscape would have been visible by looking over the low wall, with the view framed by columns. Much of the original interior decoration of the reception hall is preserved, thanks to its having been buried for more than two thousand years (fig. 4). The columns were composed of stone drums covered with stucco imitating fluted marble shafts, topped with stuccoed, painted, and gilded Corinthian capitals. The low walls of the inner rectangle and the lower part of the cliff wall of the outer rectangle were plastered and decorated with paintings in the Second Pompeian Style. Typical of this style, the paintings depict colorful panels imitating colored stone and marble plaques. An illusion of depth was created on the cliff face by constructing engaged half-columns in the middle of each panel, which seem to cut off and block the view of the panels behind. Interestingly, Josephus's description of the northern palace inaccurately refers to monolithic stone columns and colored stone panels:

> There, too, he built a palace on the western slope, beneath the ramparts on the crest and inclining towards the north. The palace wall was strong and of great height, and had four towers, sixty cubits high, at the corners. The fittings of the interior—apartments, colonnades, and baths—were of manifold variety and sumptuous; columns, each formed of a single block, supporting the building throughout, and the walls and floors of the apartments being laid with variegated stones. (*War* 7.289–90)

These and other errors in Josephus's description suggest that he never visited Masada himself.[8]

A small bathhouse was located below the eastern side of the lower terrace. Although much of it has eroded over the edge of the cliff, a stepped and plastered cold water pool (frigidarium) is still visible, with a poorly preserved mosaic on the floor in front of it, and part of the steam room, with small pillars that were part of the hypocaust heating system (see below).

The Northern Palace Complex: The Service Quarter

The northern palace was serviced by buildings located just outside (south) of the large, white-plastered stone wall. One of these is a large, Roman-style bathhouse. Bathhouses were a characteristic feature of Roman life, not just providing facilities for bathing but also serving as cultural centers with entertainment, dining, and exercise facilities. Roman cities typically had one or more public bathhouses, and the villas and mansions of the wealthy were equipped with private bathhouses, analogous to having a swimming pool or exercise room in one's home today. The large bathhouse served Herod's northern palace as well as the occupants of the small palaces.

The large bathhouse at Masada was entered through a peristyle courtyard (an open courtyard surrounded by columns) paved with a mosaic floor with black and white geometric designs, and Second Pompeian Style paintings on the walls. The first room in the bathhouse was an

apodyterium or dressing room, where guests undressed before proceeding to the baths (fig. 5). The walls were decorated with Second
Pompeian Style wall paintings and painted stucco, and the floor was
paved with black and white triangular tiles (opus sectile). Although
most of the tiles were later robbed out, their impressions are still visible
in the plaster bedding underneath. Seventy years after Herod's death, the
Jewish rebels who occupied Masada built a square plastered installation
(perhaps for storage?) in one corner of the apodyterium, covering the tile
floor and wall paintings. Against the opposite wall they added a bench
made of column drums laid side-by-side and covered with plaster.

An arched doorway led from the apodyterium to the tepidarium, a
moderately heated (tepid) room that had painted and stuccoed walls and
a tiled floor, later robbed out. At one end of the tepidarium is a small,
stepped, and plastered cold-water plunge bath (frigidarium). A doorway
in the opposite wall provided access to the largest room in the bathhouse:
the caldarium or hot (steam) room (fig. 22). Modern visitors to Masada
are immediately struck by the small pillars covering the floor of the
room, which are made of round (cut) stones that were plastered. Originally these small pillars, which are called suspensura, were not visible.
Instead they supported an upper floor, which was covered with black and
white triangular tiles like in the apodyterium (as indicated by remains
of plaster with impressions of robbed-out tiles on top of the suspensura).
Hot air from a furnace outside the caldarium circulated among the small
pillars and heated the upper floor. An arched opening leading to the furnace can still be seen in the wall of the caldarium, below the level of the
tiled floor. The walls were heated by rectangular terracotta pipes which
carried hot air upward from under the upper floor. The pipes were covered by plaster and painted, and like the suspensura would not have been
visible. Niches at either end of the room contained large tubs with water.
Steam was created by sprinkling water from the tubs onto the floor and
walls. Unlike the other rooms in the bathhouse, the caldarium was
roofed with a stone vault, as the steam would have rotted a wooden ceiling. Here we see Herod's adoption of Roman architectural forms using
local building materials (a vault made of stone instead of concrete). The
caldarium at Masada also represents an early example of this kind of
heating system (called a hypocaust), which was a hallmark of the Roman
world.

Surrounding the large bathhouse to the east and south are long, narrow storerooms which contained supplies for the northern palace (fig. 23). Ancient storerooms typically display this kind of layout, since only short wooden beams were needed for roofing a narrow room, while the elongated shape maximized the room's size. Yigael Yadin found dozens of ceramic storage jars buried in the collapse of the storerooms. These originally contained food supplies such as wine, oil, grain, and fruit, as indicated by inscriptions on the jars and analyses of their contents. In some cases, the remains of seeds, nuts, and fruits—including pomegranates, olives, dried figs—were still preserved due to the arid desert climate. Yadin also found chunks of salt, which presumably came from the Dead Sea and would have been used to preserve and flavor food.

Some of the ceramic storage jars found at Masada contained imported delicacies for Herod's table, as indicated by inscriptions in ink which describe the contents and are often dated. Greek and Latin inscriptions on several jars refer to Italian and Aegean wine, fish sauce from Spain, and pickled apples from Cumae in Italy. Some of the inscriptions mention "Herod King of Judea" as the recipient. Residue analysis identified tiny fish bones in one jar, apparently representing the remains of fish sauce. Roman fish sauces—called *garum, muria, liquamen,* and *allec*—were used as seasonings and condiments in various dishes. They were made by fermenting fish such as anchovies or mackerel together with additional ingredients including fish intestines, gills, fish blood, and salt. The taste would have been similar to today's southeast Asian fish sauces.[9]

The Synagogue

One of the rooms in the casemate wall, located on the northwest side of the mountain, is larger than the others (fig. 24). Originally, the room consisted of a porch or anteroom and a main hall with five columns to support the roof. At the time of the First Revolt, it was modified and converted to a synagogue by the Jewish rebels (see chapter 8). The function of this room in Herod's time is disputed. Yadin proposed that it was a synagogue from the start, serving as a place of worship for the Jewish members of Herod's family. However, Ehud Netzer argued that a layer of dung covering the original plastered floor of the room indicates it was used as a stable. Yadin associated the dung with the garrison that occupied the mountain between Herod's death and the outbreak of the First Revolt. The notion that Herod's family members would have needed their own synagogue as a place of worship (as assumed by Yadin) is anachronistic, as synagogues in Herod's time were Jewish assemblies for the public reading of the Torah. If the layer of dung is associated with the room's use as a stable after Herod's death, then perhaps it originally functioned as a reception room, as suggested by its size and the anteroom.

Proceeding south from the synagogue, one reaches the top of the Roman siege ramp, and just to the east of it, the entrance to Herod's western palace complex.

The Western Palace Complex

The western palace complex is situated at the point where the western route reaches the top of Masada. The location reflects the western palace's public function, in contrast to the more isolated and private northern palace. The complex was accessed by way of a guardroom, which, like the other guardrooms at Masada, has benches along the walls and was decorated with stucco molded in imitation of marble panels. From the guardroom, an elongated corridor bisected the administrative offices, servants' quarters/workshops, and storerooms (long, narrow rooms like in the northern palace complex). The corridor provided access to the royal wing of the western palace, which consisted of a large courtyard surrounded by rooms that were decorated with Second Pompeian Style wall paintings. The throne room was located on the far side of the courtyard. Holes sunk into the floor in the corner of the room presumably held the legs of a throne or a table on which bronze vessels found here were displayed. Layers of ash suggest that the floor was covered with carpets, and tapestries or curtains were hung on the walls. A staircase led to a second-story level—a more private area with living quarters.

A waiting room or reception hall adjacent to the throne room is decorated with the most elaborate mosaic floor found at Masada (fig. 6). The mosaic is made of colored tesserae (cut stone cubes) and displays a rosette surrounded by bands decorated with geometric and floral motifs. The floral motifs include olives, pomegranates, and grapes, which are among the "seven species" of agricultural produce that symbolized the fertility of the Land of Israel according to biblical tradition. The seven species are depicted frequently in Jewish art of the late Second Temple period, when many Jews refrained from using the figured images that are so common in Roman art, in strict observance of the Second Commandment which prohibits the making of images for worship. It is interesting that despite Masada's remote location, Herod chose typically "Jewish" motifs to decorate his palaces and refrained from using figured images. This likely reflects Herod's concern to avoid offending Jewish visitors to Masada rather than expressing his own religious observance or leanings, as outside of Judea he dedicated pagan temples (at Caesarea and Samaria, for example).

Across the courtyard from the throne room was a suite of rooms that included another bathhouse. Instead of a hypocaust, this bathhouse had an earlier type of heating system, consisting of a bathtub supplied with heated water. The rooms of the bathhouse were paved with simple colored mosaics. One mosaic depicts a rosette and is located by the entrance to a deep but narrow stepped pool that was either a cold-water bath (frigidarium) or a *miqveh* (Jewish ritual bath). During the First Jewish Revolt, the rebels who occupied Masada installed a small, square bin (for storage or rubbish?) in the corner of this room, which cut through the mosaic with the rosette.

The Southern Part of Masada and the Water System

Just south of the western palace complex (and next to Building 11) is a large, wide, and deep, stepped and plastered pool that was installed in a quarry and is enclosed by stone walls containing square niches (fig. 25). The date of this pool—from the time of Herod or the First Revolt—and its function—as a swimming pool or *miqveh*—are debated. The niches apparently were used to store clothing while visitors were swimming or immersing. We will consider this pool again in chapter 8. Another large pool, which dates to the time of Herod and resembles swimming pools in his palaces at Jericho and Herodium, is located near the southern tip of the mountain.[10]

The southern half of Masada is less built-up than the northern part. In Herod's time, the southern half of Masada was cultivated with gardens and food crops, as Josephus describes: "For the actual top, being of rich soil and softer than any plain, was given up by the king to cultivation; in order that, should there ever be a dearth of provisions from outside, those who had committed their lives to the protection of the fortress might not suffer from it" (*War* 7.287–88).

Today the top of Masada is barren and brown, with rocky outcrops and bare stone walls, but two thousand years ago the open spaces were green and the outsides of the buildings were plastered and whitewashed.

A peculiar structure located to the south and east of the swimming pool consists of a circular stone wall with no openings. Inside, the walls contain rows of small square niches. This structure is a columbarium (dovecote). Two casemate rooms north of the Roman siege ramp also contained columbaria. Columbaria are common at Hellenistic and early Roman sites in Idumaea and Judea, attesting to the importance of pigeons and doves as sources of food (grilled pigeon is still a delicacy in many parts of the Middle East today); fertilizer (guano); communication (carrier pigeons); and for cultic purposes (doves were common offerings in the Jerusalem temple and in other ancient temples).

Close to the southern tip of Masada is a large underground cistern (fig. 26). Accessed by means of a narrow, steeply descending staircase, it is hewn entirely out of the natural hard limestone. The inside of the cistern is an enormous cavern with the staircase on one side. The staircase and the walls and floor of the cistern are covered with thick coats of plaster that prevented water seepage into the cracks of the hard stone. Horizontal lines visible on the walls of the cistern reflect fluctuations in the water level over time. The steps made it possible to descend and draw water as the level dropped and facilitated access to allow for the silt to be cleaned out from time to time. The bottom of the cistern is still covered with a thick layer of silt.

There are at least fourteen large cisterns at Masada and numerous smaller pools for storing water. The main group of cisterns is located on the northwest side of the mountain (below the northern palace), where they are arranged in two rows, one above the other. They were supplied by aqueducts that brought flash flood waters from the riverbeds on the cliffs opposite (west) of Masada. The aqueducts were at the same level as the cisterns but were buried and put out of use by the Roman assault ramp. The upper row of cisterns was accessed by a path originating in the area of the northern palace (through a gate called the "Water Gate" by the excavators), while the lower row was accessed by a path that encircled the northern end of the mountain and connected to the Snake Path gate on the east.[11] There are also cisterns on the eastern and southeastern sides of the mountain (one is by the top of the Snake Path). The cisterns on the eastern and southeastern sides of the mountain and the one on top were too high in elevation to be filled by aqueducts. Plastered channels led rainwater into these cisterns, but there is so little rainfall that most of the water was brought manually, carried by people and pack animals from other cisterns and pools.

According to Yadin, each of the large cisterns at Masada had a capacity of up to 140,000 cubic feet, with a total capacity of almost 1,400,000 cubic feet of water.[12] It has been estimated that each cistern held enough drinking water to sustain a thousand people for one year! Josephus mentions that Herod provided Masada with plenty of pools for storing water: "Moreover, at each spot used for habitation, both on the summit and about the palace, as also before the wall, he had cut out in the rock numerous large tanks, as reservoirs for water, thus procuring a supply as ample as where springs are available" (*War* 7.290–91). The abundance of fresh water on top of this remote desert mountain allowed Herod to equip his palaces with bathhouses, swimming pools, and lush gardens.

At the southern tip of Masada, Herod built a fort (designated the "southern fort" by the excavators) which blocked access by way of a steep path that ascended this side of the mountain.[13] This spot provides a spectacular view over the dry riverbed and waterfall of Nahal Masada below and Mount Eleazar rising on the other side, as well as part of the Roman siege works (including the circumvallation wall and Camps G, H, A, and B). The sheer rock face of Mount Eleazar opposite acts as a sound barrier that makes anything shouted from the southern fort echo.

JERUSALEM

History and Topography of the City

Jerusalem sits atop the watershed between the wooded Judean hills and fertile lowlands (Shephelah) to the west and the barren wilderness of Judea (Judean desert) to the east, at an elevation of 800 meters above sea level, compared with the Dead Sea at 400 meters below sea level.[14] Jerusalem's earliest settlement—some five thousand years ago—was established on a small hill that forms a spur to the south of the Temple Mount (Hebrew *har ha-bayit*; Arabic, *al-haram al-sharif* [the Noble or Sacred Enclosure]), the great esplanade in the southeast corner of the modern Old City. This small hill came to be known by several names: the City of David; the eastern hill; and the lower city. Despite its size (only about 11 acres) and relatively low elevation, Jerusalem's first inhabitants settled on this hill because of its proximity to the only perennial source of fresh water in the area: the Gihon spring, which gushes forth at the foot of the eastern slope of the City of David. The City of David offered early inhabitants the additional advantage of natural protection, consisting of the Kidron Valley to the east and, to the west, the Tyropoeon [pronounced tie-rho-PEE-un] Valley (an ancient Greek name meaning the "Valley of the Cheesemakers"; it is sometimes called the Central Valley because it begins at the modern Damascus Gate and runs south through the center of the Old City today). The Kidron and Tyropoeon valleys meet at the southern tip of the City of David. The Mount of Olives, which is the highest mountain ridge in Jerusalem, rises to the east of the Kidron Valley before dropping steeply down toward the Dead Sea. The configuration of bedrock in the City of David is such that the bedrock is lowest at the southern tip and rises steadily toward the north, culminating in a rocky outcrop that eventually became the Temple Mount.

The original settlement in Jerusalem was confined to the small hill south of the later Temple Mount, which became known as the City of David after David conquered the city (ca. 1000 BCE). David reportedly brought the Ark of the Covenant to Jerusalem and made it the capital of his kingdom. David's son and successor Solomon expanded the city to the north, building the first temple (Solomon's temple) on the Temple Mount. The temple apparently stood on a natural outcrop of bedrock (today enshrined in the Muslim Dome of the Rock), which physically dominated the City of David and transformed the Temple Mount into the city's acropolis.

By the latter part of the eighth century Jerusalem's population could no longer be accommodated on the small hill of the City of David alone. The city expanded to the west, across the Tyropoeon Valley. This area, called the western hill, is larger and higher in elevation than the City of David, and therefore is known as the upper city (in contrast to the City of David, which is the lower city). The western hill had the advantage of natural protection on three of four sides. On the east, the western hill is bounded by the Tyropoeon Valley, which separates it from the Temple Mount and City of David. On the west and south, the western hill is encircled by the Ben-Hinnom Valley, which begins by the modern Jaffa Gate (the main gate in the middle of the western side of the Old City today) and joins the Kidron and Tyropoeon valleys at the southern tip of the City of David. Only the north side of Jerusalem was not protected by deep natural valleys. Instead, a shallow ravine called the Transverse Valley marks the northern end of the western hill, running east from the modern Jaffa Gate to the Temple Mount, where it joins the Tyropoeon Valley. In antiquity Jerusalem usually was attacked from the north because of the lack of natural defenses there. For example, when the Romans besieged Jerusalem in 70 CE, they attacked from the north, although this side of the city was protected by three successive walls.

The area we have just described—the City of David, Temple Mount, and western hill—constituted the city of Jerusalem until its destruction by the Romans in 70 CE (though by then settlement had expanded to the north) (fig. 27). Nowadays many visitors to Jerusalem have the mistaken impression that the Old City is the ancient city. In fact, the current walls of the Old City date to the Ottoman period (sixteenth century CE) and they enclose only part of the original ancient city but leave outside the City of David and the southern part of the western hill (now known as Mount Zion). In other words, the walled city has shifted to the north since antiquity. This shift occurred when the Roman emperor Hadrian rebuilt Jerusalem in the second century CE as a pagan Roman city called Aelia Capitolina. The line of the current Ottoman walls reflects this later shift to the north.

Herod's Palace and the Three Towers

When Jerusalem fell to Herod in 37 BCE, the walled settlement consisted of the Temple Mount (with the second temple), the City of David, and the western hill. On the northwestern side of the western hill, Herod built a palace for himself, as he could not use the existing palace belonging to the Hasmonean family. Josephus describes Herod's palace as consisting of two wings separated by pools and gardens. Herod named the wings the Caesareum, in honor of Augustus, and the Agrippaeum, in honor of Marcus Agrippa, Augustus's son-in-law and designated heir (who died in 12 BCE, predeceasing Augustus).[15] Herod formed a close friendship with Marcus Agrippa, who visited Judea and toured Herod's kingdom in 15 BCE. Although excavations have been conducted in the area where Herod's palace was located (the modern Armenian Garden), almost no remains of the superstructure have survived.[16]

At the northwest corner of the First Wall and on the north side of his palace, Herod erected three large towers. These towers served two purposes: (1) to reinforce the city's vulnerable northern flank, which was not bounded by a deep natural valley like the other sides; and (2) to protect Herod's palace, which was surrounded by its own fortification system. Josephus tells us that Herod named the largest tower Phasael (after his older brother); the middle-sized tower Hippicus (after a friend); and the smallest tower Mariamme (after his beloved Hasmonean wife). When Jerusalem fell to the Romans in 70 CE, Titus razed two of the towers to the ground but left one standing.

Today the sole surviving Herodian tower lies inside a large fortified enclosure (called the Citadel) next to Jaffa Gate, in the middle of the western wall of the modern Old City (fig. 28). Most of the remains in the Citadel are much later than the Roman period, dating to medieval and Ottoman times. However, some earlier remains are enclosed within the Citadel, including the northwest corner of the First Wall, into which the Herodian tower is set. Only the lower part of the original tower is preserved, which is constructed of characteristic Herodian style masonry: large ashlar stones with smooth, drafted margins and a flat, paneled boss. The upper part of the tower was reconstructed later using visibly smaller stones. The current moniker, "David's Tower," reflects a popular (and incorrect) association with King David which stems from a later tradition. The tower is visible immediately to the right after entering Jaffa Gate, within the walls of the Citadel, as well as inside the courtyard of the Citadel. The tower is thought to be either Phasael or Hippicus.

The Western Hill

In the late Second Temple period, the western hill was Jerusalem's upper-class residential quarter.[17] This is where the Hasmonean and Herodian palaces were located, and where Jerusalem's wealthiest Jews lived. In addition to offering a stunning view across the Tyropoeon Valley to the Temple Mount, the western hill remains cooler in summer thanks to its relatively high elevation. Although the Hasmonean palace has not been found, excavations in the Jewish Quarter in the 1970s by the Israeli archaeologist Nahman Avigad brought to light densely packed urban villas belonging to the Jerusalem elite. The largest villa, which Avigad dubbed "the Mansion," covers an area of some 600 square meters (ca. 6,500 square feet) (fig. 29). Each villa consisted of 2–3 stories of rooms (including a basement for storage) surrounding a central courtyard. The urban villas were decorated in Roman fashion with mosaic floors, wall paintings (frescoes) in the Second Pompeian Style (a style popular in Italy in the first century CE), and stucco (plaster molded in imitation of marble panels and other architectural shapes). They were furnished with expensive Roman-style stone tables and sets of imported pottery dishes. The Mansion's occupants owned a beautiful, mold-made glass vase signed by Ennion, a famous Phoenician glassmaker.

The large size and lavish decoration of these urban villas indicate that the residents were members of the Jerusalem elite. Clearly these wealthy Jews were "Romanized"—that is, they had adopted many aspects of the Roman lifestyle. At the same time, there is evidence that they observed Jewish law. For example, the interior decoration is Roman in style but lacks the figured images that characterize Roman art. Furthermore, each villa was equipped with one or more *miqva'ot* (ritual baths) and yielded large numbers of stone (chalk) dining dishes and other stone vessels, attesting to the observance of biblical purity laws (see chapter 8). Many Jews of the late Second Temple period believed that in contrast to pottery, stone cannot contract ritual impurity. Priests were especially concerned with purity observance, as they had to be ritually pure to serve in the temple.

The large number of ritual baths and stone vessels suggests that some of the wealthy residents of the Jewish Quarter villas were priests, which is not surprising since we know that priestly families (and especially high priestly families) were members of the Jerusalem elite. Avigad discovered additional evidence of priestly presence in a villa that he dubbed "the Burnt House." This villa is so-called because the ground floor rooms (the only part of the house that survived) were covered with layers of ashy soot from its destruction at the time of the siege of Jerusalem in 70 CE. The vats, ovens, tables, and numerous stone vessels and weights point to commercial activity or workshop production. One stone weight is inscribed with the name of a known priestly family—Bar Kathros—presumably the villa's owners. On a step leading down into a kitchen, Avigad found the skeletal arm of a young woman about twenty-five years of age, who was crushed when the burning house collapsed on top of her.

The Temple Mount

The centerpiece of Herod's building program in Jerusalem was his reconstruction of the second temple, which had been consecrated in 516 BCE (fig. 30).[18] Herod rebuilt the temple itself as well as the esplanade or open platform surrounding it (the Temple Mount). Although no identifiable remains of the temple building survive, today's Temple Mount is a product of Herod's building program. Work on the temple building was carried out circa 23/20–15 BCE, but construction on the massive complex surrounding it continued until 64 CE, a situation alluded to by the author of the Fourth Gospel: "Jesus answered them, 'Destroy this temple, and in three days I will raise it up.' The Jews then said, 'This temple has been under construction for forty-six years, and will you raise it up in three days?'" (John 2:18–19).

Herod monumentalized the temple building by expanding the esplanade on which it stood (the Temple Mount), creating one of the largest sacred precincts in the ancient world (ca. 140,000 square meters or 1,507,000 square feet or 34.5 acres). To level the platform, the bedrock had to be cut back on the north, where it rises. To the south, where the bedrock drops toward the City of David, the expanded platform was supported on a series of underground arches or vaults called a cryptoporticus. Herod enclosed the expanded platform with a temenos wall (the Greek word *temenos* refers to a sacred precinct). The upper part of the temenos wall was decorated with engaged pilasters (square pillars built into the wall), which broke up the monotony of the masonry by creating a play of light and shadow in the bright sunlight. The Western ("Wailing") Wall is part of Herod's temenos wall around the Temple Mount, not part of the temple building itself (which was located on top of the platform, approximately where the Dome of the Rock sits today).

A number of gates in the temenos wall provided access to the Temple Mount, several of which are still visible today, specifically (from north to south): Wilson's Arch, Barclay's Gate, Robinson's Arch (all on the west side of the Temple Mount), and the Hulda Gates (on the south side of the Temple Mount). The Herodian Temple Mount was a huge, open, paved space surrounded on the east, north, and west sides by colonnaded porches that provided shelter from sun and rain for the masses of pilgrims. A monumental, two-story-high building called the Royal Stoa or Royal Basilica occupied the southern end (encompassing the area occupied today by al-Aqsa mosque, but much larger). In the Roman world, a basilica was a rectangular structure with rows of columns inside, which functioned as an all-purpose public building to accommodate various kinds of assemblies. The temple building—of which nothing survives—stood in the center of the Temple Mount, apparently on a natural outcrop of bedrock that is enshrined today in the Dome of the Rock. The temple building was surrounded by its own fortification wall and towers, and was approached through two successive courtyards, the outer one accessible to Jewish women and men and the inner one to Jewish men (fig. 31). Only priests were allowed beyond this into the temple building.

Among the remains surviving from the second temple are two Greek inscriptions that originally were set into a low stone fence or barrier (called the *soreg*) which surrounded the temple's fortifications on the Temple Mount. They were discovered at different times and locations near the Temple Mount. The complete inscription is in the Istanbul Archaeological Museum, and a second, fragmentary inscription is in the Israel Museum in Jerusalem (fig. 32). They were among a series of Greek and Latin inscriptions warning gentiles not to enter the temple on pain of death. The complete inscription says: "No foreigner is to enter within the balustrade and forecourt around the sacred precinct. Whoever is caught will himself be responsible for (his) consequent death." Josephus provides remarkably similar descriptions of the *soreg* inscriptions: "Proceeding across this towards the second court of the temple, one found it surrounded by a stone balustrade, three cubits high and of exquisite workmanship; in this at regular intervals stood slabs giving warning, some in Greek, others in Latin characters, of the law of purification, to wit that no foreigner was permitted to enter the holy place, for so the second enclosure of the temple was called" (*War* 5.193–94; also see *Ant.* 15:417).[19]

Although today we tend to think of the Temple Mount exclusively in religious terms, it was a center of commercial activity as well. The thousands of visitors included not only Jewish pilgrims but gentiles (who could access the Temple Mount but not the temple). The enormous esplanade, with the Royal Stoa and porticoes, bustled with merchants and vendors, many of them selling sacrificial animals and birds. In fact, Herod's Temple Mount was analogous to ancient agoras or forums (marketplaces), which typically consisted of a large, open paved space surrounded by public buildings such as stoas, basilicas, and theaters, and a temple to the patron deity in the center. For example, the Capitolium (temple of Capitoline Jupiter) dominates the forum at Pompeii, with Mount Vesuvius towering above in the distance.[20]

The Antonia Fortress and Via Dolorosa

At the northwest corner of the Temple Mount, Herod erected a massive fortress that he named the Antonia in honor of Mark Antony (indicating it was built before Antony's defeat at the battle of Actium in 31 BCE).[21] The fortress, which was garrisoned with gentile soldiers, sat on a natural high point overlooking the Temple Mount. Herod knew that he was not popular among the Jewish population, and he considered the masses of pilgrims on the Temple Mount a potential threat and source of unrest. The Antonia was intended to deter such activity and housed troops to quell any uprisings or trouble.

Although Josephus provides a description of the Antonia, its dimensions have been the subject of debate. Today, the area where the Antonia was located is bisected by a road called the Via Dolorosa, which is parallel to the northern side of the Temple Mount. The Via Dolorosa (Italian for Way of Sorrow) is so named because, according to Christian tradition, this is the route along which Jesus carried his cross, beginning with his sentencing by Pontius Pilate and ending with his crucifixion and burial (now enshrined within the Church of the Holy Sepulcher). A convent called the Church of the Sisters of Zion lies along the north side of the Via Dolorosa today. During the construction of the convent in the late nineteenth century, a series of ancient remains came to light. The remains consist of large pools or cisterns called the Struthion (Greek for sparrow) pools, which are overlaid by a stone pavement (today identified as the Lithostratos pavement), and a monumental, triple-arched gateway sitting on top of the pavement (today called the arch of Ecce Homo). The pavement and arched gateway are identified with places where, according to the Gospel of John, Jesus was sentenced by Pontius Pilate and clothed with a purple robe and a crown of thorns:

> When Pilate heard these words, he brought Jesus outside and sat on the judge's bench at a place called The Stone Pavement (*lithostratos*). (John 19:13)

> So Jesus came out, wearing the crown of thorns and the purple robe. Pilate said to them, "Behold the man" (*ecce homo*)! (John 19:5)

These remains were long thought to be part of the Antonia, with the pools used for water storage inside the fortress, the pavement belonging to an inner courtyard, and the arched gateway providing access to the fortress. If these remains were part of the Antonia, there would be no contradiction with current Christian tradition, since the Antonia was built more than half a century before Jesus's death. However, scholars now agree that the Antonia was much smaller than previously thought and did not extend to the area north of the Via Dolorosa, thereby excluding the remains in the Church of the Sisters of Zion. Furthermore, only the Struthion pools antedate 70 CE, and they were located in an open moat outside the Antonia fortress. The arch and pavement are part of a forum that the emperor Hadrian established on this spot in the second century CE. The so-called Lithostratos pavement and arch of Ecce Homo cannot be identified with the places mentioned by John because they did not exist in the time of Jesus.

Today the Via Dolorosa begins on the north side of the Temple Mount because, according to current Christian tradition, this is where Jesus took up the cross after being sentenced to death by Pontius Pilate. In other words, modern Christian tradition identifies the Antonia as the place where Jesus was sentenced to death. However, the Gospel accounts refer to the praetorium, not the Antonia: "Then the soldiers of the governor took Jesus into the praetorium" (Mt 27:27). The praetorium—the palace of the Roman governor in Jerusalem—was Herod's palace, not the Antonia fortress. Therefore, Jesus would have been sentenced to death and taken up the cross not in the area to the north of the Temple Mount, but on the western side of the city. This means that the route walked by Jesus is different than the one walked by modern pilgrims (the Via Dolorosa). Today's route is based on later Christian tradition.

Caesarea Maritima

History of the City

The small town of Straton's Tower was established during the Persian period, when the Palestinian coast was governed by the Phoenician kings of Tyre and Sidon. The town was part of the territory that Herod received after the battle of Actium in 31 BCE, when Octavian reconfirmed Herod as king of Judea and increased the size of his kingdom. Herod rebuilt Straton's Tower as a showcase Greco-Roman port city and renamed it Caesarea—a brilliant move demonstrating his loyalty to his new patron.[22] Herod's city of Caesarea had two components: the land settlement, called Caesarea, and the harbor, called Sebaste (*sebastos* is Greek for Augustus) (fig. 33). Because Palestine's coastline lacks large natural harbors and anchorages, Caesarea quickly became the country's major port city.

Caesarea had a long history and flourished for centuries. Its importance increased after Herod's son Herod Archelaus was removed from rule in 6 CE and it became the seat of the local Roman governor (prefect or procurator) in Palestine. After he was arrested, Paul was imprisoned in the Roman governor's palace at Caesarea for two years, before being shipped off to Rome for trial and (presumably) execution (Acts 23:23–24, 33). Caesarea was a Greco-Roman city with a large gentile population and a minority of Jews. By Paul's time, the inhabitants also included some members of the early church (Acts 21:8, 15–16). The First Revolt erupted at Caesarea in 66 CE as a result of tensions between Jews and gentiles there (see chapter 7).

Vespasian made Caesarea the headquarters of his operations during the First Jewish Revolt. After the revolt, Vespasian raised Caesarea to the rank of a Roman colony. In the centuries that followed, Caesarea continued to grow, reaching its maximum extent during the fifth and sixth centuries CE (the Byzantine period). Caesarea was the last major city in Palestine to fall to the Muslims, surrendering in 640 CE after a seven-month-long siege. Although Caesarea contracted in size after the Muslim conquest, it remained an important commercial hub, as indicated by large quantities of pottery imported from around the Mediterranean. Caesarea was conquered during the First Crusade (1101) and became a key stronghold of the Crusader kingdom in the Holy Land. The Genoese found a green-colored glass vessel in the city and declared it to be the Holy Grail, the goblet used by Jesus at the Last Supper. The goblet was taken to Genoa and placed in the Church of San Lorenzo. Caesarea fell to Saladin in 1187 and was retaken by the Crusaders in 1191. When the Mamluke ruler Baybars conquered Caesarea in 1265, he razed it to the ground, ending the city's long history. In the 1880s, the Ottomans settled Bosnian refugees at Caesarea (Kaisariyeh). This settlement existed until the establishment of the state of Israel in 1948; some descendants of the Bosnian families still live in the nearby Israeli town of Hadera. After 1948, the Israeli authorities cleared and restored the Crusader fortification walls and moat.

The Harbor (Sebastos)

Herod's harbor at Caesarea (ca. 23–15 BCE) was an amazing engineering feat that resulted in the largest artificial harbor ever built in the open sea to that point (fig. 7).[23] It consisted of a large outer harbor and a smaller, more sheltered inner harbor with two basins (a middle basin and an inner basin). The harbor was created by building two breakwaters extending out into the sea. The breakwaters protected boats from rough waters and created a barrier against the prevailing currents, which come from the south and bring sand from the Nile Delta. For this reason, the southern breakwater was much longer (ca. 600 meters or 2,000 feet) than the northern one (ca. 250 meters or 800 feet). Passage through the breakwaters was from the northwest. Silting was a constant problem, kept at bay only by the repeated dredging of the harbor in antiquity. By the early

Islamic period, the inner harbor had silted up and was covered with buildings. Since then, earthquakes, the rising level of the Mediterranean, and a possible tsunami have submerged both breakwaters.

Underwater excavations at Caesarea indicate that the breakwaters were constructed using the latest innovations in Roman concrete technology. Herod imported hydraulic concrete from Italy, which contained a special type of volcanic ash that allowed the concrete mixture to harden underwater. To make the breakwaters, Herod's engineers constructed enormous wooden boxes or formworks, which were towed out into the open sea. The concrete mixture was poured into the formworks, causing them to sink to the sea floor, where the concrete hardened. A series of buildings were constructed on top of the breakwaters, including *horrea* (sgl. *horreum*), which were warehouses for storing the goods brought in and out of the harbor. Towers at the ends of the breakwaters marked the entrance to the harbor. One of them was a lighthouse that Herod modeled after the Pharos of Alexandria—one of the seven wonders of the ancient world—and that he named the Drusion, in honor of Augustus's stepson Drusus (and father of the emperor Claudius). *Horrea* continued to the south of the harbor, where one was converted into a Mithraeum in the late first century CE (a Mithraeum is a shrine dedicated to Mithras, a Near Eastern deity whose cult was especially popular among Roman soldiers).

Caesarea's Temples

Towering over Caesarea's harbor, Herod built a temple dedicated to Roma (the goddess of the city of Rome) and Augustus—another demonstration of Herod's loyalty to his new patron. The temple stood on an elevated artificial platform (called the Temple Platform or Area TP by the expedition team) overlooking the inner harbor. Herod's temple to Roma and Augustus was constructed in an Italic rather than Hellenistic style. The Italic features include the placement of the temple on a tall, raised podium accessed by steps only on the west (with the porch facing the harbor and Rome), creating an axiality and frontality that differ from Greek temples. The few surviving fragments of the superstructure indicate that the temple was built of kurkar (local sandstone) covered with stucco. The column capitals were Corinthian.

Herod's reconstruction of the Jerusalem temple presumably was motivated by genuine piety as well as by political considerations (an attempt to win the loyalty of the Jewish population). Similarly, Herod's dedication of the temple at Caesarea was intended to demonstrate his loyalty to Augustus and Rome. Although we tend to think of Herod as a Jewish (or, at least, half-Jewish) king, he apparently had no qualms about establishing a pagan temple at Caesarea. Herod dedicated other temples to Roma and Augustus at Samaria (see below) and at Banyas (Paneas), and according to Josephus, he built or restored pagan temples in Tyre, Berytus (Beirut), and on Rhodes (the temple of Pythian Apollo). In other words, Herod dedicated numerous temples within his kingdom and abroad, to the Jewish God (in Jerusalem) as well as to pagan deities and the Roman emperor. All these projects likely were motivated as much by piety as by political concerns, and they hint at Roman influence on Herod's worldview as the Romans believed that all gods should be treated with respect.[24]

Statues discovered around Caesarea indicate that there were other temples, the locations of which are still unknown. In 1961, an Italian expedition made a chance discovery in the ancient theater (see below). During the excavations, they dislodged a stone that was in secondary use (reused). The stone's underside bears a dedicatory inscription referring to an otherwise unknown temple that was dedicated by Pontius Pilate to Tiberius, the emperor at the time (fig. 34). As the Roman prefect (governor) of Judea from 26–36 CE, Pontius Pilate's main palace and administrative base were at Caesarea. According to the Gospel accounts, Pilate sentenced Jesus to death by crucifixion. The Caesarea inscription is the only archaeological artifact discovered so far that is associated directly with Pontius Pilate, aside from small bronze coins which he minted (but do not bear his name).

By the fifth and sixth centuries, most of Caesarea's population was Christian. At this time, Herod's temple to Roma and Augustus was replaced by an octagonal church, perhaps dedicated to St. Procopius, the city's first martyr. At some time during the early Islamic period, this church was destroyed or abandoned and replaced by a Great Mosque. Later, when the Crusaders occupied Caesarea, they established the Cathedral of St. Peter on the Temple Platform, the apses of which still stand today (an apse is a curved niche at the end of a basilical hall).

Jerusalem's Temple Mount and the Temple Platform at Caesarea illustrate a well-known archaeological principle called the continuity of cult, which means that once a spot becomes holy or sacred, it tends to retain its sanctity over time even if the religions change.

The Palaces

A palace built by Herod was spectacularly situated on a natural promontory jutting out into the sea south of the harbor and the Crusader city. The centerpiece of the promontory palace was a large fish pool. Rows of columns surrounded the pool on all four sides, creating a peristyle porch with the open-air pool in the center. The pool was on the lower part of the promontory, with another part of the palace located on a higher terrace to the east.

The area between the Crusader city and the promontory palace was filled with spacious, richly decorated villas or mansions that belonged to the Roman and Byzantine governing elite. The villas were abandoned after the Muslim conquest and buried under sand dunes. Long before large-scale excavations began in this area in the 1990s, the discovery of an "archives building" immediately to the south of the Crusader city hinted that this was an elite quarter. The archives building consists of seven rooms surrounding a central courtyard. Inscriptions in the mosaic floors identify this as the office where accountants of the imperial governor's tax department kept their records. The inscriptions remind citizens of their civic duty by citing passages from the New Testament such as Paul's Letter to the Romans (13:3): "Do you wish to have no fear of the authority [the governor]? Then do what is good, and you will receive its approval." Another villa nearby was paved with a beautiful mosaic floor depicting personifications of the four seasons. During the Byzantine period, new buildings were erected in this quarter, including a large public bathhouse, a palace, and a basilica (perhaps a church).

The Entertainment Arenas and City Walls

Large-scale excavations in the 1990s to the south of the Crusader city brought to light a hippodrome from the time of Herod the Great. The hippodrome was located alongside the sea, north of and adjacent to

Fig. 1. Aerial view of Masada looking north.

Fig. 2. Aerial view of Masada looking east, with the assault ramp visible on its western side.

Fig. 3. View of Machaerus, with Masada visible across the Dead Sea to the left.

Fig. 4. The lower terrace of the northern palace at Masada.

Fig. 5. The apodyterium in Herod's large bathhouse at Masada.

Fig. 6. Mosaic floor in Herod's western palace at Masada.

Fig. 7. Aerial photo of the harbor at Caesarea.

Fig. 8. View of Herodium.

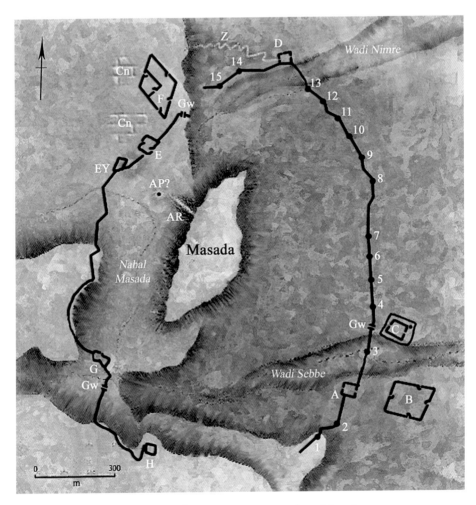

Fig. 9. Plan of the Roman siege works at Masada.

Fig. 10. View of Camp F at Masada looking west.

Fig. 11. Painted amphoriskos from the praetorium in Camp F at Masada.

Fig. 12. Contubernium in Camp F at Masada, with a book on the bench for scale.

Fig. 13. Iron arrowhead from Yadin's excavations at Masada.

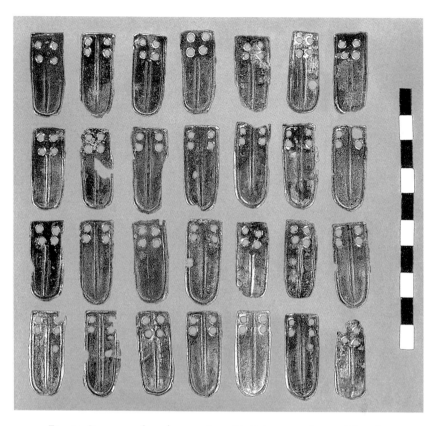

Fig. 14. Bronze scales of armor from Yadin's excavations at Masada.

Fig. 15. Scabbard chape from Yadin's excavations at Masada.

Fig. 16. View of Cave 4 at Qumran.

Fig. 17. A *miqveh* (ritual bath) at Qumran.

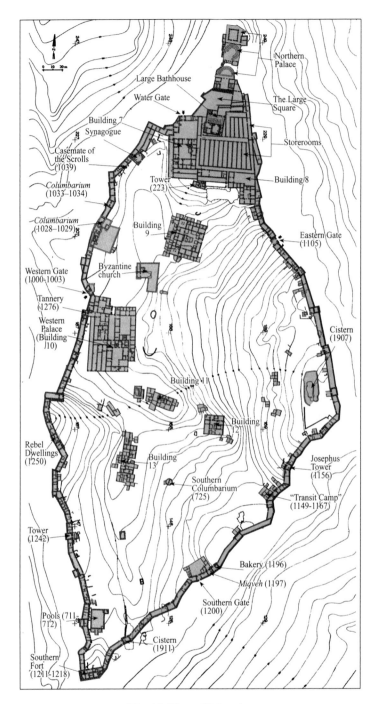

Fig. 18. Plan of Masada.

Fig. 19. Plan of Masada and its surroundings.

Fig. 20. View of the northern palace complex at Masada looking south.

Fig. 21. The massive, white-plastered stone wall that separated Herod's northern palace at Masada from the rest of the mountain.

Fig. 22. The caldarium in Herod's large bathhouse at Masada.

Fig. 23. Aerial view of the storerooms in Herod's northern palace at Masada.

Herod's promontory palace. It was bordered on the east by the palatial villa quarter, which overlooked it—an arrangement reminiscent of Rome, where the imperial palaces on the Palatine Hill overlooked the Circus Maximus. The hippodrome was a long, narrow arena with starting gates (*carceres*) at the north end and a curved southern end, surrounded by banks of seats. It was used for chariot races and perhaps foot races as well.

In the second century CE, apparently during Hadrian's reign, a new hippodrome was built at some distance to the east (the Herodian hippodrome continued to function but was used for various purposes, including as an amphitheater for animal and gladiator fights). Although it is now covered by agricultural fields of the local kibbutz, the outline of the Hadrianic hippodrome is clearly visible in aerial photographs. Parts of the spina (spine)—the wall that ran down the middle of the race course and around which the horses and chariots raced—still survive in the kibbutz fields, together with stone monoliths and obelisks that originally stood on it.

To the south of the promontory palace, Herod built a Roman-style theater overlooking the sea. The theater seated about five thousand people on banks of seats supported by stone arches and vaults. The theater and hippodrome were an integral part of Caesarea's elite quarter, which included the palaces of the Roman and Byzantine governors. Although most of the Herodian city is still unexcavated, there are indications that it had an orthogonal layout, with a grid of north-south and east-west streets. The fortification wall of the Herodian city extended from two pre-Herodian round towers on the north to the theater on the south. By the fifth century, a new wall encompassing a much larger area was built, attesting to the continued growth of the city. After the Muslim conquest, the elite quarter was abandoned and eventually covered with sand dunes, as mentioned above. By the Crusader period the settlement had contracted to a fraction of the Herodian city, centering on the Temple Platform and inner harbor.

On the northeastern side of the city, the outlines of an amphitheater are visible among the agricultural fields. The amphitheater lies at the edge of the Herodian city, but well within the expanded walls built in the fifth century CE. The oval arena must have been used for animal and gladiator fights.

Aqueducts

Roman cities were characterized by an abundance of fresh running water, sometimes brought from great distances by aqueducts. Fountains dotted the streets of Roman cities, and the water that overflowed carried garbage and debris into underground sewers. Water also supplied the public and private bathhouses that were a feature of Roman life. Although many people visualize Roman aqueducts as huge bridges carried on arches (like the Pont du Gard in France), in reality an aqueduct is simply a water channel. Although sometimes Roman aqueducts employed siphons to pump water upward, in most cases the water flowed naturally through the channel along a gentle downward slope. To maintain the level of the flow (in cases where the ground level dropped), an arched bridge was built to support the channel. If there were hills or mountains in the way, the channel could be cut as an underground tunnel. Water channels usually were covered with stone slabs, which could be removed from time to time to clean out accumulations of silt and lime.

Like a typical Roman city, Herod provisioned Caesarea with plenty of fresh water brought by aqueduct. The water came from springs in the Carmel Mountains to the northeast. To maintain a gentle downward slope, with the steep drop from the mountains to the sea, Herod's aqueduct (the high-level aqueduct) was carried on an arched bridge built of stone. Long stretches of this aqueduct still survive on the beach north of Caesarea (fig. 35).[25] The aqueduct entered the city as a water channel running under the gate between the two round towers. As Caesarea's population grew, so did the need for water. In the second century CE, Hadrian doubled the amount of available water by building a second channel alongside Herod's, supported by another arched bridge that abutted Herod's original aqueduct. Dedicatory inscriptions set into Hadrian's aqueduct indicate that it was constructed by Roman legionary soldiers stationed in the vicinity.

In the fourth century CE, a new aqueduct (the low-level aqueduct) was constructed. Unlike the high-level aqueduct, this channel originated in the marshy delta of the Tanninim (Crocodile) River, just a few miles north of Caesarea. The low-level aqueduct was created by damming the river, which was diverted into the channel. The aqueduct is so-called because an arched bridge was not necessary in this case to maintain the level of the water. Instead, the channel ran just above ground level.

Sprawling country villas belonging to wealthy families were scattered throughout the rich agricultural landscape outside Caesarea's walls. Part of one such villa was discovered accidentally and excavated in 1950 to the northeast of Caesarea. It included a lavish mosaic with medallions containing depictions of exotic animals, apparently the floor of a large peristyle courtyard. In the same area a luxurious bathhouse dating to the end of the Byzantine period was found, which included a fish pond (*piscina*) for freshwater fish that could be caught and served to the bathers.

SAMARIA-SEBASTE

After the Samarians (the Yahwistic population of the district of Samaria) revolted against Alexander the Great, he banished them from the city of Samaria, the former capital of the northern kingdom of Israel, and settled Macedonian veterans there. Therefore, by Herod's time Samaria, like Caesarea, was a non-Jewish city. Like Caesarea, Herod rebuilt Samaria after the battle of Actium, naming it Sebaste (Sebastos) in honor of Augustus (fig. 36).[26] There are many other parallels between Herod's cities of Caesarea and Samaria. For example, atop the ancient Israelite acropolis at Samaria, Herod established an Italian-style temple dedicated to Roma and Augustus. The temple stood on an elevated podium with steps on the front and was oriented to the south like typical Roman temples. It was located in the center of a large, open platform that was supported along the sides by underground arches and vaults. A small theater on the north side of the acropolis had seating on the natural slope of the hill. A temple dedicated to Kore was located on a terrace to the north, just below the acropolis. Kore (or Persephone) was the daughter of the goddess Demeter, and her cult was associated with fertility.

The city was surrounded by a wall, with a main gate on the west flanked by round towers. The gate led to a (later) colonnaded street that bisected the city from west to east and was overlooked by the acropolis to the north. A stadium (or, according to a more recent theory, a peristyle courtyard) lay in a flat plain at the northern edge of the city. An inscription on an altar found in the stadium or courtyard was dedicated to Kore by a high priest. To the east of the acropolis was a forum with a basilica along the west side. An aqueduct brought water into the city from springs to the east.

HERODIAN JERICHO (ARABIC NAME: TULUL ABU AL-ʾALAYIQ)

Jericho is a desert oasis to the northwest of the Dead Sea. The Hasmonean kings established a series of winter palaces at Jericho because of its warm climate, abundance of freshwater springs, and proximity to Jerusalem (only 17 miles or 27 kilometers away). The Hasmonean palaces included luxuriously appointed living quarters (decorated with frescoes, stucco, and mosaics), lush gardens, and swimming pools, as well as numerous *miqvaʾot*—not surprising since the Hasmonean kings also served as high priests. Herod followed suit by constructing three successive palace complexes adjacent to those of the Hasmoneans. Herod's Third Palace at Jericho—the largest and most elaborate of the series—straddled the banks of Wadi Qelt, a riverbed fed by perennial freshwater springs. The palace itself was located on the north bank and included an enormous reception hall decorated with frescoes, mosaics, *opus sectile* (colored tile) pavements, and a Roman-style bathhouse (fig. 37). Across the riverbed, on the south bank, was a large garden with stoas (colonnaded porches) on either side, which was connected to the north bank by a bridge. Flowerpots were discovered in the excavations in the garden. A huge swimming pool lay to the east of the garden, overlooked by a building on a nearby hill, the function of which is unknown.

Herod's Third Palace at Jericho was constructed by combining Roman concrete technology with the local building material—mud brick. The walls were built of concrete faced with mud bricks laid in a distinctive net pattern called *opus reticulatum* (reticulate work) (fig. 38). The mud bricks were covered with plaster and then painted with frescoes. This distinctive Roman construction technique has been discovered in only three places in Israel: Herod's Third Palace at Jericho; a Herodian palace at Banyas (in Upper Galilee); and a mausoleum (apparently associated with Herod's family) north of the Damascus Gate in Jerusalem. Because Roman concrete technology was unfamiliar to the local population, architects or workmen from Italy must have participated in these projects. The Israeli archaeologist Ehud Netzer, who excavated the

Hasmonean and Herodian palaces at Jericho, suggested that this exchange occurred in the wake of Marcus Agrippa's visit to Herod's kingdom in 15 BCE.[27]

About one mile from the palaces, Herod established a public arena that included a stadium with theater seating at one end. To protect the palaces, Herod built a fortress atop a mountain overlooking the outlet of Wadi Qelt, which he named Cypros in honor of his mother. Like Herod's other fortified desert palaces (such as Masada, Machaerus, and Hyrcania), Cypros was equipped with lavishly decorated palatial quarters, storerooms for food and cisterns for water, and a Roman-style bathhouse.

HERODIUM

Unlike his other building projects, Herod named Herodium after himself, apparently because he planned it as his final resting place and everlasting memorial.[28] And indeed, the distinctive, cone-shaped mountain (which Josephus describes as breast-shaped) still dominates the landscape around Bethlehem and is visible from Jerusalem and Machaerus (fig. 8). Herodium was a sprawling complex consisting of a fortified palace atop the mountain (Upper Herodium), and another palace and administrative complex at its base (Lower Herodium). It was established at a spot where, in 40 BCE, Herod and his family successfully fought off an attack by local villagers as they fled to Masada in the wake of the Parthian invasion (Josephus, *War* 1.265; *Ant.* 14.359–60). Years later, Herod commemorated the victory by building Herodium.

Herodium is a feat of engineering: an artificial mountain created by piling huge quantities of earth around two concentric stone walls that were built on a natural hill. The concentric walls were several stories high, with vaulted stone passages one above another inside them. Four stone towers oriented toward the cardinal points were set into the towers, the eastern one round and the others semicircular. The palace atop Upper Herodium was set into a huge depression inside the circular walls, resembling the mouth of a volcano. Within the depression, the palace was laid out axially, with the eastern half consisting of a large peristyle garden with *exedrae* (semicircular niches which perhaps contained statues) in the north, east, and south walls. The western half of the palace was divided into two equal parts: a bathhouse on the north and palace rooms on the south. The bathhouse is a modest-sized but well-equipped Roman-style facility with a hypocaust heating system, while the centerpiece of the palace rooms was a large triclinium. At the time of the First Revolt, Jewish rebels converted the triclinium into a synagogue. Only bits and pieces of the original décor of the palace—frescoes, stucco, and mosaics—survive. However, the tepidarium (warm room) of the bathhouse is still covered by the original stone dome.

A large administrative palace complex is located on the lower slope of Herodium facing Jerusalem. It was built on a terrace above a long, narrow hippodrome that was dominated by a monumental building at one end. The complex overlooks an enormous pool (ca. 69 × 45 meters or 225 × 150 feet) which was surrounded by a peristyle with extensive gardens. The pool had a circular pavilion in the center and was used for boating as well as bathing. It was supplied by aqueducts that brought water from springs in the area of Bethlehem. The lush green of the gardens and sparkling water in the pool would have created a stark contrast with the arid desert environment—a visual statement of power and abundance.

Upper and Lower Herodium were connected by a broad staircase that ascended the northwest side. Josephus relates that when Herod died in his palace at Jericho in 4 BCE, a procession brought his body to Herodium for burial. Netzer, who began excavating at Lower Herodium in the 1970s, spent decades searching for Herod's tomb, the location of which remained a mystery. Some scholars believed that Herod was buried at the top of the mountain or inside it, while Netzer thought it might be in or around the monumental building by the hippodrome. Finally, in 2007, Netzer found the tomb about midway down the north slope of the mountain, on the side facing Jerusalem (fig. 39).[29] The tomb (described by the excavators as a mausoleum) was marked by a massive stone tholos (circular structure) on a raised square podium. The high quality of the carved stone decoration of the tholos and the stone sarcophagus (coffin) fragments found nearby is unparalleled elsewhere in Israel, leaving little doubt that this is the tomb of Herod, despite the absence of inscriptions confirming the identification.[30]

Netzer's excavations on the slope around the tomb have indicated that it was part of a much larger complex of buildings that included a small theater. One room behind the theater (called the Royal Room by the excavators) is decorated with an exquisite fresco depicting figures in a sacro-idyllic landscape, painted in a trompe l'oeil window on the wall—a Roman-style painting of the highest quality that has no parallels in Israel. According to Netzer, upon Herod's death all the structures on the side of the mountain except the tomb were buried in earth, creating a gigantic burial mound (tumulus) visible for miles around. Netzer suggested that Herod's sarcophagus was smashed to bits by angry Jews shortly after his death. Josephus's failure to refer to the exact location of Herod's burial—or indeed, provide any description of the tholos marking it—indicate that it might have been forgotten by his time.

CHAPTER 5

JUDEA BEFORE HEROD

In this chapter we review the history of Judea leading up to Herod's reign, including the beliefs and customs of its inhabitants—the Judeans or "Jews." The events described here provide background for understanding the story of Masada.[1]

THE BACKGROUND: ISRAELITES, JEWS, AND THE JERUSALEM TEMPLE

The Israelite tribes are thought to have settled in Canaan around 1200 BCE. Scholars disagree about whether or to what degree the biblical account of the early Israelite settlement is historical, and many believe that some of the Israelites were Canaanites who had been in the country all along. Nevertheless, archaeological and literary evidence indicates that the next couple of centuries witnessed the emergence of a people called Israel who eventually united under the rule of a monarch and worshipped a patron deity named YHWH (usually vocalized Yahweh)—the God of Israel. According to the Hebrew Bible, the Israelite king Solomon built a house for YHWH—the first temple—on Jerusalem's sacred mountain, the Temple Mount. After Solomon's death circa 930 BCE, his kingdom split into two. The southern part became the kingdom of Judah, with its capital at Jerusalem. The northern part became the kingdom of Israel, with its capital (eventually) at the city of Samaria. In 722 BCE, the Assyrians conquered the northern kingdom of Israel and uprooted the elite. These exiles were absorbed among other peoples and became known as the "Ten Lost Tribes." In 586 BCE, Judah fell to the Babylonians, who destroyed Solomon's temple and exiled the Jerusalem elite. Sixty years later, the Persians (who took over the Babylonian Empire) granted the Judahite exiles permission to return to their homeland and rebuild the Jerusalem temple. This temple—the second temple—was consecrated in 516 BCE and destroyed by the Romans in 70 CE.

The religion of the Judahite exiles and their descendants is generally referred to as early Judaism, as opposed to Israelite religion before 586 BCE, although both are characterized by the worship of YHWH as the God of Israel. Our post-Enlightenment worldview, contemporary Western lifestyle, and lumping together of "Judeo-Christian" into one tradition have obscured the differences between Israelite religion and early Judaism on the one hand, and modern Judaism and Christianity on the other. In fact, Israelite religion and early Judaism had much more in common with other religions of the ancient Mediterranean world and Near East (modern Middle East).[2] Although ancient peoples worshiped many different gods and goddesses, usually one deity was worshiped above all others as a special protector. For example, Athens was named after the city's patron goddess, Athena. Archaeological, biblical, and epigraphic (inscriptional) evidence indicates that the early Israelites worshiped other gods in addition to the God of Israel as their chief deity.[3] Eventually some Israelites (and later, all Jews) came to believe that the God of Israel is a jealous deity who will not tolerate the worship of other gods alongside him. This does not necessarily mean they were monotheistic, which is the belief that only one God exists. Instead, at least some of them were monolatrous, meaning they worshiped only one God without denying the existence of other gods. To turn their backs on other deities, the Israelites and Jews had to believe that the God of Israel was omnipotent—more powerful than all the others combined—and therefore would protect them if they obeyed his will.

Today many Westerners believe that God is everywhere around us all the time and always accessible through prayer. But ancient peoples—including the Israelites and most Jews in the Second Temple period—did not believe that the gods dwelled among them. Instead, gods inhabited the heavens (celestial deities) or lived underground (chthonic deities). The God of Israel was a celestial deity as indicted by his epithet "the Most

High God," which is why Israelites and Jews interacted with him on mountaintops such as Mount Sinai and Jerusalem's Temple Mount.[4] To induce the gods to help humans, for example to provide protection or bring rain, they had to be enticed to leave their celestial or underground settings. This was done by offering sacrifices of the most costly and desirable foods. Celestial deities typically were offered meat—the most precious food in antiquity—which was burned on an altar so the smoke would reach the heavens and attract the god. Liquid offerings such as wine and oil usually were poured into the ground for chthonic deities.

Once the deity was enticed by sacrificial offerings, it was necessary to provide a means of interaction with humans. Priests served as intermediaries between humans and gods, and serviced the needs of the gods by feeding, clothing, and bathing them.[5] Cult statues were not deities but instead embodied the god's presence, thereby providing the means for human interaction. The cult statue was kept in a temple—literally the deity's house—which generally was larger and more elaborate than human dwellings. The Hebrew term for the Jerusalem temple is "the house," and the Temple Mount is "the mountain of the house." Ancient temples were the opposite of modern synagogues, churches, and mosques, which are congregational halls of prayer and worship. Most ancient people never entered the temple building because it was the deity's house. Only priests went inside to service the deity's needs. Everyone else congregated outside around an altar where priests offered sacrifices on their behalf. The decoration on ancient Greek temples such as the Parthenon is concentrated on the outside because that is the part of the building most people saw.

This is exactly how the first and second Jerusalem temples operated: as the house of the God of Israel, which only priests could enter, with sacrifices offered by priests on an altar outside the building. Sacrifices were offered in the Jerusalem temple around the clock to keep the God of Israel dwelling in his people's midst. However, unlike other ancient religions, Israelites and Jews came to believe that the God of Israel was too powerful to be represented in physical form or embodied within a statue. Therefore, there was no cult statue in the Jerusalem temple; instead, God's presence was simply thought to dwell within the innermost room, the Holy of Holies.[6]

Typically, each ancient god was worshiped at more than one temple. For example, numerous temples around the Roman Empire were dedicated to the Romans' chief deity, Capitoline Jupiter. In contrast, Deuteronomy—the fifth book of Moses—mandates that there should be only one temple to the God of Israel, which Jews came to locate on Jerusalem's Temple Mount. Nevertheless, other temples dedicated to the God of Israel existed in antiquity, including two in Egypt, one of which operated until 73 CE (see below).[7]

THE MACCABEES

By 331 BCE, Judea (the district around Jerusalem, which was the core of the former kingdom of Judah), together with the rest of the Persian Empire, had come under the rule of Alexander the Great. After Alexander's death in 323 BCE, Judea became part of the kingdoms of his Greek successors: the Ptolemies (based in Egypt) and the Seleucids (based in Syria). Administratively, Judea was a semi-autonomous unit within these kingdoms, with the Jews governed by a council of elders (*Gerousia*), and biblical Jewish law (the laws in the Torah/Pentateuch/Five Books of Moses) constituting the law of the land by royal command.[8] The Greeks referred to the native population of Judea as *Ioudaioi*, a term that can be translated as Judeans (emphasizing the geographical dimension of their origin) or Jews (emphasizing the religious dimension of their lifestyle).[9] This means that by royal mandate the inhabitants of Judea were obligated to worship the God of Israel as their national deity and observe his laws (the laws in the Torah). Although many Greeks and Romans considered Jewish customs such as circumcision, abstention from pork, and Sabbath observance peculiar, they respected Judaism as an ancient religion and referred to the laws in the Torah as "the ancestral laws of the Jews."[10]

Despite the freedom (and indeed the obligation) to observe biblical law, Jews were influenced to varying degrees by Greek culture.[11] Under Alexander and his successors, Greek customs spread throughout the Near East, affecting all aspects of life including language, religion, architecture and art, entertainment, education, governance, dress, and food. Local elites eagerly embraced the Greek lifestyle in emulation of the ruling class. The Jerusalem elite—primarily wealthy priestly families—were not immune to these influences, despite the fact that the Greek way of life often contradicted biblical law or Jewish customs. For example, a Greek education was key to upward mobility under Alexander's successors. Young, upper-class Greek men (and only men!) were educated in a gymnasium with a curriculum that included military training, exercise, and athletic competitions.[12] In fact, the word gymnasium derives from the Greek word *gymnos*, which means naked, because Greek athletes exercised and competed in the nude even at international events such as the Olympics (which of course originated in Greece). In contrast, in Jewish tradition public nudity is considered an affront to God.[13]

Despite enjoying semi-autonomous status, the Jews were still subject to the Greek king, who had the right to appoint priests throughout his realm. In the Greek and Roman worlds, the priesthood was an office that could be bought and sold to the highest bidder, giving wealthy elites an opportunity to compete for the honor while enriching the royal coffers. Judaism differed from most other ancient religions in having a caste system that required all priests to be Jewish males born into a priestly family.[14] The Ptolemies and Seleucids, however, treated the Jewish priesthood like all others by claiming the right to approve the appointment and requiring the high priest to pay for his office. In 175 BCE, the Seleucid king Antiochus IV Epiphanes allowed Jason (Hebrew name Jeshua), the brother of the high priest Onias III, to purchase the office for himself. Until that point, Jason had been acting as interim high priest while his brother was away in Antioch in Syria.[15]

Jason also paid Antiochus IV for permission to re-found Jerusalem as a Greek city (*polis*) named Antiochia.[16] Having the status of a polis entitled the city's citizens to certain benefits and status, including tax breaks and the right to send athletes to international competitions. It also meant that Greek law replaced the Torah as the law of the land, although the practice of Judaism was still permitted and the Jerusalem temple remained dedicated to the God of Israel. Jerusalem's conversion to a polis was not imposed on the Jews by the Greek king but was initiated by Jason and his supporters, and our ancient sources give no indication of opposition within the Jewish community at the time.[17] The author of the apocryphal work 2 Maccabees, who was opposed to

Hellenization (the adoption of Greek culture), condemned Jason and the scandalous behavior (in his view) of the Jerusalem high priests:

> He [Jason] took delight in establishing a gymnasium right under the citadel, and he induced the noblest of the young men to wear the Greek hat. There was such an extreme of Hellenization and increase in the adoption of foreign ways because of the surpassing wickedness of Jason, who was ungodly and no true high priest, that the priests were no longer intent upon their service at the altar. Despising the sanctuary and neglecting the sacrifices, they hurried to take part in the unlawful proceedings in the wrestling arena after the signal for the discus-throwing, disdaining the honors prized by their ancestors and putting the highest value upon Greek forms of prestige. (2 Mc 4:12–15)

In 172 BCE, Jason sent a man named Menelaus to Antioch in Syria (the Seleucid capital) with the cash for the required annual payment to the king. Menelaus took advantage of the opportunity to outbid Jason, offering Antiochus IV Epiphanes more money for the office of high priest. Jason fled to Ammon, the area around modern Amman in Jordan. Onias III, who was still in Antioch, was assassinated by a hit man hired by Menelaus. His son, Onias IV, fled to Egypt, where he established a Jewish temple at Leontopolis (Heliopolis), over which he and his descendants (the Oniads) presided until it was shut down by Vespasian in 73 CE. The Oniads were Zadokite high priests, so-called because they traced their ancestry back to Zadok, the high priest appointed by Solomon to officiate in the first Jerusalem temple. The Zadokites controlled the high priesthood in the Jerusalem temple until the office was usurped by Menelaus (who was from a priestly family but not of Zadokite descent).[18]

Four years later, in 168 BCE, Antiochus IV invaded Egypt, taking advantage of the weakness of the Ptolemies. Afraid that Antiochus's annexation of Egypt would make the Seleucid kingdom too powerful, the Romans intervened. The Romans were monitoring the situation because they had begun to expand their control into the eastern Mediterranean. A Roman embassy was sent to Egypt to issue Antiochus an ultimatum, ordering him to withdraw. Antiochus, humiliated, had no choice but to obey. In the meantime, false rumors spread that Antiochus was dead.

Jason took advantage of the opportunity to return to Jerusalem from Ammon. In the ensuing civil war Menelaus defeated Jason, who fled to Egypt and made his way to Sparta in Greece, where he later died. Antiochus traveled from Egypt to Jerusalem to restore order and reconfirmed Menelaus as high priest. He established a fortified citadel in Jerusalem called the Akra, where he stationed a permanent garrison of gentile soldiers to keep order in the city.[19]

The following year—167 BCE—Antiochus IV Epiphanes issued a decree, as reported by the author of the apocryphal work 1 Maccabees:

> Then the king wrote to his whole kingdom that all should be one people, and that all should give up their particular customs. All the Gentiles accepted the command of the king. Many even from Israel gladly adopted his religion; they sacrificed to idols and profaned the sabbath. And the king sent letters by messengers to Jerusalem and the towns of Judah; he directed them to follow customs strange to the land, to forbid burnt offerings and sacrifices and drink offerings in the sanctuary, to profane Sabbaths and festivals, to defile the sanctuary and the priests, to build altars and sacred precincts and shrines for idols, to sacrifice swine and other unclean animals, and to leave their sons uncircumcised. They were to make themselves abominable by everything unclean and profane, so that they would forget the law and change all the ordinances. He added, "And whoever does not obey the command of the king shall die." (1 Mc 1:41–50)

The Jerusalem temple was re-dedicated to Olympian Zeus (the chief deity of the Greek pantheon) and the Samaritan temple on Mount Gerizim (where the God of Israel was also worshipped) was re-dedicated to Zeus Hellenios. Shrines and altars to Greek gods were established elsewhere around Jerusalem and the countryside. The Roman historian Tacitus, writing in the late first–early second century CE, attributed Antiochus's decree to a desire to eradicate the Jewish religion (*Hist.* 5.8:2). This is probably a more accurate reflection of Tacitus's own anti-Jewish biases than Antiochus's motivations (whether anti-Judaism or anti-Semitism in the modern sense existed in antiquity is debated by scholars).[20] Perhaps Antiochus's decree was an attempt to use Hellenization as a means of quelling the ongoing unrest in Judea and uniting the Jews with other peoples in his kingdom.[21]

Opposition to the new reality soon came from members of a priestly family called the Hasmoneans from the town of Modiin (about midway between Tel Aviv and Jerusalem). The family's patriarch, Mattathias, defied the king's order to participate in a Greek sacrifice and killed a Jew who was complying as well as one of the king's officers. He and his five sons fled to the wilderness, attracting recruits to their cause. Mattathias's third son, Judah Maccabee (a nickname meaning Judah "the hammer"; in Greek, Judas Maccabeus), led the rebels in a bloody civil war aimed at eliminating internal opponents and an external war against the Seleucids, successfully employing guerilla tactics.[22]

In 164 BCE, Antiochus IV Epiphanes died. His son, Antiochus V, canceled his father's decree, issuing an edict granting the Jews full religious freedom and amnesty. Judah and his brothers seized the Jerusalem temple, which they re-dedicated to the God of Israel in mid-December. According to tradition, they found only a one-day supply of ritually pure oil to light the temple's seven-branched lampstand or candelabrum (menorah). Miraculously, the lamp burned for eight days, until they were able to obtain more oil. The re-dedication of the temple in 164 BCE became the basis for the holiday of Hanukkah, which is celebrated by lighting a "Hanukkah menorah" with eight branches—one for each day the oil burned (plus an additional branch to light the others).[23]

Although nowadays Hanukkah is probably the best-known Jewish holiday owing to its proximity to the Christmas season, it is a minor Jewish holiday because it has no scriptural basis. In contrast to Hanukkah, the major Jewish holidays—Rosh Hashanah (the New Year), Yom Kippur (the Day of Atonement), Sukkot (the Festival of Booths), Passover, and Shavuot (Pentecost)—are biblically mandated.[24] These biblically mandated holidays occur in the fall and spring because they were agricultural festivals associated with planting and harvesting. They were related later to specific events in the history of Israel, such as Passover's commemoration of the exodus from Egypt and Shavuot's celebration of the giving of the Torah on Mount Sinai. Sukkot, Passover, and Shavuot were the three great pilgrimage holidays to the Jerusalem temple. Jews now celebrate the major holidays in various ways, including abstaining from work and attending synagogue services, and participating in festive meals (or, on Yom Kippur, fasting). In contrast, although it is customary to light a Hanukkah menorah while reciting blessings, Jews do not attend synagogue or abstain from work on this holiday.[25]

Even after the temple's re-dedication, Jewish rebels continued to wage war against the Seleucids, with the goal of gaining independence. During the war, Judah and his brother Eleazar lost their lives in battle. In 152 BCE, the Seleucid king appointed Judah's brother Jonathan governor of Judea and high priest. In 142 BCE, Jonathan was killed and was succeeded by his brother Simon, who died in 134 BCE. Over the course of three decades, these five remarkable brothers led the Jews in a successful uprising and eventual independence from Seleucid rule. During this period, they captured the Akra fortress in Jerusalem and razed it to the ground. Judah and his brothers also signed a treaty of friendship and alliance (in Latin, *amicitia*) with the Romans, who supported the Jews in an attempt to weaken Seleucid control over the region.[26]

Not all Jews, however, were thrilled with the Maccabees' success and their rise to power. Among these were the Maccabees' opponents, many of whom were members of the Jerusalem elite, including priestly families. Even many of the Maccabees' supporters opposed the appointment of Jonathan and his successors as high priests. For one thing, although the Hasmoneans were a priestly family, they were not Zadokites.[27] No less important, since earliest times the offices of high priest and king had been separated, with no one man serving in both capacities. The Hasmoneans' break with precedent alienated some Jews and contributed to growing divisions among the population.[28] By around 100 BCE, a number of Jewish groups, sects, and movements had emerged, the best-known of which are the Sadducees, Pharisees, and Essenes (and later, Jesus's movement).

ANCIENT JEWISH SECTARIANISM: SADDUCEES, PHARISEES, AND ESSENES

The Jewish groups of the late Second Temple period are often described as sects.[29] Today the word sect is used in a pejorative sense to denote a group that has severed itself from a larger or more established religion because of disagreements over beliefs or ideologies. In contrast, a denomination is a legitimate subgroup of a church. The word heresy also has a negative meaning today, referring to an inauthentic or illegitimate religious doctrine that contradicts accepted orthodoxy. In other words, sects and heresies are religious groups and doctrines of which we disapprove. However, originally the Latin word *secta* and the Greek word *haireseis* were neutral terms meaning "school" (a collection of people) or "school of thought." These words came to have negative connotations after the rise of Christianity, when the Church Fathers used them to denigrate groups and doctrines they criticized.[30]

Josephus describes the major Jewish sects of the late Second Temple period as philosophical schools.[31] "Jewish philosophy, in fact, takes three forms. The followers of the first school are called Pharisees, of the second Sadducees, of the third Essenes" (*War* 2.119).

In the ancient world (including among the Jews), the worship of god(s) was effected through practice, involving offerings and sacrifices, often made by priestly intermediaries on behalf of the people. Even today Judaism focuses on the correct observance of the laws in the Torah, in contrast to Christianity, which emphasizes faith. Whereas divisions among Jews center on matters of practice such as the observance of the sabbath and dietary laws, Christians are divided by doctrines and dogma. In the ancient world, religion—the worship of god(s)—was a matter of practice, not faith in the Christian sense of the word. It was through the study of philosophy (Greek for "love of wisdom"), not religion, that Greeks and Romans sought answers to big questions about morality and immorality, good and evil, human existence, and so on. This is the reason Josephus refers to the Jewish sects of the late Second Temple periods as philosophical schools. Unlike the Greeks and Romans, however, Jews sought answers to life's big questions in the Torah rather than in the works of philosophers such as Aristotle and Plato.[32]

All the Jewish sects—including Jesus's movement—worshiped the God of Israel as their national deity and took for granted the obligation to live according to his laws (the Torah). Their disagreements centered on the correct interpretation and practice of these laws. Correct practice was necessary for the survival of the Jews, as any offense to God potentially could cause him to abandon his people. This is the reason why, as petty or minor as some of the disagreements may seem to us today, ancient Jews considered them a matter of life or death.

Although in post-Enlightenment Western society politics and religion are separated (in theory, if not in practice), no such distinction existed in the ancient world.[33] For example, as we have seen, among the Greeks and Romans priests were appointed or approved by kings, and the priesthood was an office that could be sold to the highest bidder. Similarly, although we tend to think of the Jewish sects only in religious terms, they were involved in politics. In particular, the Sadducees and Pharisees acted as political parties, siding with different Hasmonean rulers in attempts to influence them.[34]

The Sadducees

When Jason and Menelaus (and later the Hasmoneans) usurped the high priesthood, the Zadokites lost control of this office and never regained it.[35] The Zadokite line split into three branches:

1. The Oniads: After the high priest Onias III was assassinated in Antioch, his son Onias IV fled to Egypt, where he established a temple at Leontopolis (Heliopolis), over which he and his descendants officiated until it was shut down by Vespasian in 73 CE (see above).

2. The Essenes/Qumran sect: Another branch of the Zadokite family was involved with the sect that eventually became known as the Essenes, members of which established the settlement at Qumran (see below).

3. The Sadducees: A third branch of the Zadokite family remained in Jerusalem, forming an alliance with the ruling powers and becoming an integral part of Jewish society for the next two centuries. They were called Sadducees, a term apparently derived from the name Zadok/Zadokite.[36]

We know less about the Sadducees than the Pharisees and Essenes because they left us no writings of their own. Instead, all our information comes from sources that were hostile to them: Josephus (who identifies himself as a Pharisee); the New Testament; and rabbinic literature (the writings of later sages whose approach to the interpretation of biblical law is similar to that of the Pharisees). The Sadducees were the wealthy members of Jewish society—and in particular the Jerusalem elite—including the higher ranking priestly families and aristocracy. Because the Sadducees wanted to maintain their status by preserving the status quo, they were political conservatives who accommodated with the ruling powers. They were also religious conservatives who opposed religious innovations. They recognized only the authority of written law as divinely ordained, and adhered to it literally, rejecting Pharisaic oral tradition which opened the door to human innovation and interpretation. For example, the Sadducees rejected the Pharisaic doctrine of individual, physical resurrection of the dead because it is not explicitly mentioned in the Torah.

The Pharisees

Although the Pharisees are familiar to many westerners today from the Gospel accounts, our information about them is sketchy and incomplete.[37] We do not even know why they were called Pharisees. The name appears to derive from the Hebrew word *parash*, which means "to separate." But separate from what? Some scholars speculate that the Pharisees were so-called because they kept themselves apart from other Jews, who they considered lax in their observance of ritual purity laws, and held themselves to a higher standard. It is not clear whether the Pharisees referred to themselves by this term or if it was a name used by others to describe the group.[38] In writings associated with the Pharisees, they usually refer to themselves by other names including friend (*haver*), scribe, or sage (*rabbi*). Interestingly, the only two ancient Jews who are self-identified in our sources as Pharisees were Diaspora Jews: Saul/Paul of Tarsus, and Flavius Josephus, who spent the last three decades of his life in Rome (see chapter 1).[39]

Although Pharisees sometimes addressed each other as rabbi, the term was not exclusive to them. Rabbi simply means "my master" or "one who is greater than me." Jews used it as an informal title of respect to address men who were considered experts in the Torah. Unlike today, ancient rabbis did not undergo a formal process of ordination or officiate over synagogue congregations. The occasional references to Jesus as a rabbi in the Gospel accounts do not mean he was a Pharisee, but rather that his followers respected him as an expert in Jewish law.[40]

The Pharisees came from diverse backgrounds in urban and rural areas.[41] They are known for an innovative approach to the Torah called *oral law* because it allows for human interpretation and expansion on the written law, in contrast to the Sadducees, who accepted only the authority of written law as divinely ordained. Josephus compares as follows the positions of the Pharisees and Sadducees:[42]

> Though they [the Pharisees] postulate that everything is brought about by fate, still they do not deprive the human will of the pursuit of what is in man's power . . . They believe that souls have power to survive death and that there are rewards and punishments under the earth for those who have led lives of virtue or vice. (*Ant.* 18.13–14)

> The Sadducees hold that the soul perishes along with the body. They own no observance of any sort apart from the laws. (*Ant.* 18.16)

Similarly, in Acts 23:8 we read: "The Sadducees say that there is no resurrection, or angel, or spirit; but the Pharisees acknowledge all three."

In other words, whereas the Pharisees believed in a future, physical resurrection of the dead and an afterlife of the soul, the Sadducees rejected both. And whereas according to the Sadducees humans enjoy complete free will, the Pharisees believed in a combination of human free will and divinely ordained fate. A famous sage named Rabbi Akiba reportedly expressed this view as follows: "All is foreseen, but freedom of choice is given" (Mishnah Avot 3:16).[43] In other words, although humans have free will, God foresees our choices. Ultimately, Pharisaic beliefs including the innovation of oral law prevailed, as they were shared by the rabbis—a group of sages who became the leaders of Judaism in the centuries following the destruction of the second temple, who are responsible for the "rabbinic Judaism" that is normative today. In fact, it was the flexibility of the Pharisaic approach to the interpretation of the Torah that enabled Judaism to survive the temple's destruction, an event that made it impossible to continue to offer sacrifices as required by biblical law.

Although Sadducees are mentioned in the Gospel accounts (as well as a group called scribes whose identity is debated by scholars), references to Pharisees are much more common. Jesus is repeatedly portrayed as debating the Pharisees on points of law. It is possible that the numerous references to Pharisees reflect the post-70 composition date of the Gospel accounts, as they survived in some form the trauma of the temple's destruction, whereas the Sadducees apparently did not. However,

I agree with scholars who believe that this reflects the situation in Galilee before 70, when the Pharisees reportedly were influential among the local Jewish population.[44] It therefore makes sense that of the different Jewish groups, Jesus had the most contact with the Pharisees.

But could Jesus have been a Pharisee himself? In my opinion, despite some similarities (such as a belief in resurrection), the Pharisees' repeated criticisms of Jesus and his disciples as reported in the Gospels indicate he was not a Pharisee.[45] In one famous episode, Jesus is portrayed as explicitly rejecting the Pharisaic innovation of oral law:

> Now when the Pharisees and some of the scribes who had come from Jerusalem gathered around him, they noticed that some of his disciples were eating with defiled hands, that is, without washing them. (For the Pharisees, and all the Jews, do not eat unless they thoroughly wash their hands, thus observing the tradition of the elders; and they do not eat anything from the market unless they wash it; and there are also many other traditions that they observe, the washing of cups, pots, and bronze kettles.) So the Pharisees and the scribes asked him, "Why do your disciples not live according to the tradition of the elders, but eat with defiled hands?" He said to them, "Isaiah prophesied rightly about you hypocrites, as it is written,
>
> This people honors me with their lips,
>   But their hearts are far from me;
> in vain do they worship me,
>   teaching human precepts as doctrines.
>
> You abandon the commandment of God and hold to human tradition." (Mk 7:1–8; also see Mt 15:1–20)

In this passage, the Pharisees criticize Jesus and his disciples for not washing their hands ritually before eating. However, there is no law in the Torah requiring the washing of hands before meals. Instead, as the Gospel authors correctly describe, this was a "tradition of the elders"— that is, a Pharisaic innovation which became customary. When the Pharisees ask Jesus why he and his disciples do "not live according to the tradition of the elders," they are referring to observing oral law. Jesus calls his critics hypocrites who honor God with their lips but not their hearts, supporting his position by citing scripture (Is 29:13): "in vain do they worship me, teaching human precepts as doctrines." He concludes by criticizing the Pharisees for not observing written (divinely ordained) law (the Torah) and accepting instead the authority of oral law ("human tradition").[46]

The Essenes

The site of Qumran was inhabited by members of the Essene sect (see chapter 3).[47] The sect apparently was established by dispossessed Zadokite priests, as reflected by the founder's nickname or sobriquet: the Teacher of Righteousness (Hebrew *tzedek* [righteousness] is a pun on *tzadok* [Zadok/Zadokite]).[48] This branch of the Zadokite family regarded the non-Zadokite priests in control of the Jerusalem temple as usurpers who polluted the temple and the sacrifices offered there. They withdrew, apparently refusing to participate in the sacrificial cult, and awaited the day when they would regain control of the temple. In the interim, the sect constituted itself as a substitute temple (or, more precisely, the wilderness tabernacle), with each full member living his everyday life as if he were a priest (although not all members were from Zadokite or other priestly families).

The Dead Sea Scrolls belonged to the inhabitants of Qumran, who deposited them in caves surrounding the site. The remains of approximately one thousand different scrolls were found in eleven caves, all of which represent Jewish religious writings. They include the earliest copies of the books of the Hebrew Bible (Old Testament) that have ever been found; Aramaic translations of biblical books (*targumim*; singular: *targum*); commentaries on biblical—and especially prophetic—books (*pesharim*; singular: *pesher*); apocryphal works such as Tobit and Ecclesiasticus/the Wisdom of Ben Sira (books that are included in the Catholic canon of sacred scripture but not in the Hebrew Bible and Protestant Bible); and pseudepigrapha (books such as Enoch and Jubilees, which were not included in the Jewish, Protestant, or Catholic canons of sacred scripture but are sometimes preserved in the canons of other churches). The Dead Sea Scrolls also include sectarian works, which were composed by members of the sect and describe or reflect their distinctive outlook, beliefs, and practices. Sectarian works include the Damascus Document, the Community Rule (Manual of Discipline), the War

Scroll, and perhaps the Temple Scroll. There are no copies of the New Testament among the Dead Sea Scrolls, nor do the scrolls contain references to Jesus or anyone in his circle.

Members of the Essene sect lived in towns and villages around Palestine, including in Jerusalem, but some practiced desert separatism—that is, some lived apart in the wilderness, as at Qumran (the only such community identified so far). Although many members were married and had families, only physically and mentally unblemished adult men were eligible to apply for full membership (the same qualifications required for priests serving in the Jerusalem temple). Applicants were required to undergo a process of initiation that lasted two to three years. After a candidate passed the initial stages of initiation, he surrendered all personal property, as the sect practiced the pooling of possessions.

The sect attracted members because it promised salvation to them alone, for this was an apocalyptic group that anticipated the imminent arrival of the end of days, which would be ushered in by a forty-year war between the Sons of Light (= good = themselves) and the Sons of Darkness (= evil = everyone else). In contrast to the Pharisees and Sadducees, the Essenes believed in predeterminism, meaning everything is preordained by God and there is no human free will at all. Therefore, the forty-year-long war and its outcome—victory for the Sons of Light— were preordained by God. Another peculiarity of this sect is their expectation of not one but two messiahs: in addition to the usual royal messiah of Israel descended from David, they anticipated a second, priestly messiah descended from Aaron (and, possibly, a third, prophetic messiah).

Contrary to widely publicized claims, Jesus was not an Essene despite some similarities between these groups.[49] For example, both Jesus's movement (as described in the New Testament) and the Essenes pooled their possessions and held communal meals. And, of course, both were apocalyptic movements which anticipated the imminent arrival of the end of days (or even thought it was already under way). However, there are also important differences between these groups. For example, Jesus did not preach that there is no human free will because everything is preordained by God, nor does the New Testament indicate that Jesus's followers anticipated the arrival of more than one messiah. The major differences between the two groups concern their approaches to purity observance and membership. Whereas the Essenes observed the highest level of Jewish ritual purity due to their priestly lifestyle, the Gospel accounts suggest that Jesus was unconcerned about coming into contact with the most severely impure members of Jewish society, including hemorrhaging women, lepers, and even corpses. And whereas the Essenes were an exclusive movement, with only a small sector of the Jewish population eligible to apply for full membership, Jesus reportedly welcomed everyone to join his followers. In other words, despite some similarities, including an apocalyptic outlook, Jesus and his movement were diametrically opposed to the Essenes in fundamental ways.

Although Jesus was not an Essene, it is possible that John the Baptist was a member of the sect at some point. After all, according to the Gospel accounts John was active in the wilderness near Qumran; he reportedly was from a priestly family and lived an ascetic lifestyle (similar to the Essenes); and his emphasis on baptism recalls the Essenes's concern with purification through immersion in water (as reflected in the large numbers and sizes of the *miqva'ot* at Qumran). Therefore, John might have had some contact with the Qumran community and perhaps even was a member at one point in his life. Even if this is the case—and it is completely speculative—by the time we read about John in the Gospel accounts, he could not have been an Essene, as indicated by differences in his clothing (he reportedly wore camel hair clothing with a leather belt, whereas full members of the Essene sect wore linen like priests); his diet (John reportedly consumed locusts and wild honey whereas full members of the Essenes consumed the pure food and drink of the sect); and his theology of baptism (which differs from that of Essene ritual purification).

Qumran was destroyed by the Romans in June 68 CE, while Vespasian was subduing Jericho. In his excavations at Masada, Yigael Yadin discovered some of the same works as those found among the Dead Sea Scrolls (in particular, the Songs of the Sabbath Sacrifice). Although scholars do not believe these works are Essene compositions, they are compatible with their distinctive outlook. Yadin therefore suggested that some members of the Qumran community fled in advance of the Romans in 68 and joined the rebels holding out atop Masada. Since then, other scholars have noted that the same scribal hand (handwriting) can be identified on scrolls from Masada and Qumran, and other finds from Masada (such as the same type of cylindrical pottery jars distinctive to Qumran) suggest sectarian presence. It therefore seems likely that Essenes were among the Jews who took refuge at Masada (see chapter 8).[50]

THE HASMONEANS

John Hyrcanus I (134–104 BCE)

After Simon died, he was succeeded by his son John Hyrcanus I.[51] Until this point, the Maccabees had governed only the district of Judea. John Hyrcanus I embarked on a campaign of expansion through military conquest, adding territories to the east (Transjordan = ancient Peraea), south (Idumaea), and north (Samaria). Idumaea was the area of the northern Negev desert (map 1). Before 586 BCE it had been the southern part of the biblical kingdom of Judah. After Judah was conquered by the Babylonians, Edomites (who lived to the southeast of the Dead Sea) settled in southern Judah. This district became known as Idumaea, and the inhabitants as Idumaeans. The Edomites/Idumaeans were a Semitic people who worshiped a god named Qos as their national deity, alongside other gods. John Hyrcanus I forced the Idumaeans and other non-Jewish inhabitants of conquered territories to convert to Judaism or go into exile, as Josephus reports:

> Hyrcanus also captured the Idumaean cities of Adora and Marisa, and after subduing all the Idumaeans, permitted them to remain in their country so long as they had themselves circumcised and were willing to observe the laws of the Jews. And so, out of attachment to the land of their fathers, they submitted to circumcision and to making their manner of life conform in all other respects to that of the Jews. And from that time on they have continued to be Jews. (*Ant.* 13.257–58)

Many Jews today are surprised to learn that the Hasmoneans forcibly converted conquered peoples to Judaism, as this practice and even proselytizing are discouraged in rabbinic Judaism. However, this prohibition did not exist in antiquity, and there is plenty of evidence of ancient Jewish proselytism. In my opinion, the Hasmoneans employed a policy of forced conversion for the same reasons that Alexander's successors imposed Greek culture on their subjects: as a means of unifying the diverse peoples under their rule. In other words, Hasmonean "Judaization" is the Jewish analogue to Greek "Hellenization."[52]

Unlike the other territories, Samaria was not Judaized by John Hyrcanus I because of the makeup of its population, which was descended from the poorer Israelites who were left behind after the Assyrian conquest in 722 BCE. The Samarians or Samaritans continued to worship the God of Israel as their national deity, eventually building a temple on a sacred mountain in their territory (Mount Gerizim), presided over by their own priesthood. This is the background to a centuries-long conflict between the Jews and Samaritans: two closely related peoples who both self-identified as the true Israel and laid claim to the same national deity.[53]

When John Hyrcanus I conquered Samaria, he could not forcibly convert the population to Judaism because they already worshiped the God of Israel as their national deity. Instead, he destroyed the temple on Mount Gerizim, thereby eliminating the Jerusalem temple's chief rival.[54] Interestingly, ancient Jewish sources never express any such hostility toward or condemnation of the Oniad temple at Leontopolis in Egypt.[55]

Aristobulus I (104–103 BCE)

After John Hyrcanus I died, his son Aristobulus imprisoned his mother and siblings and had one brother put to death so he could seize the reins of power (his mother starved to death in prison).[56] Aristobulus I was a Hellenizer who used his Greek name instead of his Hebrew name Judah. One of the great ironies of Jewish history is that although Hanukkah commemorates the Maccabean victory over Antiochus IV's attempt to Hellenize the Jews, the Hasmoneans adopted Greek customs soon after they became rulers.[57] Aristobulus I (or possibly his successor Alexander Jannaeus) was the first Hasmonean to call himself king.[58] During Aristobulus I's brief reign he conquered Galilee and the Golan, perhaps converting to Judaism the Ituraeans, a native Semitic people.[59]

Approximately one hundred years after Aristobulus I's conquest and Judaization of Galilee, Jesus was born. Only two of the four Gospels contain birth narratives about Jesus (Mt 1.18–15 and Lk 2.1–7).[60] Both place

Jesus's birth in Bethlehem in Judea (although they differ on the circumstances surrounding the birth and on other points), despite the fact that elsewhere the gospels refer to Jesus as being from Nazareth in Galilee. The differences between the birth narratives in Matthew and Luke, and their absence from the other Gospels, suggest they were inserted by the authors—but why? The answer is clear, as Matthew and Luke both indicate: to establish Jesus's lineage from King David:

> An account of the genealogy of Jesus the Messiah, the son of David. (Mt 1:1)

> Joseph also went from the town of Nazareth in Galilee to Judea, to the city of David called Bethlehem, because he was descended from the house and family of David. (Lk 2:4)

This indicates that whoever they were, the Gospel authors took for granted the biblical principle that the messiah will be descended from David (see, e.g., Is 11:1; Jer 23:5–6; 2 Sm 7:16). Clearly, Matthew and Luke inserted the birth narratives to provide Jesus's bona fides as a legitimate Jewish messiah of the line of David.[61] No less important, the birth narratives also established Jesus's connection to Judea. Since Galilee had been Judaized by the Hasmoneans only a century before Jesus's birth, Jews could have questioned whether he came from a family of Judeans or Judaized Galileans. The birth narratives in Matthew and Luke served to establish Jesus's Judean (Jewish) origin as well as his connection to David. Even John—the latest of the canonical Gospels—expresses this expectation:

> When they heard these words, some in the crowd said, "This is really the prophet." Others said, "This is the Messiah." But some asked, "Surely the Messiah does not come from Galilee, does he? Has not the scripture said that the Messiah is descended from David and comes from Bethlehem, the village where David lived?" (7:40–42)[62]

Archaeological evidence indicates that the Hasmonean conquest of Galilee was followed by a wave of Judean colonization and settlement. Therefore, some scholars argue that Jesus's family could have been Judean anyway, if they were descended from colonists who settled in Galilee after the Hasmonean conquest.[63]

Alexander Jannaeus (103–76 BCE)

When Aristobulus I died of an illness in 103 BCE, his brothers were still imprisoned. Aristobulus's widow, Salome Alexandra freed the brothers and married one of them—Alexander Jannaeus.[64] In doing so, she and Jannaeus fulfilled one biblical law while transgressing another.[65] The law that Salome Alexandra and Alexander Jannaeus fulfilled is Deuteronomy 25:5–6, which requires a childless widow to marry her husband's brother (this arrangement is called levirate marriage, from Latin *levir* meaning a husband's brother):

> When brothers reside together, and one of them dies and has no son, the wife of the deceased shall not be married outside the family to a stranger. Her husband's brother shall go in to her, taking her in marriage, and performing the duty of a husband's brother to her, and the firstborn whom she bears shall succeed to the name of the deceased brother, so that his name may not be blotted out of Israel.

Although this legislation seems strange to us, it made sense in its original social context. Today we assume that women should have autonomy and freedom and be on equal footing with men, but such notions did not exist in the ancient world. To the contrary, it was difficult for women who were not under the protection of an adult male—first a father and later a husband—to survive. Widows and orphans are repeatedly mentioned in the Bible as the most vulnerable members of society precisely because of their independent status.[66] Once a woman was married and was no longer a virgin, she was much less desirable to other men, which is why many widows never remarried. A childless widow was the most vulnerable of all, as she did not even have children to support her. Therefore, the law in Deuteronomy was intended to protect a childless widow by maintaining her married status within her former husband's household. The perpetuation of the family's bloodline and the name of the deceased were priorities in a society organized as clans headed by patriarchs.[67]

The biblical law that Salome Alexandra and Alexander Jannaeus transgressed is Leviticus 21:7, which permits the high priest to marry only a virgin, and explicitly forbids marriage to a widow: "He shall marry only a woman who is a virgin. A widow, or a divorced woman, or a woman who has been defiled, a prostitute, these he shall not marry." Because Alexander Jannaeus, like his predecessors, served as high priest, by marrying Salome Alexandra he violated this biblical prohibition.

Alexander Jannaeus's disregard for biblical law and his cruelty made him unpopular with much of the Jewish population, especially the Pharisees. Josephus reports that one year, while Alexander Jannaeus was officiating as high priest at the altar during Sukkot, the onlookers rose up against him and pelted him with citrons (Hebrew *ethrog*—a citrus fruit resembling a large bumpy lemon that is used in the ritual of this holiday):

> As for Alexander, his own people revolted against him—for the nation was aroused against him—at the celebration of the festival, and as he stood beside the altar and was about to sacrifice, they pelted him with citrons . . . and being enraged at this, he killed some six thousand of them. (*Ant.* 13: 372–73)[68]

In 88 BCE, following a prolonged civil war during which Alexander Jannaeus eliminated thousands of his opponents, Jewish rebels turned for support to the Seleucid king Demetrius III Eukairos, who was happy to assist in the hopes of regaining control of Hasmonean territory. But when Demetrius invaded, the rebels defected back to Alexander Jannaeus and Demetrius was forced to withdraw. Alexander Jannaeus exacted revenge by crucifying approximately eight hundred of his opponents, as Josephus describes:

> and there he did a thing that was as cruel as could be: while he feasted with his concubines in a conspicuous place, he ordered some eight hundred of the Jews to be crucified, and slaughtered their children and wives before the eyes of the still living wretches. (*Ant.* 13:380)

A sectarian work from Qumran called the Pesher Nahum alludes to this civil war.[69] *Pesharim* are sectarian commentaries on or interpretations of biblical books with a couple of distinctive features: (1) the author believed that the true meaning of the biblical text had been revealed to the sect's inspired leader, the Teacher of Righteousness; and (2) the author understood the events described in the biblical text as occurring in his own time.[70] The genre is characterized by the citation of a biblical passage, followed by the author's interpretation. The Pesher Nahum's allusion to the civil war includes the real names of historical figures, as opposed to most sectarian works, which typically refer to individuals using nicknames (such as the Teacher of Righteousness and his opponent, the Wicked Priest):

> Its interpretation concerns Deme]trius, king of Yavan, who wanted to enter Jerusalem on the advice of those looking for easy interpretations, [but he did not enter, for God had not given Jerusalem] into the hand of the kings of Yavan from Antiochus up to the appearance of the chiefs of the Kittim. (4Q169 Frags. 3 + 4 cols. 2–3)[71]

This passage names Demetrius (III), king of Yavan (Hebrew for "Greece"), and the Seleucid (Greek) king Antiochus (III), who conquered Jerusalem and Judea in 198 BCE. It also refers to an invasion by the Romans (Kittim), indicating that the Pesher Nahum was composed after the Roman annexation of Judea in 63 BCE. The author says that Demetrius was invited to invade Jerusalem by a group called "those looking for easy interpretations" or "the seekers of smooth things" (Hebrew *dorshay halakot*).

This passage is followed by an allusion to Alexander Jannaeus's crucifixion of the eight hundred rebels:

> Its interpretation concerns the Angry Lion [who filled his cave with a mass of corpses, carrying out rev]enge against those looking for easy interpretations, who hanged living men [from the tree, committing an atrocity which had not been committed] in Israel since ancient times, for it is [hor]rible for the one hanged alive from the tree. (4Q169 Frags. 3 + 4 cols. 6–7)

The "Angry Lion" (or "Lion of Wrath") is a nickname or sobriquet for Alexander Jannaeus. "Those looking for easy interpretations" or "the Seekers of Smooth Things" is a derogatory nickname and Hebrew pun used by the Essenes to denote the Pharisees. Instead of referring to the Pharisees as *dorshay halakhot*—"the seekers of the law"—that is, those seeking to observe the law correctly—the Essenes derided them as *dorshay halakot*—that is, those looking for easy (or smooth) interpretations of the law. Although the Pharisees prided themselves on being scrupulous in Torah observance, the even stricter Qumran sect/Essenes considered them lax.[72]

Both Josephus and the Pesher Nahum refer to Alexander Jannaeus's crucifixion of the rebels. Josephus uses the Greek term for crucifixion, whereas the author of the *pesher* describes the procedure in typical Hebrew fashion as hanging men alive from a tree. How widely ancient Jews employed crucifixion as a method of execution is debated by scholars.[73]

Aside from the internal unrest, Alexander Jannaeus's long reign was characterized by a series of military campaigns which added to the Hasmonean kingdom the Palestinian coast and parts of Transjordan (including the Decapolis city of Pella, which he destroyed when its inhabitants refused to convert to Judaism). Under Alexander Jannaeus the Hasmonean kingdom reached its greatest extent. Josephus reports that "the high priest Jonathan" was the first to build a fortress atop Masada (*War* 7.285). There were two Hasmonean rulers named Jonathan who served as high priests: (1) Jonathan Maccabee (who assumed the office of high priest in 152 BCE); and (2) Alexander Jannaeus, whose Hebrew name was Jonathan. Scholars disagree about which Jonathan Josephus had in mind. Some argue that Josephus intended the earlier Jonathan—Jonathan the Maccabee—because elsewhere he attributes the initial fortification of Masada to "ancient kings" (*Ant.* 4.399).[74] It is unclear, however, to what extent the Maccabees/Hasmoneans controlled the area around Masada before John Hyrcanus I's conquest of Idumaea.[75] Yaakov Meshorer claimed that the rarity of second-century BCE coins at Masada indicates that Josephus's "high priest Jonathan" was, in fact, Alexander Jannaeus.[76] However, this argument, based on an absence of evidence, is inconclusive. No buildings dating to the Hasmonean period have been identified with certainty at Masada, as Herod's construction activities apparently obliterated all earlier remains.[77] So whether Masada was first fortified by Jonathan Maccabee or Alexander Jannaeus remains an open question.

Salome Alexandra (76–67 BCE)

After Alexander Jannaeus died of an illness while on campaign in Transjordan, his widow Salome Alexandra succeeded him to the throne.[78] Because she could not serve as high priest, Salome Alexandra appointed her older son John Hyrcanus II to that office. Her reign lasted almost a decade and was relatively peaceful. Salome Alexandra was a remarkable woman: the wife of two Hasmonean kings and the only woman to rule the Hasmonean kingdom as queen. Josephus, who, typical of ancient male authors, considered women inferior to men, praised her:

> she died, having reigned nine years and having lived seventy-three years in all. She was a woman who showed none of the weakness of her sex: for being one of those inordinately desirous of the power to rule, she showed by her deeds the ability to carry out her plans, and at the same time she exposed the follies of those men who continually fail to maintain sovereign power. (*Ant.* 13.430)[79]

THE END OF THE HASMONEAN KINGDOM

After Salome Alexandra died, civil war erupted between her two sons over the succession.[80] Her older son, John Hyrcanus II, was supported by the Pharisees, and her younger son, Aristobulus II, was supported by the Sadducees. Hyrcanus II secured the throne thanks to the intervention of Antipater, a wealthy and influential Idumaean Jew who, like his father (Herod's grandfather Antipas), had served as governor of Idumaea under the Hasmoneans.[81] Antipater exploited the conflict between the brothers to advance himself, supporting the weak Hyrcanus II over the ambitious Aristobulus II. When the two sides reached a stalemate, the brothers turned to the Romans for help.

This was the period of the Late Republic in Rome. During the first century BCE, a series of powerful generals seized the reins of power illegally, establishing themselves as dictators. At the time Hyrcanus II and Aristobulus II made their plea for help, the Roman general Pompey was campaigning in Asia Minor (the area of modern Turkey). As a result, Pompey invaded Judea and besieged Jerusalem, which he took with the aid of Hyrcanus II. Pompey desecrated the temple by entering the Holy of Holies in the Jerusalem temple, which was off-limits to everyone except the high priest, who went in only on the Day of Atonement (Yom Kippur). As we have seen, the Pesher Nahum refers to the fall of Jerusalem to the Romans (Kittim):

> Its interpretation concerns Deme]trius, king of Yavan, who wanted to enter Jerusalem on the advice of those looking for easy

interpretations, [but he did not enter, *for God had not given Jerusa-lem] into the hand of the kings of Yavan from Antiochus up to the ap-pearance of the chiefs of the Kittim.* (4Q169 Frags. 3 + 4 cols. 2–3; my emphasis)

Tacitus also mentions this event, and describes Pompey's astonishment at finding the Holy of Holies empty:

> The first Roman to subdue the Jews and set foot in their temple by right of conquest was Gnaeus Pompey: thereafter it was a matter of common knowledge that there were no representations of the gods within, but that the place was empty and the secret shrine contained nothing. (*Hist.* 5.9:1)[82]

Pompey rewarded Hyrcanus II for his support with the high priest-hood but punished the Jews for refusing to submit peacefully to the Romans by dismembering the Hasmonean kingdom. Only territories with high concentrations of Jews (including the Yahwistic population of Samaria) were left under the administration of the high priest: Judea, Galilee, eastern Idumaea, Samaria, and Peraea. To strengthen the pro-Roman elements within the country, the Romans formed a league of the most Hellenized cities called the Decapolis (the ten cities of the New Tes-tament), which included Beth Shean/Scythopolis, Pella, Gadara, and Abila. They were part of the newly established Roman province of Syria, which was under the administration of a military governor with the title "proconsul" or "legate" (indicating his authority to command a legion), who was based at the capital of Antioch.[83]

The three decades (63–31 BCE) following Pompey's conquest were turbulent in Rome. This period is characterized by the decline of the Republic, the struggle between Julius Caesar and Pompey; Pompey's death; Julius Caesar's ascension to power; Julius Caesar's assassination (in 44 BCE); and the struggle between Octavian (Julius Caesar's step-nephew, later called Augustus Caesar) and Mark Antony.

After Hyrcanus II and Antipater supplied Julius Caesar with Jewish soldiers during his campaign in Egypt (48–47 BCE), Caesar rewarded them by bestowing on Hyrcanus II the title "ethnarch of the Jews" and on Antipater the title "procurator."[84] Antipater entrusted his sons Phasael and Herod with the task of governing Jerusalem and Galilee. In 43 BCE,

Antipater was murdered by a supporter of Hyrcanus II named Malichus. Soon afterward, Herod had Malichus assassinated, but Malichus's brother continued to stir up trouble, seizing Masada and other fortresses:

> For Malichus' brother, having stirred up a revolt, was then guarding a good many fortresses, including Masada, the strongest of all. Accordingly when Herod had recovered from his illness, he came against him and took from him all the fortresses he held. (Josephus, *Ant.* 14.296)

Around this time (42 BCE), Cassius and Brutus, conservatives who wanted to restore the Roman Republic, were defeated at the Battle of Philippi by the Second Triumvirate, an alliance that included Octavian and Mark Antony. After the battle, the eastern Roman provinces— including Judea—were placed under the administration of Mark Antony, who established his base of operations at Alexandria in Egypt. It was in Egypt that Mark Antony became infatuated with Cleopatra VII, a Ptolemaic queen who previously had been involved with Julius Caesar, and with whom she had a son. Mark Antony eventually divorced his wife Octavia, who was Octavian's sister, to marry Cleopatra, who bore him three children.

The Parthian Invasion (40 BCE)

Expansion into the eastern Mediterranean brought the Romans into prolonged conflict with the Parthians, descendants of the ancient Persians.[85] In 40 BCE, the Parthians overran Syria and Palestine, where they were welcomed by the Jews. Antigonus II Mattathias (or Mattathias Antigonus), the son of Aristobulus II, seized the opportunity to reestablish the Hasmonean kingdom. Hyrcanus II and Phasael (Herod's older brother) were captured and turned over to Mattathias Antigonus. Phasael committed suicide, while Mattathias Antigonus disfigured Hyrcanus II to ensure he could never again serve as high priest:[86]

> Hyrcanus threw himself at the feet of Antigonus, who with his own teeth lacerated his suppliant's ears, in order to disqualify him for ever, under any change of circumstances, from resuming the high priesthood; since freedom from physical defect is essential to the holder of that office. (Josephus, *War* 1.270)

Hyrcanus II was led away in captivity to Parthia, and Mattathias Antigonus became high priest and king of Judea. Herod escaped capture by fleeing south to Idumaea, depositing his family for safekeeping atop Masada. There Herod left his mother and sisters, his younger brother Joseph, his fiancée Mariamme (a Hasmonean princess), and her mother well-provisioned and under the protection of a garrison of eight hundred soldiers.[87] While Herod was gone (winter–spring 40/39 BCE), Matthathias Antigonus's forces blockaded Masada. The situation became dire when the water supply on the mountain almost ran out, and Joseph made plans to escape with two hundred soldiers to seek aid: "But he was stopped by a rain which God sent in the night, for once the cisterns were filled with water, they no longer needed to flee" (Josephus, *Ant.* 14.390). Emboldened by their good fortune, Joseph and his troops went on the offensive and began to attack the besiegers in ambushes and open skirmishes.

In the meantime, Herod had traveled from Masada to Nabataea on the southeastern side of the Dead Sea to seek assistance. The Nabataeans were an Arab people who prospered by trading in luxury goods such as incense, which they transported through the desert on caravans from the Arabian Peninsula to the port at Gaza. By the first century BCE the Nabataeans had established a large kingdom that bordered the Hasmonean kingdom, and was annexed by the Romans in 106 CE. Herod sought aid from the Nabataean king because his father had lent the king money in the past, and his mother Cypros was a Nabataean.[88]

When the Nabataean king refused to assist, Herod continued to Egypt, where he was greeted with "a magnificent reception from Cleopatra, who hoped to entrust him with the command of an expedition which she was preparing" (Josephus, *War* 1.279). Herod refused Cleopatra's offer as he did not trust her, and with good reason. Because Judea had once been part of the Ptolemaic kingdom, Cleopatra considered the territory her birthright, and wanted to use Herod to gain control of it. Instead, Herod set sail for Rome, where he appeared before the Senate. Thanks to Mark Antony's support, the Senate unanimously bestowed upon Herod the title "king of Judea" and sent him back to Judea to wage war against the Parthians and Mattathias Antigonus.

CHAPTER 6

FROM HEROD TO THE FIRST JEWISH REVOLT AGAINST ROME

(40 BCE–66 CE)

In 40 BCE the Roman Senate appointed Herod client king of Judea, granting him the Jewish and Judaized territories of Judea, Galilee, Idumaea, and Peraea. Herod was a cruel and ruthless ruler who, ironically, is best-known for an atrocity he probably did not commit: the massacre of the innocents (Mt 2:16–18). This chapter provides an overview of Herod the Great's reign and the deteriorating conditions in Judea after his death, culminating with the outbreak of the First Jewish Revolt against Rome in 66 CE.[1] This turbulent period is characterized by a number of factors that are thought to have contributed to the outbreak of the revolt, including:

* Mounting tensions between various sectors of the population (e.g., urban versus rural; elites versus lower classes; Jews versus gentiles; Samaritans versus Galileans and Judeans)
* Diverse movements and splinter parties, often violently opposed to one another
* Inept and greedy Roman governors
* Ineffective native leadership, decimated by Herod's elimination of members of the Hasmonean family and his most capable sons
* The Jewish struggle for autonomy or independence
* Messianic aspirations and apocalyptic visions which gave rise to self-appointed and follower-proclaimed leaders

Although scholars agree that the causes of the revolt are complex, there is no consensus about which of the above factors contributed to its outbreak. This is because our main source of information is Josephus, whose writings are biased and open to different interpretations (see chapter 1). Recently, for example, Martin Goodman has identified the tensions leading up to the revolt as "largely internal to Jewish society rather than symptoms of widespread resentment of Roman rule," with little or no evidence of messianic fervor.[2] Steve Mason argues that the revolt was not the result of long-simmering animosity between the Jews (Judeans) and Rome, but instead was triggered by local conditions and specific events that occurred in the mid-60s under the emperor Nero and his governor Gessius Florus.[3] The following overview is based on Josephus's testimony and modern scholarship without taking sides in the debate over the causes of the revolt.

HEROD THE GREAT

Herod's War with Mattathias Antigonus (40–37 BCE)

Soon after appearing before the Senate, Herod returned to Judea from Rome to wage war against Mattathias Antigonus, with the assistance of forces provided by Sosius, the legate of Syria.[4] Herod landed at Ptolemais (Akko/Acre) and subdued Joppa (Jaffa) before proceeding to Masada, where his family was still under siege. After freeing his family and depositing them for safekeeping in the city of Samaria, Herod mounted a campaign in Galilee. Herod's war against Mattathias Antigonus lasted three years, during which time he married Mariamme, the Hasmonean princess to whom he had been engaged for five years. The war ended in 37 BCE when Jerusalem fell after a prolonged siege, culminating with a massacre of the city's inhabitants:

> And soon every quarter was filled with the blood of the slain, for the Romans were furious at the length of the siege, while the Jews on Herod's side were anxious not to leave a single adversary alive. And so they were slaughtered in heaps, whether crowded together in alleys and houses or seeking refuge in the temple; no pity was shown either to infants or the aged, nor were weak women spared. (Josephus, *Ant.* 14.479–80)

Mattathias Antigonus surrendered to Herod, throwing himself at So-sius's feet and begging for mercy:

> In this scene Antigonus, regardless alike of his former fortune and that which now was his, came down from the castle and threw himself at the feet of Sossius. The latter, far from pitying his changed conditions, burst into uncontrollable laughter and called him Antigone. He did not, however, treat him as a woman and leave him at liberty; no, he was put in irons and kept under strict guard . . . Sossius, after dedicating to God a crown of gold, withdrew from Jerusalem, taking with him to [Mark] Antony Antigonus in chains. This prisoner, to the last clinging with forlorn hope to life, fell beneath the axe, a fitting end to his ignominious career. (Josephus, *War* 1.353, 357)

Sossius mocked Antigonus for his cowardly behavior by calling him Antigone—the female version of the name Antigonus. Josephus reports that Mark Antony "was the first Roman who decided to behead a king, since he believed that in no other way could he change the attitude of the Jews so that they would accept Herod, who had been appointed in his place" (*Ant.* 15.9).[5]

Herod's Reign: The Early Years (37–31 BCE)

During the early years of Herod's reign, members of the Hasmonean family and Cleopatra attempted to usurp his kingdom.[6] After the bloody massacre in Jerusalem, Herod also faced widespread opposition among the Jewish population, who refused to accept him as a legitimate king because he was not a Hasmonean despite his marriage to Mariamme. Altogether Herod had ten wives, as was common in antiquity, many of his marriages were intended to cement political and social alliances among elite families.[7] Ironically, Herod's main threat from the Hasmoneans was because of his marriage to Mariamme, whose ambitious mother Alexandra attempted to use her position within Herod's household to reestablish Hasmonean rule. Ultimately, however, Alexandra's schemes backfired and things ended badly for her and Mariamme.

In the meantime, the aging and physically disfigured Hyrcanus II was released from Parthian captivity and returned to Jerusalem. Because Herod was neither Judean nor from a priestly family, he could not serve as high priest, but as king he had the right to appoint the high priest.[8] Afraid of bolstering Hasmonean claims by installing Mariamme's younger brother Aristobulus III, Herod instead chose a high priest named Hananel from a relatively unknown Babylonian priestly family. Infuriated, Alexandra contacted Cleopatra, who she hoped could convince Mark Antony to intervene on Aristobulus III's behalf. After Mark Antony showed interest, Herod became alarmed and replaced Hananel with the seventeen-year-old Aristobulus III.[9] When Aristobulus III made an appearance as high priest on the holiday of Sukkot, the crowd's response confirmed Herod's worst fears:

> For Aristobulus was a youth of seventeen when he went up to the altar to perform the sacrifices in accordance with the law, wearing the ornamental dress of the high priests and carrying out the rites of the cult, and he was extraordinarily handsome and taller than most youths of his age, and in his appearance, moreover, he displayed to the full the nobility of his descent. And so there arose among the people an impulsive feeling of affection toward him, and there came to them a vivid memory of the deeds performed by his grandfather Aristobulus. Being overcome, they gradually revealed their feelings, showing joyful and painful emotion at the same time, and they called out to him good wishes mingled with prayers, so that the affection of the crowd became evident, and their acknowledgement of their emotions seemed too impulsive in view of their having a king. (Josephus, *Ant.* 15.51–52)

As a result, Herod promptly had the young Hasmonean prince drowned in a swimming pool in his palace at Jericho:

> For Herod had not spared even this poor lad; he had bestowed upon him in his seventeenth year the office of high-priest, and then immediately after conferring the honor had put him to death . . . he was, consequently, sent by night to Jericho, and there, in accordance with instructions, plunged into a swimming-bath by the Gauls and drowned. (Josephus, *War* 1.437)

Whereas previously the Jewish high priesthood had been a lifetime appointment, throughout his reign Herod replaced high priests in rapid succession for political purposes.[10]

Herod's attention now turned to Mariamme, the beautiful Hasmonean princess with whom he was madly in love (and who reportedly despised him in equal measure). While Herod's love for Mariamme was exceeded only by his jealousy—he imagined that every man desired her as much as he did—Alexandra attempted to use her daughter as a means of recovering the throne for the Hasmoneans. Herod's jealousy and paranoia led him to give his brother-in-law Joseph secret orders to kill Mariamme if anything ever happened to him, so no other man could have her.

At the same time Herod was faced with threats from the Hasmonean members of his household, he had to deal with Cleopatra's ambitions. Cleopatra considered Herod's kingdom her birthright, as Judea had once been under Ptolemaic rule. In 37/36 BCE, Mark Antony divorced his wife Octavia (Octavian's sister), reportedly a great beauty, to marry the seductive Cleopatra. Cleopatra manipulated Mark Antony into granting her large sections of territory, including the Decapolis cities, most of the Palestinian coast, the eastern shore of the Dead Sea, and the valuable balsam and date palm plantations at Jericho (which Herod had to pay to lease from her!). Herod watched helplessly as Cleopatra whittled away at his kingdom, powerless to stop her due to his dependence on Mark Antony.

Mark Antony's involvement with Cleopatra led to growing tensions with his co-ruler Octavian, which culminated in 31 BCE in a naval battle at Actium off the coast of Greece. Octavian's forces decisively defeated the forces of Mark Antony and Cleopatra, who fled to Egypt and soon thereafter committed suicide. Mark Antony's death paved the way for Octavian to assume sole rule of Rome. Four years later (27 BCE), the Roman Senate bestowed upon Octavian the title "Augustus," an event that marks the transition from the Roman Republic to the Empire.

Herod's Reign: The Middle Years (31–ca. 10 BCE)

The middle years of Herod's reign were a time of prosperity and success but with continuing domestic troubles. The battle of Actium was a mixed blessing for Herod. On the one hand, Mark Antony and Cleopatra's defeat and subsequent deaths removed Cleopatra's threat to Herod's kingdom. On the other hand, Mark Antony had been Herod's patron, championing his cause before the Roman Senate in 40 BCE. Therefore, after the battle of Actium Herod wasted no time in requesting an audience with Octavian. Before departing, Herod had Hyrcanus II executed, apparently because he considered the elderly Hasmonean a possible contender to the throne.[11] Herod's meeting with Octavian took place on the island of Rhodes. There Herod acknowledged his past connections to Mark Antony but pledged loyalty to Octavian, who he asked to be concerned not with "whose friend, but how loyal a friend" he had been (Josephus, *War* 1.390). Herod was so convincing that not only did Octavian reconfirm him as king, but soon thereafter he increased the size of Herod's kingdom, granting him additional territories and returning the plantations at Jericho that Mark Antony had given to Cleopatra. Over time, Herod's kingdom was expanded to include Samaria, the Golan, and territories northeast of the Golan, until it was almost as large as the Hasmonean kingdom had been at its greatest extent (map 2).[12]

At the same time, Herod continued to be plagued by problems with the Hasmonean members of his household. Before departing for Rhodes, Herod left his brother Pheroras in charge, and placed Mariamme and Alexandra under armed guard at Alexandrium-Sartaba, a palace-fortress north of Jericho perched on a mountain overlooking the Jordan Valley. Herod considered these measures necessary because he feared, perhaps justifiably, that Alexandra might take advantage of his absence to incite a revolt. The rest of Herod's family—including his mother Cypros, his sister Salome, and all his children including Mariamme's—were taken to Masada for safekeeping. The sequestration of groups of family members at different fortresses was due to the animosity between Mariamme and Alexandra on one hand, and Herod's mother and sister on the other, who detested each other.[13]

When Herod returned from Rhodes, Salome and Cypros conspired to eliminate Mariamme. Well-aware of Herod's extreme jealousy of her, they falsely accused Mariamme of having been unfaithful in his absence. Enraged, Herod had Mariamme executed, an act that he immediately regretted and that nearly drove him mad:[14]

> And he would frequently call out for her and frequently utter unseemly laments . . . And so he put aside the administration of his

kingdom, and was so far overcome by his passion that he would actually order his servants to summon Mariamme as if she were still alive and able to heed them. (Josephus, *Ant.* 15.241–42)

Alexandra took advantage of Herod's unstable emotional state to seize control of Jerusalem's fortresses.[15] Her actions were reported to Herod, who immediately had Alexandra put to death.

Even after Mariamme's and Alexandra's deaths, Herod's household troubles continued. Before her execution, Mariamme bore Herod five children: two daughters and three sons. The sons—Alexander and Aristobulus—were educated in Rome (the third son died at a young age in Rome). Sending native princes to Rome for an education was common practice, as the Romans governed their empire through a top-down approach by "Romanizing" the local aristocracies and elites.[16]

After his sons returned to Jerusalem in 17 BCE, Herod arranged marriages for the two princes. Alexander married Glaphyra, a daughter of Archelaus, king of Cappadocia. As we have seen, arranged marriages were a means of cementing political and social alliances among ruling and elite families. Intermarriage among relatives (endogamy) was also common; for example, Herod's wives included a cousin and a niece (see *War* 1.563).[17] Herod's son Aristobulus married Berenice, a daughter of Herod's sister Salome (his first cousin). As offensive as intermarriage among close relatives might seem to us, it was common among the upper classes, who used the arrangement to retain power within their families. This is how Mariamme came to be the granddaughter of two brothers: Hyrcanus II and Aristobulus II.[18] The Ptolemies in Egypt practiced a more extreme version of endogamy: brother-sister marriage (which biblical law prohibits). This is the reason many of the Ptolemaic kings were known by the epithet *Philadelphos*, a Greek term meaning "lover of my brother/sister," and it is why some of the cities they founded were called Philadelphia.

Some of Herod's non-Hasmonean relatives, especially Salome and Antipater, the son of Herod's first wife Doris, were jealous of Alexander and Aristobulus and led a campaign of slander against them. For the most part, the animosity and intrigues among members of Herod's household had little to do with whether Herod actually liked some more than others, but instead stemmed from their ambitions to succeed him to the throne (or have their side of the family succeed him to the throne). Anyone given preferential treatment by Herod was considered a potential heir-designate and therefore a threat to other sides of the family.

Herod's Reign: The Late Years (ca. 10–4 BCE)

The last years of Herod's reign (until his death in 4 BCE) were characterized by continuing domestic turmoil within his household and around Judea. The slanderous rumors about Alexander and Aristobulus, spread mostly by Antipater, eventually swayed Herod, who accused his two sons of treason and imprisoned them. In 7 BCE, he had them put to death: "He then sent his sons to Sebaste [Samaria], a town not far from Caesarea, and ordered them to be strangled" (Josephus, *War* 1.551).

Antipater also fell victim to Herod's paranoia. Hearing that Antipater was plotting to murder him and take over the throne, Herod ordered him executed just five days before his own death. The turmoil in Herod's household, the elimination of his most capable sons, and Herod's production of three different wills in the last two years of his life (with the last one issued after Antipater's execution) made his last years very unstable.[19]

Augustus reportedly quipped, "It is better to be Herod's pig (*hus*) than his son (*huios*)" (Macrobius, *Saturnalia* 2.4.11). If Augustus did say this, the statement is interesting for several reasons. First, it reflects Herod's widespread reputation for having his sons put to death. Second, it indicates that Augustus knew Greek well enough to make a pun on the words *hus* and *huios*, which sound similar. Third, the statement suggests that Herod observed biblical law prohibiting the consumption of pork, meaning that unlike his own sons, pigs were safe from slaughter.[20] Herod's reputation for executing his sons might have given rise to the story of the massacre (or slaughter) of the innocents as reported in Matthew 2:16:

> When Herod saw that he had been tricked by the wise men, he was infuriated, and he sent and killed all the [male] children in and around Bethlehem who were two years old or under, according to the time that he had learned from the wise men.

Ironically, although this story is the reason for Herod's lasting infamy as a cruel and ruthless ruler, it is an atrocity he probably did not commit. This episode is not mentioned in any sources aside from the Gospel of Matthew, where it is presented as part of Jesus's birth narrative. As we have seen, only two of the four Gospel accounts contain birth narratives, and they differ significantly from each other. This means there is no independent confirmation that this event ever occurred. Furthermore, Herod's command echoes Pharaoh's order to have all firstborn Hebrew males put to death (Exodus 1:22), thereby presenting Jesus as a new Moses. In fact, Matthew's account is filled with allusions to the exodus, as Herod's edict is immediately preceded by the story of Joseph and Mary's flight to Egypt (Mt 2:13–15). For these reasons, many scholars believe that the massacre of the innocents never occurred, but instead was inspired by Herod's reputation for executing his own sons.[21]

Shortly before Herod died, he fell ill. As rumors spread that he was dying, two Jewish educators (Greek *sophistai*) incited a crowd of youths to pull down a golden eagle that Herod had erected over one of the gates of the Jerusalem temple. Herod had the educators and those who assisted them burned alive (see Josephus, *War* 1.648–55). Josephus seems to indicate that the educators were Pharisees by calling them sophists, a term he uses as equivalent to rabbi.[22] Why these educators and their followers found the golden eagle offensive and tore it down is unclear, nor do we know over which gate of the temple it was placed. Josephus says the eagle violated biblical law: "It was, in fact, unlawful to place in the temple either images or busts or any representation whatsoever of a living creature" (*War* 1.650). It is true that Jewish art of the late Second Temple period (but not in later centuries) is almost entirely aniconic (without figured images), apparently because Jews strictly interpreted and adhered to the second commandment, which prohibits the making of images for worship. Nevertheless, there are a few examples of figured images in Jewish art of the late Second Temple period, including in Jerusalem.[23] Some scholars have speculated that the Jews found the eagle offensive because it was a symbol of the Roman Empire. However, images of eagles appear on Tyrian tetradrachmas (or sheqels), which were the only coins accepted as payment for the annual temple tax required of all Jewish adult men.[24] Even Solomon's temple had been decorated with figured images such as cherubs (1 Kgs 6:23–35). Therefore, the motivation for pulling down the golden eagle remains obscure.

Herod suffered from an agonizing disease in the final days of his life, for which he sought relief in the hot springs at Callirrhoe:

> He had fever, though not a raging fever, an intolerable itching of the whole skin, continuous pains in the intestines, tumors in the feet as in dropsy, inflammation of the abdomen and gangrene of the privy parts, engendering worms, in addition to asthma, with great difficulty in breathing, and convulsions in all his limbs . . . Thus he crossed the Jordan to take the warm baths at Callirrhoe, the water of which descend into the Lake Asphaltitis and from their sweetness are also used for drink. There, the physicians deciding to raise the temperature of his whole body with hot oil, he was lowered into a bath full of that liquid. (Josephus, *War* 1.656–57)

Many scholars have speculated on the nature of Herod's disease, with proposed diagnoses ranging from syphilis to kidney failure.[25] Although Herod apparently perished due to an illness, we cannot be certain that Josephus's description is accurate, as it was surely motivated by a desire to show that a horrible man was punished at the end of his life by suffering a horrible death. Herod died in his palace at Jericho in 4 BCE. His body was carried in a procession to Herodium, where he was laid to rest. Josephus brought *War* Book 1 to a close with an account of Herod's death and burial:

> Around the bier were Herod's sons and a large group of his relations; these were followed by the guards, the Thracian contingent, Germans and Gauls, all equipped as for war. The remainder of the troops marched in front, armed and in orderly array, led by their commanders and subordinate officers; behind these came five hundred of Herod's servants and freedmen, carrying spices. The body was thus conveyed for a distance of two hundred furlongs to Herodion, where, in accordance with the directions of the deceased, it was interred. So ended Herod's reign. (*War* 1.671–73)

The Division of Herod's Kingdom among His Sons

Upon Herod's death in 4 BCE, riots and uprisings erupted throughout Judea. Peace was restored only after Varus, the Syrian legate, moved in with three legions and brutally suppressed the unrest (sometimes called "the war of Varus"), reportedly crucifying about two thousand rebels. Herod left a will dividing the kingdom among three of his sons, which was subject to the emperor's approval. Augustus confirmed the division of Herod's kingdom, but gave each of the three sons lesser titles than king:[26]

1. Herod Archelaus, the elder son of Malthace the Samaritan, was made ethnarch of Judea, Samaria, and Idumaea (4 BCE–6 CE)
2. Herod Antipas, his youngest son and offspring of Malthace, was made tetrarch of Galilee and Peraea (4 BCE–39 CE)
3. Philip, the son of Cleopatra of Jerusalem, was made tetrarch of the northern territories of Trachonitis, Batanaea (biblical Bashan), Auranitis (biblical Hauran), Gaulanitis (Golan), Paneas (Banyas), and Ituraea (4 BCE–33/34 CE)[27]

Herod Archelaus

Herod Archelaus inherited the parts of his father's kingdom that were thoroughly Jewish/Judaized and Yahwistic/Samaritan.[28] He had the shortest reign of Herod's three sons, due to his inability to rule effectively. The Jews and Samaritans complained so bitterly about his cruelty that in 6 CE Augustus removed Archelaus and banished him to Gaul (France).

Philip

Philip is the only one of Herod's three sons who ruled until his death (33/34 CE).[29] His territory—consisting of the Golan and areas farther to the north and east—was populated mostly by gentiles. Philip established a new capital for his territory by the springs of Paneas (Banyas), one of the sources of the Jordan River, naming the city Caesarea Philippi in honor of the emperor and himself. Philip died childless after a reign of thirty-seven years, although he was married to Herodias, the daughter of Herod's sister Salome (his first cousin).[30] After his death, Philip's territory was placed under the direct administration of the legate in Syria.

Herod Antipas

Herod Antipas, who had the longest reign of the three brothers, inherited the Judaized territories of Galilee and Peraea.[31] Antipas initially chose Sepphoris, a Jewish town in the heart of Lower Galilee, as his capital. He renamed the town *Autokratoris* (Latin *Imperatoria*) in honor of Augustus, and reportedly rebuilt it as a Greco-Roman city. Sepphoris figures prominently in debates about the historical Jesus, as the small hamlet of Nazareth is only four miles (6.5 kilometers) away. Although Sepphoris is not mentioned in the Gospel accounts in connection with Jesus, many scholars believe that Jesus likely visited the town and there was exposed to Greco-Roman institutions and culture.[32] Around 20 CE, Antipas moved his capital to a newly established city on the western shore of the Sea of Galilee, which he named Tiberias in honor of the Emperor Tiberius (Augustus's successor).

Antipas's marriage to the daughter of the Nabataean king ended when he fell in love with Herodias, the wife of his brother Philip.[33] Antipas and Herodias divorced their spouses and married each other, violating a biblical law that prohibits marriage to a brother's wife. Antipas is probably best-known for his execution of John the Baptist, which the Gospels attribute to his condemnation of his unlawful marriage to Herodias: "For Herod [Antipas] had arrested John, bound him, and put him in prison on account of Herodias, his brother Philip's wife, because John had been telling him, 'it is not lawful for you to have her' " (Mt 14:3; also see Mk 6:14–29; Lk 3:1–2).

However, Josephus indicates that Antipas executed John the Baptist because he feared that John's movement might lead to unrest:[34] "Herod [Antipas] decided therefore that it would be much better to strike first and be rid of him before his work led to an uprising, than to wait for an upheaval, get involved in a difficult situation, and see his mistake" (*Ant.* 18.118).

Of course, the Herod mentioned in these passages in the Gospels and Josephus is Antipas, not Herod the Great. According to these accounts, Antipas executed John the Baptist at Machaerus in Peraea—one of Herod the Great's fortified desert palaces. A few decades later, Machaerus, like Masada, held out against the Romans after the fall of Jerusalem in 70 CE. Antipas's marriage to the ambitious Herodias eventually caused his downfall (see below).

The Roman Governors and Later
Successors of Herod

After Archelaus was deposed in 6 CE, his territory (Judea, Samaria, and Idumaea) was placed under the administration of Roman governors based at Caesarea Maritima. These governors—titled prefects or procurators—administered Judea independently on behalf of the emperor, but ultimately were subordinate to the legate in Syria.[35] Because they did not have the authority to command a legion, the main military force in the region remained stationed in Antioch, where the legate was based. Only one cohort (approximately 500 soldiers) was stationed permanently in Jerusalem, in the Antonia fortress.[36] Whereas Jerusalem had been the capital city and administrative base of Herod the Great and Archelaus, the Roman governors chose to reside at Caesarea Maritima, which had a harbor that facilitated communication with Rome and offered the amenities of a Greco-Roman city. As the administrators of Judea, the Roman governors were responsible for appointing the high priests in the Jerusalem temple.[37]

Pontius Pilate (26–37 CE)

The fifth prefect is the most infamous: Pontius Pilate, who Philo describes as "naturally inflexible, a blend of self-will and relentlessness," and speaks of his conduct as full of briberies, insults, robberies, outrages, and wanton injuries, executions without trial constantly repeated, ceaseless and supremely grievous cruelty (*Embassy to Gaius* 301–302 [38]).[38] Pilate's disregard for Jewish religious concerns became evident early in his administration, when he sent troops into Jerusalem with standards decorated with portraits of the emperor, in contrast to his predecessors who had refrained from doing so to avoid offending the Jews. After being confronted by crowds of protestors, Pilate withdrew the troops.

Pilate, of course, is notorious for having sentenced Jesus to death.[39] Interestingly, Luke is the only Gospel that describes Pilate handing Jesus over to Herod Antipas for judgment, as Jesus came from Galilee, the territory that was under Antipas's administration at the time:[40]

Then Pilate said to the chief priests and the crowds, "I find no basis for an accusation against this man." But they were insistent and said, "He stirs up the people by teaching throughout all Judea, from Galilee where he began even to this place." When Pilate heard this, he asked whether the man was a Galilean. And when he learned that he was under Herod's jurisdiction, he sent him off to Herod, who was himself in Jerusalem at that time . . . Even Herod with his soldiers treated him with contempt and mocked him; then he put an elegant robe on him, and sent him back to Pilate. That same day Herod and Pilate became friends with each other; before this they had been enemies. (Lk 23:4–12)

Of course, the Herod named in this passage is Herod Antipas, not Herod the Great.

Ultimately, Pilate's inability to govern the local population effectively led to his removal from office. A large group of armed Samaritans followed their leader to Mount Gerizim, expecting to find the sacred tabernacle vessels hidden there by Moses. Alarmed by the crowd, Pilate had his troops block the procession. A battle ensued with casualties, and Pilate executed the leader and the most influential Samaritans. The Samaritans appealed to the legate in Syria, who ordered Pilate to Rome for a trial and replaced him with another prefect.

Herod Agrippa I (Marcus Julius Agrippa)

Herod Agrippa I (37–44 CE) was the grandson of Herod the Great and Mariamme.[41] Like other native princes around the empire (including his father Aristobulus IV, who was executed by Herod in 7 BCE), Herod Agrippa I was raised and educated in Rome.[42] There he grew up in the company of members of the imperial family, and later befriended Gaius (better known by his nickname Caligula). When Gaius became emperor in 37 CE, he appointed Herod Agrippa I king of the territories that had belonged to Philip.

On his way to Judea in 38 CE, Agrippa I passed through Egypt. Upon arrival he was given a royal reception by the Jews of Alexandria, which was home to a large and prosperous Jewish population, including the famous philosopher Philo (ca. 20 BCE–50 CE). Thanks to his family's immense wealth, Philo was able to devote himself to the study of philosophy, a common pursuit among his elite male peers. As a Jew, however, Philo sought the answers to life's questions in the Torah rather than in the writings of Greek philosophers, although his approach was influenced by middle Platonic thought (a type of Platonism). For example, Philo used allegory as a means of resolving apparent contradictions in the text of the Hebrew Bible, or when the literal meaning of the text did not make sense to him. He believed that a divine intermediary being called the Logos bridged the gap between God's perfection and the imperfect material world. Philo's extensive writings were preserved by Christians, who adopted his allegorical approach in their appropriation of the biblical tradition and applied his concept of the Logos to Jesus Christ, the son of God.

At the beginning of his reign, Gaius governed moderately and enjoyed great popularity, but as time went on he came to believe he was a god and acted accordingly:

> He [Gaius] administered the empire quite high-mindedly during the first and second years of his reign. By exercising moderation, he made great advances in popularity both with the Romans themselves and with their subjects, he ceased to think of himself as a man, and, as he imagined himself a god because of the greatness of his empire, he was moved to disregard the divine power in all his official acts. (*Ant.* 18.256)

Gaius's increasingly delusional and autocratic behavior made him unpopular throughout the empire. Although his predecessors had been deified after their deaths, Gaius's demand to be worshiped as a god contrasted with Augustus's attempts to present himself as *primus inter pares*—"first among equals" and his adoption of the title *princeps* ("leader" or "first citizen"). Furthermore, the Jews had been exempted from participating in emperor cult because the Romans recognized Judaism as an ancient religion and allowed Jews to observe their ancestral laws (the Torah). Instead, twice daily sacrifices were offered in the Jerusalem temple on behalf of Rome and the emperor.[43]

Agrippa I's enthusiastic reception by the Jews of Alexandria and their refusal to worship Gaius as a god inflamed already tense relations with the gentile inhabitants of the city. A pogrom erupted: Jewish property was plundered, synagogues were destroyed, and the Jews were herded into one of the city's quarters, effectively creating a ghetto.[44] Not only did the Roman legate Flaccus fail to protect the Jews during the pogrom, but he punished them by dissolving their semi-autonomous civic organization (*politeuma*), effectively reducing them to the status of aliens. In protest, the Alexandrian Jews sent a delegation to Rome to appeal to Gaius under the leadership of their most distinguished representative, Philo. The gentiles sent a counter-delegation led by a Hellenized Egyptian and Jew-hater named Apion. Several decades later, Josephus wrote a work called *Against Apion* in which he attempted to refute Apion's anti-Jewish claims (see chapter 1).[45] According to Philo, the meetings with Gaius (which he documents in *Against Flaccus* and *On the Embassy to Gaius*) did not go well, and the question of the status of the Jews of Alexandria was not resolved until Claudius became emperor.

When Gaius proclaimed himself a god, he ordered the Syrian legate, Petronius, to convert the Jerusalem temple into a shrine for the imperial cult, with a statue of himself set up in it. Petronius stalled, realizing that carrying out Gaius's orders would likely incite a Jewish revolt. In the meantime, Agrippa I had arrived in Rome and learned of Gaius's order (40 CE). Agrippa I intervened with his old friend, and Gaius rescinded his order, thereby averting an almost certain disaster.[46]

Agrippa I's sister was Herodias, who had divorced Philip to marry his half-brother, Antipas (the ruler of Galilee and Peraea who had John the Baptist beheaded). In 37 CE, Gaius made Agrippa I ruler of the former territories of Philip and bestowed upon him the title of king, whereas Antipas had the lesser title of tetrarch. This rankled Herodias, who goaded her husband into asking Gaius for the title of king. Agrippa I countered by accusing Antipas of conspiracy against the emperor. As a result, Gaius removed Antipas from rule and gave his territories to Agrippa I (39 CE). Antipas and Herodias were banished to Gaul.

In 41 CE, Gaius, who had become increasingly unpopular, was assassinated. Agrippa I played a significant role in convincing the Roman Senate that Claudius should become the next emperor. Claudius rewarded Agrippa I by confirming him as king and added to his kingdom Archelaus's former territories (Judea, Samaria, and Idumaea). As a result, an enlarged version of Herod the Great's kingdom was reunited under the rule of his grandson, Agrippa I. Ancient Jewish sources speak in glowing terms of Agrippa I's piety and devotion to his people and the Torah.

As a descendant of the Hasmoneans, Agrippa I was fantastically popular with the Jews, although he had been raised in Rome and was not an observant Jew.[47] For example, most of his coins depict human images, including Gaius, Claudius, himself, and even pagan temples and deities. He had statues of his daughters displayed at Caesarea and Samaria-Sebaste. In contrast, Christian tradition describes Agrippa I as a persecutor of the developing Church. He had James the son of Zebedee beheaded and Peter arrested, although the latter escaped from prison:[48]

> About that time King Herod laid violent hands upon some who belonged to the church. He had James, the brother of John, killed with the sword. After he saw that it pleased the Jews, he proceeded to arrest Peter also. (Acts 12:1–3)

Notice that the author of Acts refers to Agrippa I as King Herod.[49] After Agrippa I died suddenly in Caesarea at the age of fifty-four, Claudius decided not to appoint his oldest son, Herod Agrippa II—who was only seventeen—to succeed him.[50] Instead, Agrippa I's kingdom was made part of the Roman province of Syria and placed under the administration of procurators. Their inability to deal with the diverse populations and unstable conditions exacerbated the deteriorating situation, and they often overreacted to perceived threats by employing military force. The following are some of the highlights—and lowlights—of the administrations of these procurators.[51]

Cuspius Fadus (44–46 CE)

Cuspius Fadus's administration is known for the appearance of a messianic figure named Theudas, who persuaded his followers to go to the Jordan River, where he would part the waters and lead them across. Fadus, alarmed by the crowd, attacked and killed many of them. Theudas was captured and decapitated, and his head was carried to Jerusalem:

> Then he said to them, "Fellow Israelites, consider carefully what you propose to do to these men. For some time ago Theudas rose up, claiming to be somebody, and a number of men, about four hundred, joined him; but he was killed and all who followed him were dispersed and disappeared." (Acts 5:35–36; also see Josephus, *Ant.* 20.97–99)

Tiberius Julius Alexander (46–48 CE)

Tiberius Julius Alexander was the nephew of Philo of Alexandria. He inherited Roman citizenship from his father and repudiated or abandoned Judaism, rising high in the ranks of the Roman administration. Claudius appointed him procurator of Judea from 46 to 48, and from 66 to 69 he served as prefect of Egypt under Nero, during which time he brutally suppressed the Jewish unrest in Alexandria that accompanied the First Revolt. Tiberius Julius Alexander played an instrumental role in Vespasian's elevation to emperor, and advised Titus as second-in-command during the siege of Jerusalem in 70 CE. His younger brother, Marcus Julius Alexander, was married to Berenice, the daughter of Agrippa I and sister of Agrippa II.[52] After Marcus Julius Alexander's premature death in 44 CE, Berenice married twice more (her second husband died and she abandoned her third husband). Later, Berenice became the mistress of Titus, who was eleven years her junior. Titus eventually had to send Berenice away due to the Roman public's disapproval of his involvement with an eastern Jewish princess, as the Roman historian Cassius Dio, writing in the early third century CE, reports:

> Berenice was at the very height of her power and consequently came to Rome along with her brother Agrippa. The latter was given the rank of praetor, while she dwelt in the palace, cohabiting with Titus. She expected to marry him and was already behaving in every respect as if she were his wife; but when he perceived that the Romans were displeased with the situation, he sent her away.[53]

Similarly, many Romans had frowned upon Cleopatra's affairs with Julius Caesar and Mark Antony about a century earlier.[54]

Ventidius Cumanus (48–52 CE)

During Ventidius Cumanus's administration, local unrest increased, as reflected by an incident that occurred during Passover (one of the three pilgrimage holidays), involving a Roman soldier posted on one of the porches overlooking the temple:

The usual crowd had assembled at Jerusalem for the feast of unleavened bread, and the Roman cohort had taken up its position on the roof of the portico of the temple . . . Thereupon one of the soldiers, raising his robe, stooped in an indecent attitude, so as to turn his backside to the Jews, and made a noise in keeping with his posture. (Josephus, *War* 2.224)

The insult was even worse than it seems, as Roman soldiers wore no undergarments under their tunics. Offended, the crowd of worshipers called on Cumanus to punish the soldier. When they began to throw stones, he called in reinforcements. Josephus reports that in the ensuing stampede, 20,000–30,000 Jews were killed. Although ancient crowd estimates are notoriously unreliable and often exaggerated (as happens even today), Josephus's account indicates that a large number of pilgrims lost their lives that day.

The worst incident—a conflict involving Samaritans and Jews (Galileans and Judeans)—cost Cumanus his post.[55] The conflict broke out when Galilean Jews on their way to the Jerusalem temple were murdered in Samaria. After appealing unsuccessfully to Cumanus to investigate the matter, armed Judeans joined with Galileans to exact revenge on the Samaritans, attacking and burning their villages. Cumanus led his troops against the Jews, killing and capturing many. The Jews and Samaritans appealed to the Syrian legate, who punished both sides before referring them to Claudius in Rome for further adjudication. Thanks to the intervention of Agrippa II (the son of Agrippa I), Claudius decided in favor of the Jews. He executed the Samaritan leaders and sent Cumanus into exile.

Marcus Antonius Felix (52–60 CE)

Marcus Antonius Felix (or Claudius Felix) was known in Roman circles for his three marriages, all to members of royal families. His first wife was the granddaughter of Mark Antony and Cleopatra. Felix's second wife was Drusilla, the daughter of Herod Agrippa I. As a young teenager, Drusilla was married to the king of Emesa (in Syria). When Felix became procurator of Judea, she was about fourteen years old. Felix was so taken by Drusilla's great beauty that he persuaded the sixteen-year-old to divorce her husband and marry him (54 CE), in violation of biblical law.[56]

Conditions grew increasingly anarchic during Felix's administration. Jewish urban terrorists called *sicarii* assassinated their compatriots by concealing daggers (Latin *sica*) under their cloaks and mingling in crowds, then sneaking up on their targets and stabbing them:[57]

> But while the country was thus cleared of these pests, a new species of banditti was springing up in Jerusalem, the so-called *sicarii*, who committed murders in broad daylight in the heart of the city. The festivals were their special seasons, when they would mingle with the crowd, carrying short daggers concealed under their clothing, with which they stabbed their enemies. Then, when they fell, the murderers joined in the cries of indignation and, through this plausible behavior, were never discovered. (Josephus, *War* 2.254–55)

Messianic and prophetic figures contributed to the unrest. One Egyptian Jew attracted thousands of followers, promising them that he would destroy the walls of Jerusalem with a command while standing on the Mount of Olives.[58] Felix sent his troops against the crowds, killing or capturing hundreds, but the Egyptian Jew escaped. According to Acts 21:38, a Roman tribune confused Paul with this Egyptian: "Then you are not the Egyptian who recently stirred up a revolt and led the four thousand assassins out into the wilderness?"

This episode occurred after Paul was arrested while on pilgrimage to the Jerusalem temple. Acts (21:26–36) reports that the Jews of Asia (that is, the Roman province of Asia, meaning Asia Minor, not the Far East!) saw Paul (who was from Tarsus in Asia Minor) in the company of a Greek named Trophimus of Ephesus (also in Asia Minor). Believing that Paul had brought his companion into the area within the *soreg* (a charge never directly refuted by Paul), which was off-limits to gentiles (see chapter 4), the Jews of Asia sounded the alarm. Inscriptions set into the *soreg* warned trespassers of punishment by death—and indeed, the Jewish mob was attempting to lynch Paul when he was taken into protective custody by the Romans:

> Then all the city was aroused, and the people rushed together. They seized Paul and dragged him out of the temple, and immediately the

doors were shut. While they were trying to kill him, word came to the tribune of the cohort that all Jerusalem was in an uproar. (Acts 21:30–31)

Because he was a Roman citizen, Paul eventually was escorted by five hundred troops to Caesarea Maritima, where it was up to the procurator to determine his fate.[59] Felix held Paul in custody at Caesarea for nearly two years, during which time they reportedly spoke frequently: "Some days later when Felix came with his wife Drusilla, who was Jewish, he sent for Paul and heard him speak concerning faith in Christ Jesus" (Acts 24:24).

Herod Agrippa II (Marcus Julius Agrippa)

Herod Agrippa II, the son of Agrippa I and brother of Drusilla and Berenice, was born in Rome and educated there as a teenager.[60] Although Agrippa II was too young to inherit the throne upon his father's death in 44 CE, a few years later Claudius made him king of Chalcis in Lebanon and gave him oversight of the Jerusalem temple and the right to appoint the high priests.[61] During Felix's administration, Claudius made Agrippa II king of Philip's former territories. When Nero became emperor in 54 CE, he added parts of Galilee and Peraea to Agrippa II's kingdom.

After her second husband died, Berenice moved into the palace at Caesarea Philippi with her bachelor brother, leading to rumors that the two had an incestuous relationship. Writing in the early second century CE, the Roman poet Juvenal lambasted the royal siblings in one of his satires:

> Then in the winter time, when the merchant Jason is shut out from view, and his armed sailors are blocked out by the white booths, she will carry off huge crystal vases, vases bigger still of agate, and finally a diamond of great renown, made precious by the finger of Berenice.
>
> It was given as a present long ago by the barbarian Agrippa to his incestuous sister, in that country where kings celebrate festal sabbaths with bare feet, and where a long-established clemency suffers pigs to attain old age. (*Satires* 6.153–60)[62]

When they were in Jerusalem, Agrippa II and Berenice stayed in the old Hasmonean palace on the western hill, which overlooked the Temple Mount. Agrippa II added another floor to the palace with a dining room that provided a view of the activities in the temple, including the sacrifices. This aroused the ire of the priests and Sanhedrin, who responded by erecting a high wall around the temple precincts. Because the wall also blocked the view of the Roman soldiers standing guard on the temple porticoes, Festus became involved in the dispute. Both sides appealed to the emperor (Nero), who allowed the Jews to leave the wall up, a decision attributed to the influence of his mistress (and later wife) Poppaea, who Josephus describes as "God fearing."

When the revolt broke out in 66 CE, Agrippa II's attempts to keep the peace were rebuffed and he was forced to leave Jerusalem. He sided with the Romans, providing military assistance and accompanying Titus during the siege of Jerusalem in 70. Agrippa II died around 92 CE, unmarried and childless.[63]

Porcius Festus (60–62 CE)

When Porcius Festus replaced Felix in 60 CE, he found Paul still in custody at Caesarea. Shortly after Festus's arrival, Agrippa II and his sister Berenice visited Caesarea to greet the newly installed procurator. Festus took the opportunity to consult with them about Paul's case:

> So on the next day Agrippa and Bernice came with great pomp, and they entered the audience hall with the military tribunes and the prominent men of the city. Then Festus gave the order and Paul was brought in. (Acts 25:23)

Although the Jews demanded to try Paul in Jerusalem, as a Roman citizen Paul invoked his right to be judged by the emperor. Therefore, Festus sent Paul to Rome, where he probably was executed a couple of years later.

Festus died in office (62 CE), leaving an interval when there was no procurator in Judea. In the interim, the high priest Ananus (or Annas) took advantage of the opportunity to have James "the Just," brother of Jesus and leader of Jesus's followers in Jerusalem, brought before the Sanhedrin on a charge of breaking biblical Jewish law. This was almost certainly a trumped-up charge, as James was known for being a pious and Torah-observant Jew. James's arrest likely was because of his outspoken opposition to and condemnation of the lifestyle of the wealthy Jerusalem elite, which included Ananus and other priests. The exact charge is unknown, but the fact that Ananus was found guilty and sentenced to death by stoning suggests he was accused of blasphemy:

> And so he [Ananus the high priest] convened the judges of the Sanhedrin and brought before them a man named James, the brother of Jesus who was called the Christ, and certain others. He accused them of having transgressed the law and delivered them to be stoned. (Josephus, *Ant.* 20.200)

The possibility that James's arrest and execution were motivated by political factors rather than by a violation of Jewish law is indicated by the opposition of moderate Jews and the Pharisees. These groups complained to Agrippa II and the newly installed procurator (Albinus), who deposed and replaced Ananus.

Lucceius Albinus (62–64 CE) and Gessius Florus (64–66 CE)

The last two procurators before the outbreak of the revolt are best known for their cruelty and greed.[64] Florus, whose wife's friendship with Nero's wife Poppaea secured him the post, is described by Josephus as having "stripped whole cities, ruined entire populations, and almost went the length of proclaiming throughout the country that all were at liberty to practice brigandage, on condition that he receive his share of the spoils" (*War* 2.278). Florus's most egregious act was taking money from the Jerusalem temple under the pretense that Nero wanted it. As these events unfolded, all-out war was sparked by a conflict between Jews and gentiles at Caesarea Maritima over access to a synagogue.

CHAPTER 7

THE FIRST JEWISH REVOLT
AGAINST ROME

(66–70 CE)

"The ostensible pretext for war was out of proportion to the mag-
nitude of the disasters to which it led" (*War* 2.285). Josephus's
succinct remark aptly summarizes the topic of this chapter: the First
Jewish Revolt and its aftermath.[1]

THE OUTBREAK OF WAR

By the spring of 66, the country was a tinderbox about to go up in flames.
The spark that lit the fire came not from Jerusalem but Caesarea Maritima, where tensions between Jews and gentiles had been escalating for
years. A synagogue at Caesarea adjoined a plot of land owned by a Greek,
who refused repeated Jewish offers to purchase the property. Instead, the
owner built workshops on the property, leaving only a narrow passage
to access the synagogue. Upon arrival at the synagogue one Sabbath, the
Jews found another Greek conducting a mock sacrifice of birds at the
entrance to the passage. Fighting erupted and the cavalry commander
stationed at Caesarea intervened. When the Jews appealed to Gessius
Florus, he had them arrested.[2]

Outraged at learning of the events in Caesarea, the Jews of Jerusalem
were further incensed when Florus took money from the temple. A
crowd assembled, mockingly passing around a basket to collect alms for

the "needy" governor. Enraged at the insult, Florus unleashed a cohort of soldiers, who sacked the city and massacred some of the inhabitants. Josephus writes that Florus even crucified Jews of equestrian rank—that is, high-ranking Jews who should have been immune from this method of execution. Berenice (who was in Jerusalem) and Agrippa II (who returned from Alexandria, where he was visiting Tiberius Julius Alexander, then the prefect of Egypt) tried unsuccessfully to restore peace:

> Subsequently, he [Agrippa II] endeavored to induce the people to submit to the orders of Florus until a successor was sent by Caesar [Nero] to replace him. But this exasperated the Jews, who heaped abuse upon the king and formally proclaimed his banishment from the city; some of the insurgents even ventured to throw stones at him. (Josephus, *War* 2.406)

In the meantime, a band of Jewish rebels had taken Masada from a small garrison that occupied the mountain after Herod's death (*War* 2.408). In Jerusalem, the traditional sacrifices offered in the temple on behalf of the Roman state and emperor were halted by Eleazar, son of Ananias, a young high priest who was captain of the temple. This decision was opposed by many of the high priests and members of the royal (Herodian) family, reflecting a division along lines of class and wealth, for the most affluent and prominent Jews had the most to lose in a conflict with Rome. These prominent Jews called upon Florus and Agrippa II to send troops and stop the violence before it escalated. Florus ignored their request, but Agrippa II, who was responsible for the temple (which was occupied by rebels), dispatched two thousand cavalry to Jerusalem.[3]

At this point, Josephus reports, "a certain Menahem, son of Judas surnamed the Galilean—that redoubtable doctor who in old days, under Quirinius, had upbraided the Jews for recognizing the Romans as masters when they already had God" (*War* 2.433), and some of his accomplices raided Herod's fortress at Masada, bringing the arms they plundered to Jerusalem. Thus equipped, Menahem became a leader of the rebel forces in Jerusalem, and his band was instrumental in taking Herod's palace a couple of weeks later.

After a week of fighting, the insurgents took the Upper City (Western Hill) and burned down the house of the high priest, Agrippa II's palace (the old Hasmonean palace), and the public archives office, which was targeted because it housed tax and loan records. When the rebels captured the Antonia fortress and slaughtered its garrison, Agrippa's troops and supporters took refuge in Herod's palace. They left after capitulating, but the Roman cohort, which was holed up in the three towers adjacent to Herod's palace, was massacred by the insurgents, who reneged on a promise of safe conduct after offering terms of surrender. The rebels also murdered the high priest, who had been hiding in the palace.[4]

These victories encouraged Menahem to such a degree that he became, Josephus says, "inflated and brutalized" (*War* 2.442). Unable to tolerate his behavior, the followers of Eleazar (the captain of the temple) captured, tortured, and executed Menahem, and massacred the members of his band. Among the few who managed to escape was Eleazar ben Yair, a relative of Menahem's, who made his way to Masada, where he became the leader of the rebels holding out there.[5]

By August–September 66 CE, violence between Jews and gentiles had erupted throughout the country, resulting in massacres and atrocities in many cities. Finally, Cestius Gallus, the Syrian legate, took action. He marched south from Antioch at the head of some 30,000 soldiers: four legions (III Gallica; VI Ferrata; X Fretensis; XII Fulminata—only the last was at the full strength of 5,250 soldiers), six infantry cohorts (a cohort is about 500 men), four *alae* of cavalry (each ca. 500 men), and a sizable number of auxiliary forces supplied by local kings, including 15,000 troops accompanied by Agrippa II. The Roman forces followed the coast by way of Akko (Ptolemais), Caesarea Maritima, and Aphek-Antipatris, reaching Lydda (Lod) at Sukkot (the Feast of Tabernacles), when Jerusalem was teeming with pilgrims. Along the way, Cestius dispatched troops to subdue Galilee, which submitted for the most part peacefully, following the lead of Sepphoris. From Lydda, the army proceeded inland to Jerusalem, where Cestius set up camp on Mount Scopus.[6]

Cestius began his assault on Jerusalem by burning the northern suburb of Bezetha, but his troops were repelled when they attacked the Temple Mount. For reasons that are unclear, Cestius then ordered his army to retreat to the coast. Pursued by the Jews and unable to regroup, the Roman soldiers were ambushed in the mountain pass at Beth-Horon. Cestius made it back to Antioch with his life and only a fraction of his army, having lost six thousand soldiers (more than a legion) and much of his equipment and animals. The battle at Beth-Horon went down in history as one of the most humiliating defeats ever suffered by the Roman army. The Jewish rebels plundered the corpses, collected the abandoned military equipment, and returned victorious to Jerusalem.[7]

With Cestius's defeat, all-out war became inevitable. Strongly pro-Roman Jews fled Jerusalem, and moderate pro-Romans now had to cast their lot with the anti-Roman rebels: "After this catastrophe of Cestius many distinguished Jews abandoned the city as swimmers desert a sinking ship" (Josephus, *War* 2.556). Because the country was no longer under Roman rule, the Jews set up a government with moderates and high priests in control—although by the end of the revolt, extremists had taken over. The country was divided into seven districts under the administration of military governors: Jerusalem, Idumaea, Peraea, Jericho, Western Judea, Northeast Judea, and Galilee (including Gamla in the Golan). Josephus was put in charge of Galilee, a challenging task as this region lay directly in the path of the Roman advance from Syria. Furthermore, Galilee's Jewish population was divided into pro- and anti-war factions, with some cities (such as Sepphoris) supporting the Romans. Josephus's bitterest enemy was John, son of Levi of Gischala (Gush Halav) in Upper Galilee, who became the leader of a powerful rebel band. Another band of extremists was led by Simon bar Giora of Gerasa, who early in the revolt terrorized the wealthy by raiding their houses. After the high priest Ananus, who was in charge of Jerusalem, sent forces against Simon, he and his followers fled to Masada, where they remained until later in the revolt when Ananus was killed (Josephus, *War* 2.653) (see chapter 8). Both John and Simon played prominent roles in the siege and fall of Jerusalem in 70.[8]

The Subjugation of the Country Outside of Jerusalem

The emperor Nero, who was in Greece when he learned of Cestius's defeat, sent his general Vespasian to Syria to restore order. In the spring of 67, Vespasian assembled his forces in Antioch and dispatched his older son Titus to Alexandria to bring an additional legion. Altogether Vespasian had about 60,000 troops under his command: two legions based in Antioch (V Macedonica and X Fretensis) and the Alexandrian-based legion (XV Apollinaris); twenty-three auxiliary cohorts; six *alae* of cavalry; and troops provided by local kings including Agrippa II, who was in Antioch when Vespasian arrived.[9]

Vespasian pushed southward with his troops along the coast toward Galilee. When he reached Ptolemais (Akko), he was met by a delegation from Sepphoris requesting Roman protection. And so it was that even before the army took the field, the major city in Galilee had surrendered.[10] From Ptolemais, Vespasian moved with his army into Galilee, where Jewish forces abandoned many of the towns without a fight. Josephus had taken refuge in the fortified town of Jotapata (Hebrew Yodefat), which held out against a Roman siege for forty-seven days. Excavations in the mid-1990s uncovered light arrowheads and ballista stones connected with the siege and suggest that the Romans launched their main assault from the northwest—the town's most accessible side. When Jotapata finally succumbed in June or July 67, the inhabitants were slaughtered or enslaved. Josephus, who was hiding in a cistern with forty companions, survived and was taken into custody by Vespasian (see chapter 1).[11]

Vespasian established permanent military bases at Caesarea and Scythopolis (Beth-Shean), both of them gentile cities with a mild winter climate. He now turned his attention to Lower Eastern Galilee and the Golan, marching on Tiberias, which surrendered voluntarily, and then marched northward along the shore of the Sea of Galilee to Taricheae (Magdala or Migdal—the hometown of Mary Magdalene). Both Tiberias and Taricheae were under Agrippa II's jurisdiction but had been overtaken by rebels. Although the Jewish defenders at Taricheae put up a brave defense, they were no match for the Romans. The townspeople fled by taking to fishing boats and rafts on the lake, where they were pursued by the Romans, who slaughtered so many that, according to Josephus, the water turned red with blood:

> One could see the whole lake red with blood and covered with corpses, for not a man escaped. During the following days the district reeked with a dreadful stench and presented a spectacle equally horrible. The beaches were strewn with wrecks and swollen carcasses; these corpses, scorched and clammy in decay, so polluted the atmosphere that the catastrophe which plunged the Jews in mourning inspired even its

authors with disgust. Such was the issue of this naval engagement. The dead, including those who fell in the previous defense of the town, numbered six thousand seven hundred. (*War* 3.530–31)

The surviving Jews were executed or enslaved by Vespasian, who shipped six thousand of the fittest to Corinth to work on the construction of the Isthmian Canal, recently begun by Nero.[12]

With the fall of Taricheae, all the other settlements in the region surrendered to the Romans, except for Gischala and Mount Tabor in Galilee, and Gamla in the Golan. Gischala (Gush Halav), the hometown of John, son of Levi, surrendered after John and his followers fled to Jerusalem under cover of night. Mount Tabor was taken by a Roman detachment during the siege of Gamla. Gamla was a large fortified Jewish town perched on the steep slopes of a mountain overlooking the northeast shore of the Sea of Galilee (the town's name means "camel," from the mountain's hump-like shape) (fig. 40). Like Tiberias and Taricheae, it was under Agrippa II's jurisdiction but supported the revolt. Gamla fell after a heroic resistance by the inhabitants. During the month-long siege, the Romans breached the walls but suffered heavy losses when the roofs of houses on which the soldiers were crowded collapsed beneath their weight, burying them. Other soldiers were picked off by the town's defenders as they tried to flee through the narrow alleys. After the Romans succeeded in entering the town a second time, some of the inhabitants chose to take their own lives by flinging themselves over the steep slopes on which the town was built—for which reason Gamla is sometimes referred to as "the Masada of the Golan":

> Despairing of their lives and hemmed in on every side, multitudes plunged headlong with their wives and children into the ravine which had been excavated to a vast depth beneath the citadel. Indeed, the rage of the Romans was thus made to appear milder than the frantic self-immolation of the vanquished, four thousand only being slain of the former, while those who flung themselves over the cliff were found to exceed five thousand. (Josephus, *War* 4.79–80)[13]

Shmaryahu Gutman's 1976–1988 excavations at Gamla brought to light vivid evidence of the Roman siege, in which three legions participated: the XV Apollinaris, the V Macedonica, and the X Frentensis. The town was fortified only on the east as the other sides are protected by deep ravines. When the revolt broke out in 66, the fortifications consisted of a row of houses abutting each other, running down the east slope, dominated at the top by a circular stone tower. Narrow alleyways between the houses had been blocked with stones to create a continuous line of defense. Large concentrations of ballista stones and projectiles (iron catapult bolts and arrowheads) indicate that the Romans employed heavy artillery and focused their initial assault high on the east slope (Area G, near the synagogue), while simultaneously attacking points below (Areas M and T). The tips of some catapult bolts had bent from the force of impact with their targets. Several breaches in the fortifications appear to have been made by the Romans. In a narrow alleyway near the wall, the remains of a complete set of military equipment belonging to a legionary of the V Macedonica was discovered under a stone collapse. The set includes remnants of a helmet, segmented armor, a dagger, a scabbard chape for a sword, a shield, and an ownership tag. Guy Stiebel noted that this equipment shows signs of battle damage and speculated that the soldier had been dragged wounded or dead from the collapse, leaving behind part of his gear.[14]

Warfare in antiquity was largely a seasonal affair. By November 67, when the cold, rainy season had set in, the entire northern part of the country had been subdued by the Romans. Vespasian settled his troops in their winter quarters at Caesarea Maritima and Scythopolis, planning to resume his campaign in the spring. By now, Jerusalem was filled with refugees who had poured into the city in the wake of the Roman subjugation of Galilee. Among them were extremists such as John of Gischala and his followers, creating additional factions that began fighting with each other. The extremists soon took over, eliminating moderates and anyone suspected of pro-Roman sympathies. According to the fourth-century writer Eusebius, by this time the early Christian community of Jerusalem had abandoned the city for Pella in Peraea.[15] Also by this time, sicarii had taken over Masada, using it as a base for raiding nearby settlements. One of these was the Jewish village at Ein Gedi, whose inhabitants were massacred by the sicarii during a raid at Passover.[16]

As the rainy season ended (spring 68), Vespasian renewed his campaign, intending to isolate Jerusalem by subduing the rest of the country first. He turned his attention to the coastal cities and western Judea

(Aphek-Antipatris, Lydda [Lod], Jamnia), Idumaea, Samaria, and Per-aea. In May–June 68 CE, Vespasian took Jericho and destroyed the sectarian settlement at Qumran, some of whose members may have fled south and taken refuge atop Masada. It was at this time that Vespasian had a bound Jewish captive tossed into the Dead Sea, after being told that it is impossible to sink in the water (see chapter 2).[17]

With the rest of the country subdued, Vespasian returned to his base at Caesarea and began preparations for the siege of Jerusalem. However, Nero's suicide in Rome delayed his plans, as Vespasian awaited orders from the next emperor to proceed. The delay was extended when the situation in Rome deteriorated, after a civil war erupted with a rapid succession of claimants to the throne ("the year of the four emperors").[18]

At the beginning of the revolt, when Simon bar Giora fled from the high priest Ananus in Jerusalem and took refuge atop Masada, the other rebels had regarded him with suspicion and confined him to the lower part of the fortress.[19] Eventually, however, Simon gained their trust, and he and his band joined them in raiding nearby settlements. In the meantime, the high priest Ananus had been put to death by a mob in Jerusalem, leaving Simon and his band free to depart Masada. For a while they roamed around southern Judea and Idumaea, plundering many of the same towns and villages whose inhabitants had been terrorized by the marauding sicarii from Masada.[20] Josephus describes the devastation wrought by Simon and his followers:

> Just as a forest in the wake of locusts may be seen stripped quite bare, so in the rear of Simon's army nothing remained but a desert. Some places they burnt, others they razed to the ground; all vegetation throughout the country vanished, either trodden under foot or consumed; while the tramp of their march rendered cultivated land harder than the barren soil. In short, nothing touched by their ravages left any sign of its having ever existed. (*War* 4.536–37)

While awaiting word from Rome, Vespasian subdued the rest of Judea and Idumaea aside from Jerusalem, including destroying the ancient town of Hebron. By the late spring of 69 CE, the only remaining holdouts were Herod's fortified palaces at Herodium, Machaerus (in Peraea), and Masada, which were in the hands of Jewish rebels. By this time Simon and his followers were camped outside the walls of Jerusalem, killing anyone they caught leaving the city. The situation inside the city was equally dire, with various rebel factions including John of Gischala's followers terrorizing the population.[21]

The Siege of Jerusalem

Eventually the people of Jerusalem admitted Simon into the city, hoping he could rid them of John—a solution that only worsened the situation by escalating the sectarian violence. As a result, the city was divided among three extremist factions: John of Gischala's band held the outer court of the temple and part of the City of David; a faction led by Eleazar ben Simon occupied the inner court of the temple; and Simon bar Giora's band, which was the largest and most powerful (and included about 5,000 Idumaeans [*War* 5.249]), controlled the Upper City and part of the City of David. The Roman historian Tacitus describes as follows the conditions in Jerusalem:

> There were three generals, three armies: the outermost and largest circuit of the wall was held by Simon, the middle of the city by John, and the temple was guarded by Eleazar. John and Simon were strong in numbers and equipment, Eleazar had the advantage of position: between these three there was constant fighting, treachery, and arson, and a great store of grain was consumed. (*Histories* V.12.3)[22]

As the factions continued to battle each other in Jerusalem, the situation in Rome eventually stabilized when Vespasian was proclaimed emperor and assumed the throne. In the summer of 70 CE he departed for Rome, leaving his older son Titus to oversee the siege of Jerusalem. In the meantime, during the ongoing violence in Jerusalem, much of the grain stores—a critical food supply for the upcoming siege—was consumed by fire as buildings around the city went up in flames:

> At all events the result was that all the environs of the temple were reduced to ashes, the city was converted into a desolate no man's land for their domestic warfare, and almost all the corn, which might have sufficed them for many years of siege, was burnt up. (Josephus, *War* 5.25)

Written centuries later, the Babylonian Talmud recalls the famine caused by the senseless destruction of Jerusalem's grain supply:

> The *biryoni* [Zealots] were then in the city. The Rabbis said to them:
> Let us go out and make peace with them [the Romans]. They would
> not let them, but on the contrary said, Let us go out and fight them.
> The Rabbis said: You will not succeed. They then rose up and burnt
> the stores of wheat and barley so that a famine ensued. (b. Gittin 56a)
> (Soncino translation)

After assembling his forces at Caesarea, Titus reached Jerusalem and
set up camp on Mount Scopus and the Mount of Olives just before Passover (April–May) 70 CE—that is, at the time of the spring harvest season.
He commanded four legions—the three headed by his father (V Macedonica; X Fretensis; XV Apollinaris) and the reconstituted XII Fulminata
(which had been decimated at Cestius's defeat); five thousand supplementary legionaries brought from Egypt and Mesopotamia; a large
number of Syrian auxiliaries; and troops provided by local kings. Tiberias Julius Alexander (Philo's nephew) accompanied Titus as his chief
advisor. As a former procurator of Judea, he was intimately familiar
with Jerusalem.[23]

Yet the infighting within the city continued. When Eleazar opened
the gates to the inner court of the temple for the Passover celebration,
John's band launched a surprise attack and took over, reducing to two
the number of factions in the city: his and Simon's. However, once the
Roman assault began, the factions united. Titus launched his offensive
against the northern side of the city, which, although enclosed by three
successive walls, lacks the natural protection of a deep valley like the
other sides. The outermost (Third) wall, which enclosed a large but relatively undeveloped area (the suburb of Bezetha) was breached after fifteen days of being assaulted with battering rams. The Romans breached
the Second Wall after five days, but they were repelled by the defenders
and took it only after another four days of fighting. Each of the four legions now began raising earth ramps for battering rams against the First
Wall (on the north side of the Upper City) (which was defended by Simon
bar Giora) and the Antonia Fortress (which was defended by John of
Gischala).[24]

While the Roman troops were busy erecting the siege works, Titus
dispatched Josephus in an unsuccessful attempt to persuade the defenders to surrender:

Josephus, accordingly, went round the wall, and, endeavoring to keep out of range of missiles and yet within ear-shot, repeatedly implored them to spare themselves and the people, to spare their country and their temple . . . Josephus, during this exhortation, was derided by many from the ramparts, by many execrated, and by some assailed with missiles. (Josephus, *War* 5.362, 375)[25]

As food supplies within the city dwindled, famine spread and the inhabitants fought each other for every scrap. Poor people, the very young, and the elderly suffered the most.[26] Those unfortunates caught trying to flee the city were tortured and put to death by John and Simon, or by the Romans. The Romans tried to intimidate the Jews into submission by returning prisoners to the city with their hands cut off and by crucifixion near the walls:

They were accordingly scourged and subjected to torture of every description, before being killed, and then crucified opposite the walls . . . The soldiers, out of rage and hatred amused themselves by nailing their prisoners in different postures; and so great was their number, that space could not be found for the crosses nor crosses for the bodies. (Josephus, *War* 5.449, 451)

When Syrian auxiliaries found a refugee picking gold coins he had swallowed for safekeeping out of his feces, the soldiers began cutting open other deserters in the hopes of finding more hidden treasure.[27]

After seventeen days, the legions finished piling four massive earthen ramps against the wall. The defenders promptly destroyed these by tunneling underneath, buttressing the tunnels with timbers smeared with pitch and bitumen which they set on fire, causing the mounds of earth to collapse. Titus commanded his men to construct a siege wall encircling the city (the same kind of wall erected by the Romans three years later around the base of Masada), to ensure that none of the besieged could escape, and that no supplies or assistance could reach them.[28] The wall—completed in only three days—worsened the famine within the city:

For the Jews, along with all egress, every hope of escape was now cut off; and the famine, enlarging its maw, devoured the people by households and families. The roofs were thronged with women and babes completely exhausted, the alleys with the corpses of the aged; children and youths, with swollen figures, roamed like phantoms through the market-places and collapsed wherever their doom took them. (Josephus, *War* 5.512–13)

As the famine became more severe, Josephus reports that a starving mother slaughtered and cannibalized her infant son.[29] Discussing Josephus's descriptions of the atrocities committed in Jerusalem during the siege, the modern historian Emil Schürer remarked, "Josephus's imagination was fertile, but even if only half of what he says is true, it was still horrible enough."[30]

After another three weeks, the Romans re-erected the ramps against the Antonia, which they took and razed to the ground after fierce fighting.[31] Unbelievably, despite the famine, fighting, and atrocities, the daily sacrifices in the temple had continued until now. But Josephus reports that on the day the Antonia was razed, the sacrifices ceased, probably because there were no more lambs.[32] Later, the rabbis lamented this disastrous day in the Mishnah, saying, "Five things befell our fathers on the 17th of Tammuz . . . the Daily Whole-offering (Hebrew *tamid*) ceased" (m. Taanith 4.6).[33]

The Fall of Jerusalem and Destruction of the Temple

Josephus, who had been continuing his rounds outside the walls, again attempted to persuade the defenders to surrender but was rebuffed. Once the Antonia was razed, Titus instructed his troops to construct a ramp by the wall of the Temple Mount. After the wall was breached, fighting spread onto the roofs of the porches on the Temple Mount, which were set ablaze. The Romans raised another ramp against the fortification wall surrounding the temple (inside the Temple Mount), which they breached by setting fire to its gates. Although, according to Josephus, the temple burned down when a rogue Roman soldier flung a burning timber into it, he blames the temple's destruction on the Jewish defenders for having taken refuge inside the building. In fact, Josephus repeatedly attempts to exonerate Titus, claiming that he would never have ordered the temple's destruction, which was done against his wishes.[34]

It is true, as Josephus says, that "the Romans would never venture, except under the direst necessity, to set fire to the holy places" (*War* 6.121). However, Josephus's account of Titus's reluctance to destroy the Jerusalem temple is contradicted by Sulpicius Severus's reference to the same event: "On the other hand, others, and Titus himself, expressed their opinion that the Temple should be destroyed without delay, in order that the religion of the Jews and Christians should be more completely exterminated" (*Chronica* II.30:7).[35] Sulpicius Severus was a late fourth–early fifth century CE Christian writer from Gaul (France), which means he was far removed in time and space from the destruction of the Jerusalem temple. His account is relevant to our discussion because a mid-nineteenth-century scholar named Jacob Bernays suggested that Sulpicius's description of the temple's destruction derives not from Josephus but from a lost section of Tacitus's *Histories*. Since then, most scholars have preferred Sulpicius's version, that Titus ordered the temple destroyed on the grounds that Tacitus would be a less biased source than Josephus, whose apologetic tendencies are well-known. Commissioned by his Flavian patrons to write his histories, Josephus might have whitewashed Titus's role in the temple's destruction by absolving him of responsibility. On the other hand, Sulpicius's version presents its own difficulties, as he was hostile to the Jews and clearly modified the original text.[36] Whether or not Titus ordered the temple's destruction, this disagreement is a reminder that Josephus and other ancient sources are not always accurate or reliable and therefore must be read critically.

As the temple burned, Titus and his commanders rushed into the building and looted its treasures, including the menorah (seven-branched candelabrum) and showbread table, which were taken to Rome. Other sacred objects from the temple were turned over to Titus by priests who had held them in safekeeping and were captured or surrendered. With the temple still in flames, the Roman troops set up their standards in the temple court and sacrificed to them, hailing Titus as *imperator* (commander)—a title usually reserved for the emperor.[37]

The desecration of the Jerusalem temple by pagan sacrifices might be the desolating sacrilege mentioned in the Gospel accounts as a fulfillment of Jesus's prophecy that the temple would be destroyed, echoing earlier predictions of the end of days in the book of Daniel. The book of Daniel is believed to have been written around 167–164 BCE, that is, at

the time of the Maccabean revolt.[38] It refers to the tumultuous events
that occurred in Judea when Antiochus IV Epiphanes outlawed Judaism and re-dedicated the Jerusalem temple to the Greek god Olympian
Zeus. Daniel 9:24–27 contains the prophecy of seventy weeks, in which
Daniel ponders the meaning of Jeremiah's prediction (25:11–12 and 29:10)
that Jerusalem would remain desolate for seventy years. Daniel is told
by the angel Gabriel about various events that would take place within
a period of seventy weeks of years (each week = one year), including the
setting up of an abomination of desolation or desolating sacrilege (Hebrew *shikutz meshomem*) in the temple. Abomination is the Hebrew term
for an idol:

> After the sixty-two weeks, an anointed one [the Jewish high priest
> Onias III] shall be cut off and shall have nothing, and the troops of
> the prince [Antiochus IV] who is to come shall destroy the city and
> the sanctuary. Desolations are decreed. He [Antiochus IV] shall make
> a strong covenant with many [Hellenizing Jews] for one week, and for
> half of the week he shall make sacrifice and offering cease; and in their
> place shall be an *abomination that desolates*, until the decreed end is
> poured out upon the desolator. (Daniel 9:26–27; also see 11:31–32)

> From the time that the regular burnt offering is taken away and the
> *abomination that desolates* is set up, there shall be one thousand two
> hundred ninety days. (Daniel 12:11)

The desolating sacrilege is also mentioned in 1 Maccabees:

> Now on the fifteenth day of Kislev, in the one hundred forty-fifth year;
> they erected a *desolating sacrilege* on the altar of burnt offering. . . . On
> the twenty-fifth day of the month they offered sacrifice on the altar that
> was on top of the altar of burnt offering. (1 Mc 1:54, 59; also see 6:7)

The desolating sacrilege of Daniel and 1 Maccabees seems to refer to an
altar to Zeus erected by Antiochus IV in the Jerusalem temple.

According to the Gospel accounts, Jesus foretold the destruction of
the Temple and described signs of the end of days:

> So when you see the *desolating sacrilege* standing in the holy place, as
> was spoken of by the prophet Daniel (let the reader understand), then
> those in Judea must flee to the mountains. (Mt 24:15–16)

> But when you see the *desolating sacrilege* set up where it ought not to
> be (let the reader understand), then those in Judea must flee to the
> mountains. (Mk 13:14: also see Lk 21:20–21)

Jesus's statement implies that the prophecy of the desolating sacrilege
in Daniel 9:27 is about to be fulfilled.

What is the desolating sacrilege of the Gospel accounts? The answer
depends partly on whether they were composed before or after 70 CE.
Notice the difference between Mark and Matthew:

> But when you see the desolating sacrilege set up where it ought not
> to be . . . (Mark)

> So when you see the desolating sacrilege standing in the holy place . . .
> (Matthew)

Mark is generally thought to be the earliest Gospel, written around
the time of the First Revolt or soon thereafter, while Matthew is usually
dated circa 80–90 CE. Therefore, the authors of these Gospels did not
necessarily understand the desolating sacrilege to be the same thing. Depending on the date of composition, the author of the Gospel of Mark
might have thought the desolating sacrilege was a statue that the Romans
would set up in the temple (in the future), as Caligula had intended to
do in 39–40 CE. The author of the Gospel of Matthew might have understood the desolating sacrilege as the Roman standards set up in the
temple in 70 CE, to which Titus's troops offered sacrifices.[39]

Although the temple was destroyed on the tenth day of the month of
Av, later rabbinic tradition harmonized the destruction of both the first
and second temples on the ninth of Av (in August).[40] But the destruction of the temple in 70 CE did not mark the end of the siege of Jerusalem, which continued for another month. While the temple was ablaze,
the Romans set fire to the Ophel and the City of David (Lower City), as
the Jewish defenders had fled to the Upper City. Titus now instructed
his troops to erect ramps at the northwest and northeast corners of the
Upper City (against the First Wall)—a difficult task due to the shortage
of wood around Jerusalem, which had been stripped bare of trees during the siege. After eighteen days the Romans completed the siege works
and breached the wall but met with little resistance from the starved
and exhausted defenders, many of whom were caught fleeing through

underground sewers.[41] One such sewer was excavated recently beneath an ancient paved street along the Tyropoeon Valley, which connected the Pool of Siloam at the southern tip of the City of David with the Temple Mount.[42] John of Gischala was among those who took refuge in the sewers, but surrendered after emerging due to starvation. Simon bar Giora was captured later, after surfacing from a tunnel beneath the temple.[43]

Josephus reports that as the Romans overran the Upper City, they massacred the inhabitants, and ransacked and burned down the houses: "Pouring into the alleys, sword in hand, they massacred indiscriminately all whom they met, and burnt the houses with all who had taken refuge within" (*War* 6.404). From 1969 to 1982, the Israeli archaeologist Nahman Avigad conducted excavations in that part of the Upper City that now is in the Old City's Jewish Quarter, bringing to light richly decorated urban mansions that belonged to Jerusalem's elite in the first century CE (see chapter 4). Avigad dubbed one of these the "Burnt House" because its ruins—preserving only the basement level—were covered with soot and ash from the conflagration in 70 CE. A stone weight inscribed with the name "Bar Kathros" suggests that the house belonged to that priestly family. In a small kitchen on one side of the basement, Avigad found the skeletal arm of a young woman in her early twenties, who was trapped and crushed when the burning house collapsed on top of her. These were the first remains of a human victim of the Roman siege of Jerusalem discovered in archaeological excavations.[44]

On Titus's orders, the Roman soldiers rounded up all the survivors, executing the very young, the elderly, the infirm, and anyone who resisted or was a known insurgent. Seven hundred of the tallest and most handsome youths were selected to be paraded in the triumph at Rome, while able-bodied men were shipped off to Egypt for hard labor in mines or were saved for use in gladiator and animal fights. Women and children under the age of seventeen were sold into slavery. According to Josephus, the price of slaves in the Roman Empire dropped dramatically due to the glut created in the aftermath of the revolt. He reports that, "The total number of prisoners taken throughout the entire war amounted to ninety-seven thousand, and of those who perished during the siege, from first to last, one million one hundred thousand" (*War*

6.420). Although these numbers are unreliable and surely inflated, they give an impression of the scale of the loss of life.[45] It is at this point—the end of the siege of Jerusalem—that Josephus concludes Book 6, the penultimate book of *The Jewish War*.

THE FLAVIAN TRIUMPH AND THE AFTERMATH
OF THE REVOLT

Before departing, Titus ordered the entire city and the temple razed except for the three towers adjacent to Herod's palace (Phasael, Hippicus, Mariamme), which were left standing as a testament to the strength of Jerusalem's defenses.[46] Titus also left intact the wall encircling the western side of the Upper City (that is, the western circuit of the First Wall), which now became the camp of the Tenth Legion.[47] This reflects a major administrative adjustment that the Romans made in the wake of the First Revolt. Until now, the closest legions to Judea had been stationed in Antioch in Syria, a distance of approximately 500 miles (800 kilometers). After the revolt, the Romans made Judea an independent province and stationed the Tenth Legion permanently in Jerusalem. In the event of any future unrest, a legion with its commander would be on hand to deal with the trouble immediately.[48]

Titus departed for Rome from Alexandria after making the rounds of a number of cities in Syria, where he hosted gladiator and animal fights to the death using Jewish prisoners.[49] Upon his return to Rome (in 71), Titus and his father and younger brother Domitian celebrated a joint triumph with a parade of captives and spoils. Since the time of the Republic, Roman generals celebrating a successful foreign campaign or conquest had been entitled to a triumph, a highly ceremonial and scripted procession with religious significance.[50] Josephus provides a detailed account of the Flavian victory parade and the fullest surviving description of any imperial triumph (*War* 7.123–58). The procession set out from the triumphal gate following the Sacred Way through the Roman Forum and terminated at the temple of Capitoline Jupiter on the Capitoline Hill.[51]

John of Gischala, Simon bar Giora, and seven hundred tall and handsome young prisoners—whose wounds from fighting and maltreatment at the hands of the Romans were hidden by clothing (*War* 7.138)—marched through the streets as the spoils from the temple were displayed to the crowds lining the parade route:

> The spoils in general were borne in promiscuous heaps; but conspicuous above all stood out those captured in the temple at Jerusalem. These consisted of a golden table [the showbread table], many talents in weight, and a lampstand [the menorah], likewise made of gold, but constructed on a different pattern from those which we use in ordinary life. Affixed to a pedestal was a central shaft, from which there extended slender branches, arranged trident-fashion, a wrought lamp being attached to the extremity of each branch; of these there were seven, indicating the honor paid to that number among the Jews. After these, and last all the spoils, was carried a copy of the Jewish Law [Torah scroll]. Then followed a large party carrying images of victory, all made of ivory and gold. Behind them drove Vespasian, followed by Titus; while Domitian rode beside them, in magnificent apparel and mounted on a steed that was itself a sight. (Josephus, *War* 7.148–52)

The procession terminated at the temple of Capitoline Jupiter, where Simon was taken to be scourged and executed—the typical Roman punishment for captured generals. John, who upon surrendering to Titus in Jerusalem had begged for mercy, was sentenced to life in prison.[52]

Roman triumphs culminated with a sacrifice of thanks offered by the victorious general at the temple of Capitoline Jupiter. In the eyes of the Romans, the destruction of the Jerusalem temple meant that their gods, and in particular Jupiter—their chief deity—had defeated the God of Israel. Jews, Greeks, and Romans believed that military defeats were a consequence of the patron deity abandoning his city or people. Various ancient writers express the view that Jerusalem fell after the God of Israel abandoned the temple and his people. Tacitus describes "the gods" departing the Jerusalem temple:

> Contending hosts were seen meeting in the skies, arms flashed and suddenly the temple was illuminated with fire from the clouds. Of a sudden the doors of the shrine opened and a superhuman voice cried, "The gods are departing"; at the same moment the mighty stir of their going was heard. (*Histories* V.13:1)[53]

Josephus portrays Titus as sharing this belief: "I call the gods of my fathers to witness and any deity that once watched over this place—for now I believe that there is none" (*War* 6.127).

Josephus repeatedly expresses a view common among ancient Jews that God had temporarily deserted them, analogous to earlier instances in Jewish history when (so they believed) their failure to observe God's laws properly had resulted in their punishment, including the destruction of the first temple.[54] Early Christians believed that the second temple had been abandoned by God when Jesus expired on the cross, as indicated by the Gospel accounts of the darkening of the sky and the tearing of the temple's veil.[55]

Three years after the fall of Jerusalem, Vespasian shut down the Oniad temple at Leontopolis in Egypt, where since the second century BCE Zadokite priests had presided over sacrifices to the God of Israel. Thus, by 73 CE, the sacrificial cult to the God of Israel had been obliterated. This was an exceptional circumstance, as the Romans generally believed that all gods deserved to be treated with honor and piety (*pietas*). Usually the Romans assimilated other deities to their own pantheon, identifying them with gods they already worshiped (for example, Greek Zeus = Roman Jupiter), or incorporating wholesale more exotic deities (such as the Egyptian goddess Isis). Sometimes they enticed a patron deity to desert his city and people with the promise of an improved cult at Rome.[56] None of this happened in the case of the God of Israel—perhaps because of his reputation as a jealous God who would not tolerate the worship of other gods alongside him. Instead, from the Roman point of view, after the God of Israel was defeated by Capitoline Jupiter, his cult ceased to exist.

After 70, the cult of the God of Israel seems to have been subjugated to and replaced by that of Capitoline Jupiter. Vespasian transferred the payment of the Jerusalem temple tax (an annual half-sheqel payment by all adult Jewish men for the maintenance of the sacrificial cult) to the cult of Jupiter, using the money to finance the reconstruction of the temple of Capitoline Jupiter (which had burned down during the civil war in Rome in 69 CE).[57] The sacred objects from the Jerusalem temple were removed from a cultic context and no longer were used ritually. Vespasian placed the Torah scrolls and purple hangings in his palace on the Palatine Hill, while other spoils—including the showbread table and menorah—were housed in a new temple of Peace (Pax) that Vespasian dedicated in the Roman Forum.

Josephus says, "The triumphal ceremonies of being concluded and the empire of the Romans established on the firmest foundation, Vespasian decided to erect a temple of Peace" (*War* 7.158). In fact, the temple of Peace was not built until four years after the triumph (75 CE), and it differed from other temples in being an open enclosure planted with gardens, in which the spoils from the Jerusalem temple and treasures from Nero's Golden House (Domus Aurea) were displayed like works of art. The dedication of a temple to Pax clearly was intended to celebrate the Roman victory in the Jewish war. However, it also alluded to the end of the civil war in Rome with the establishment of the Flavian dynasty.[58]

The first—and only—dynasty in the Roman Empire before this was the Julio-Claudian dynasty, which had been established by Augustus and ended with Nero. When Vespasian became emperor, he sought to legitimize his new dynasty (the Flavians) by connecting himself with the popular (and populist) Augustus and distancing himself from the despotic, unpopular Nero. Vespasian's dedication of a temple to Pax was a conscious allusion to Augustus's Ara Pacis (Altar of Peace), while on property formerly occupied by Nero's Domus Aurea he erected a giant public arena—the Colosseum (Flavian amphitheater).[59]

Vespasian and his sons used the Jewish war to bolster their claims to legitimacy, celebrating their victory over a people who had already been under Roman rule (the Jews) as if they were newly conquered.[60] Steve Mason, who describes Vespasian and Titus's military achievements as "modest," observes, the "provincial revolt in Roman Judaea and the campaign that suppressed it in AD 67–70 received unprecedented publicity."[61] The victory was commemorated in various media, including the erection of monuments around Rome and the minting of coins emblazoned with the legend "Judea Capta" above a bound male captive and a mourning woman flanking a date palm, symbolizing the conquered province and people. Josephus's writings were commissioned by the Flavians as part of their propaganda effort, to record the achievements on which the new dynasty was founded, which were advertised as forming the basis for an era of peace in the empire.[62]

The Flavians funded a number of building projects around Rome with the spoils of the Jewish war, as indicated by the Colosseum's original dedicatory inscription, which was begun by Vespasian and completed by Titus in 80 CE: "The Emperor Titus Caesar Vespasian Augustus ordered the new amphitheater to be made from the (proceeds from the sale of the) booty [*ex manubiis*]."[63] Long after the war, Titus and Domitian kept the victory alive in the eyes of the Roman public by erecting monuments at key points along the parade route. A lost arch of Titus dedicated in 81 CE in the center of the curved end of the Circus Maxiumus seems to have marked the spot where Vespasian and Titus passed during the triumph.[64]

The better-known arch of Titus, apparently erected by Domitian after Titus's death, still straddles the triumphal route, connecting it with the Colosseum. The dedicatory inscription on the attic (at the top of the arch) refers to the deified Titus, and the relief panel at the apex of the arch's passageway depicts Titus's apotheosis (deification) on the back of an eagle (a symbol of Jupiter). The arch thus functioned as a dynastic monument to a line of deified emperors. However, the famous panels decorating the sides of the inner passageway indicate that it was primarily a triumphal monument. The panel on the north side depicts Titus riding in a chariot and crowned by Victory, while the panel on the south side shows the parade of spoils from the Jerusalem temple, with the prominence of the showbread table and the menorah mirroring Josephus's description (fig. 41). These objects provide a snapshot of the entire parade and commemorate the defining moment of the Flavian victory over the Jews.[65]

As a result of the revolt, the connection between the Jews and their homeland was severed. Beginning in the Flavian period, Roman writers refer to the country as Idumaea or Palestina instead of Judea, whereas Jews are referred to in connection with Jewish practices but not with Judea. Eventually the term *Ioudaioi* (Jews) came to denote not people from Judea but people of a certain religion, as is still the case today. The references to Idumaea and Palestina by Roman writers suggest that from their point of view, Judea ceased to exist after the elimination of the temple and sacrificial cult of the Jewish God.[66]

Sixty years after the destruction of Jerusalem and the second temple, Hadrian precipitated a second Jewish revolt (the Bar Kokhba Revolt, so-called after its leader; 132–135 CE) when he re-founded Jerusalem as a pagan Roman city called Aelia Capitolina and announced his intention to build a temple to Capitoline Jupiter—the city's new patron deity—on the Temple Mount. In the wake of the revolt, Hadrian changed the name of the province from Judea to Syria-Palestina. Although Hadrian's actions are generally (and not incorrectly) understood as anti-Jewish, they reflect a new reality that had taken hold under the Flavians: the province was already widely known as Palestine instead of Judea, and from the Roman point of view, the cult of the God of Israel had been extinguished and replaced by that of Capitoline Jupiter.[67] For the Romans, the Flavian victory over the Jews must have reinforced the view that Rome's greatness and destiny as the eternal center (*Rome aeterna*) were due to the favor of all of the gods. This concept was given physical expression by Hadrian's construction (or reconstruction) of a temple that still stands in Rome today: the Pantheon—the temple to all gods.[68]

CHAPTER 8

THE REBEL OCCUPATION
OF MASADA

(66–73/74 CE)

The monumentality and lavish decoration of Herod's palaces at
Masada are a visual statement of power and wealth. But most visitors today are drawn to the site by events that left a less visible but no
less enduring legacy: the fortress's occupation by Jewish rebels and refugees during the First Revolt. This chapter presents their story as illustrated by archaeological remains from Yigael Yadin's excavations.

WHO WERE THE JEWS AT MASADA?

Already in 66 CE, as unrest spread throughout the country, a band of
Jewish rebels seized Masada from the Roman garrison that occupied the
fortress after Herod's death, as Josephus reports: "And now some of the
most ardent promoters of hostilities banded together and made an assault on a fortress called Masada; and having gained possession of it by
stratagem, they slew the Roman guards and put a garrison of their own
in their place" (*War* 2.408).

Shortly thereafter, Josephus says that "a certain Menahem, son of
Judas surnamed the Galilean" (*War* 2.433), and some of his accomplices
raided Masada, bringing the arms they plundered to Jerusalem. Thus
equipped, Menahem became a leader of a rebel faction in Jerusalem.

However, Menahem was so brutal that he and his followers were soon massacred by other groups in Jerusalem. Among the few who managed to escape was Eleazar ben Yair, a relative of Menahem's who made his way to Masada, where he became the leader of the rebels holding out there (*War* 2.442–48). By the winter of 67/68 CE, the sicarii were using Masada as a base for raiding nearby settlements including Ein Gedi, where they massacred upwards of seven hundred villagers during the Passover festival (Josephus, *War* 4.399–405).[1]

Soon after the revolt broke out, the high priest Ananus sent forces against Simon bar Giora, who was terrorizing the wealthy by raiding their houses. As a result, Simon and his followers fled to Masada (Josephus, *War* 2.653). After the high priest Ananus was put to death by a mob in Jerusalem, Simon and his band left Masada and began to roam southern Judea and Idumaea (Josephus, *War* 4.504–8). KV

These episodes highlight the fluid nature of the population at Masada. Archaeological evidence suggests that after the Romans destroyed Qumran in 68, some of the sectarians (Essenes) might have fled south to Masada. Presumably other Jews took refuge there during the revolt and after the fall of Jerusalem in 70. By the time the Romans arrived in the winter–spring of 72/73 or 73/74, Masada was occupied by a rag-tag group of men, women, and children, totaling 967 according to Josephus. Although we cannot know if Josephus's number is accurate, archaeological remains indicate that hundreds of Jews were living on the mountain at the time of the siege.[2]

The Jews at Masada likely included unaffiliated individuals and families as well as members of groups such as the Qumran sect/Essenes.[3] However, according to Josephus, the dominant group at Masada was the sicarii, who seized the mountain at the outset of the revolt and retained control until its fall. Josephus describes the sicarii (from the Latin word for dagger) as urban terrorists who became active in the years leading up to the revolt. He identifies Eleazar ben Yair, the Jewish leader at Masada at the time of the Roman siege, as the head of the sicarii as well as a former follower and relative of Menahem's, who at the beginning of the revolt had raided Herod's armory atop Masada and soon thereafter was executed by opponents in Jerusalem due to his brutality (*War* 2.447; 7.252–53).

In one passage, Josephus describes Menahem's followers as "Zealots" (*War* 2.444). This has created confusion as Josephus generally uses the term Zealots to describe other factions that were active during the revolt, including those led by Eleazer ben Simon and John of Gischala.[4] Although many scholars have offered different solutions to reconcile these contradictions, most agree that Eleazar ben Yair and his group at Masada were sicarii. Nonetheless, Yadin's consistent use of the term Zealots rather than sicarii to describe the dominant rebel group at Masada continues to cause confusion, not least among the many tourists who are told stories of the Zealots' heroic last stand. It is unclear why Yadin chose to use the term Zealot, as he certainly knew about the contradictions in Josephus. Amnon Ben-Tor, a senior Israeli archaeologist who as a graduate student was an area supervisor on Yadin's excavations at Masada, connects Yadin's choice of terms with his aversion to a Jewish political group called *Brit Habiryonim* (the Strongmen Alliance), which was active in Palestine in the 1930s and 1940s. Members of this group considered themselves the successors of the sicarii and believed that the killing of Jews who collaborated with the British was justified—a position diametrically opposed to that of the Haganah, with which Yadin was affiliated (see chapter 9).[5]

The nature and even the very existence of the Zealots and sicarii are also debated by scholars. Steve Mason proposes that instead of being a distinct faction, the term sicarii was used by Josephus as a "scare-word" to evoke a particular kind of violence and terrorism.[6] Hanan Eshel speculated that because Josephus was a Zealot leader at the beginning of the revolt, when writing *War* years later he artificially distinguished between the "moderate" Zealots and the "extremist" sicarii, pinning on the latter the responsibility for the disastrous outcome of the revolt and thereby distancing himself.[7] Here I use the terms rebels and refugees to encompass the variety of backgrounds and affiliations represented among the Jews at Masada.

MASADA DURING THE REVOLT:
THE ARCHAEOLOGICAL REMAINS: HOUSING

Archaeologists love destruction because destruction levels yield the best-preserved remains—a snapshot frozen in time.[8] Whether or not the Jews committed mass suicide at the time of the siege, when Masada fell to the Romans, many of the buildings went up in flames. This destruction level at Masada yielded the richest assemblage of finds of any occupation period, including artifacts made of organic materials such as cloth and leather, which were buried in the collapse of the ruined buildings and were preserved thanks to the arid desert climate. Yadin describes the eerie experience of excavating these remains:

> Often, as we would clear a casemate chamber, we had the feeling that it had only just been abandoned; for there was a familiar domestic atmosphere, with the white wall above the cooking stoves smudged with soot. There were rooms we excavated which at first glance had not been burnt, but we would find in a corner a heap of spent embers containing the remains of clothing, sandals, domestic utensils and cosmetic items.[9]

These remains present a vivid picture of the lives of the refugee families, who were crowded into the casemate wall rooms, in Herod's palaces, and in shoddily built, makeshift accommodations. They modified and added onto existing buildings and constructed new ones which are easily distinguishable from Herod's. For example, in the bathhouse in the western palace, a small bin (for storage or rubbish?) added by the rebels cut through a mosaic floor. The rebels also recycled architectural fragments from Herod's buildings, as for example a bench made of column drums laid side-by-side and covered with plaster, which was laid on top of the apodyterium's tile floor in the large bathhouse in the northern palace complex.

Rebel construction is characterized by small fieldstones that are easily distinguishable from the larger stones used by Herod in his buildings. The rooms in their structures are small, with thin walls of stone or mud that could have supported only a low ceiling covered by branches or textiles. The floors are usually of bare stone, sometimes covered with a thin layer of packed earth. The archaeologists who participated in Yadin's excavations referred to the rebel dwellings as "transit camps," as they recalled the temporary quarters assigned to new immigrants to Israel in the 1950s (fig. 42).[10] Often, the rooms inside existing Herodian buildings—especially the casemate wall and the smaller palaces—were subdivided by partitions, suggesting that large numbers of refugees were crammed into these spaces. In some places, entire neighborhoods of slum dwellings were added along the inner face of the casemate wall, including one that comprised fifteen living units.[11]

The rebel dwellings were equipped with the basic necessities of daily life and survival, including stoves and ovens for cooking and baking, and silos, shelves, and cupboards for storage. Ben-Tor notes that approximately 145 ovens and 85 stoves were discovered at Masada, most of them in the casemate wall rooms—the largest number of cooking and baking installations discovered at any site in Israel.[12] The stoves are made of mud and are shaped like rectangular boxes (fig. 43). Typically, there are two holes in the top which were used as burners, with an opening below for fuel. Cooking pots would have been set on the burners and heated by wood or animal dung cakes underneath. Next to the stoves in some rooms, Yadin found unburned pieces of kindling, and cooking and storage vessels.[13]

The dome-shaped mud or clay ovens (*tabuns*) had a large opening on top and a small opening at the base to remove the ashes from fuel burned on the floor. Bread was baked by sticking pieces of dough to the inside of the heated walls. A tower in the southwestern section of the casemate wall contained three ovens of this type and a stove with two burners, leading the excavators to speculate that it functioned as a bakery.[14] Two rooms in the southern part of Herod's western palace complex contained an unusually large number of cooking installations, including ovens and two stoves with four burners each. Because this concentration points to communal cooking, while other parts of the western palace displayed relatively little evidence of modifications by the rebels, Ehud Netzer suggested that it was occupied by a group of rebel commanders, an important family, or perhaps a coherent community such as the Essenes.[15] Eshel has proposed that the evidence of communal food preparation indicates the occupants were orphans.[16]

During the revolt, workshops were installed in some of the Herodian buildings. For example, the rebels partitioned a room in the western casemate wall, creating five plastered cells separated by a corridor. One of the cells contained two large circular vats that drained into a smaller vat, leading Netzer to suggest that this was a tannery where leather was produced from animal hides.[17] Surprisingly, the rebels installed an iron arrowhead workshop in the waiting room or reception hall adjacent to the throne room of Herod's western palace—which was decorated with the most elaborate mosaic floor found at Masada—and in another room nearby. The largest concentrations of arrowheads at Masada, totaling more than two hundred, were discovered in these two rooms. The arrowheads were found together with pieces of slag, charcoal, and arrow shafts, lying in hearths where the heat was so intense it had whitened the surrounding areas. These rooms might have been selected for use as arrowhead workshops because the pools in the nearby bathhouse contained water necessary for quenching and tempering the iron. The arrowheads manufactured by the rebels were of typical Roman type, with a long tang that was inserted into a wooden shaft and three barbed wing-tips to stick in the victim's flesh.[18]

Food

According to Josephus, when the rebels took Masada, they found Herod's cisterns and pools filled with water, and his storerooms still stocked with edible food as well as weapons and other provisions:

> For here had been stored a mass of corn [grain, not maize], amply sufficient to last for years, abundance of wine and oil, besides every variety of pulse [legumes] and dates. All these Eleazar, when he with his Sicarii became through treachery master of the fortress, found in perfect condition and no whit inferior to goods recently laid in; although from the date of storage to the capture of the place by the Romans well-nigh a century had elapsed. Indeed, the Romans found what remained of the fruits undecayed. . . . There was also found a mass of arms of every description, hoarded up by the king and sufficient for ten thousand men, besides unwrought iron, brass, and lead. (War 7.296–98, 299)

These passages are one example where Josephus seems to contradict himself, as earlier in War (2.433–34) he mentions that at the beginning of the revolt, Menahem had raided Herod's armory at Masada. However, Josephus does not say that Menahem took all of the arms, and indeed, a sword and some scales of armor dating to the time of Herod were discovered in Yadin's excavations.[19] Although Yadin found unworked tin and other metals in one of the storerooms, the absence of weapons presumably is due to looting after the end of the siege. It is possible that the rebels used raw iron from Herod's stores to manufacture their own arrowheads.

The destruction level yielded a large and rich assemblage of approximately 4,500 pottery vessels, some of which might have been brought to the site in Herod's time, but nearly all of which were still in use when Masada fell to the Romans. Although there are some imports, mostly from Herod's time (such as fine red-slipped table wares and amphoras), the majority of the pottery is locally made (Judean), and most of it consists of common, utilitarian storage jars and cooking pots. The large number of these types and their concentration in the casemate wall rooms (where almost 1,600 vessels were found alongside stoves and ovens) reflect the rebels' concern with basic survival and subsistence, focusing on the storage and preparation of food.[20] The storage jars have an elongated globular body with two small loop handles on either side of the shoulder, a short neck, and a relatively small mouth that could be sealed with a lump of clay. Because they have their rounded bases, the jars would have been placed on a stand, or, more commonly, were stuck into a dirt floor, sometimes leaning against a wall. These jars were designed to store food and liquids, not transport goods. Therefore, unlike amphoras (transport jars), which have pointed bases and long necks so they could be picked up and carried easily, the storage jars—which are described as "bag-shaped"—were intended to be filled and left in one spot. Other pottery vessels from the time of the revolt include a small number of painted plates and bowls, some of which are Nabataean in origin, and oil lamps.

The storerooms are buried under heaps of stones, created when an earthquake caused the walls to collapse, as can be seen in aerial photographs. Yadin excavated a number of the storerooms in the northern palace and left the others untouched. The floors of some rooms were covered with hydraulic plaster to accommodate the storage of liquids—mostly wine and oil. In one storeroom the plastered floor slopes slightly toward both sides, where pits collected spilled liquids. Huge storage jars for wine and oil were discovered broken but still in situ, lining the walls of this room. Although the original contents of the jars might have been brought to Masada in Herod's time, the addition of Hebrew names and/or Hebrew and Aramaic inscriptions (such as bar [son of] Jason) shows they were used by the rebels.[21] Thirty-seven jars found at Masada bear inscriptions indicating their contents, twenty-four of which refer to dried figs, and most of which come from the storerooms. Dried figs were an important component of the ancient Near Eastern diet, as they are abundant, nutritious, easily carried and transported, and can be stored for long periods. Other food items mentioned in inscriptions on jars include berries or olives, fish, dough, meat, and herbs.[22]

Thanks to the arid climate, the remains of seeds, nuts, and fruits—including pomegranates, olives, and dried figs—were preserved for two thousand years. There are also chunks of salt, which presumably came from the Dead Sea and would have been used to flavor and preserve food. Although many of the food remains come from the storerooms, they were also discovered elsewhere around the mountain.[23] The food stores would have been supplemented by a limited amount of fresh produce grown in the gardens on the mountain that had been established by Herod, and by raising herds of sheep and goats.

Despite the apparent variety of food available at Masada, living conditions during the revolt were harsh. Any delicacies left from Herod's time were probably consumed early on, likely distributed among the rebel commanders and officers. Otherwise, grain, oil, and legumes were the dietary staples. The food consumed by most refugees on a daily basis would have been limited to bread dipped in oil and bean pastes (similar to hummus—chickpea dip) and meatless lentil stews. Furthermore, analyses indicate that the food remains were infested with insects and larvae, including beetles, weevils, and moths. The fruits were particularly severely affected, with the dates and figs containing large numbers of charred larvae and adult insects.[24] Thus, by the time Masada fell to the Romans, the food supplies were infested by pests.

The discovery of storage jars and food remains in the storerooms at Masada seems to contradict Josephus, who says that the rebels destroyed their food supplies to show the Romans that they did not starve to death but chose to die by committing mass suicide (*War* 7.336). Yadin, who understood Josephus's account literally, reconciled this apparent contradiction by saying that "the Zealots did not need to leave all their stores of food to the Romans. It was enough for them to leave one or two rooms with untouched victuals to show that they had not died through lack of food."[25] However, the food remains could equally support the opposite view: that Josephus's account of the mass suicide is all or partly fabricated (see chapter 9).

Fig. 24. Aerial view of the synagogue at Masada.

Fig. 25. The "swimming pool" at Masada.

Fig. 26. Southern cistern on the Masada summit.

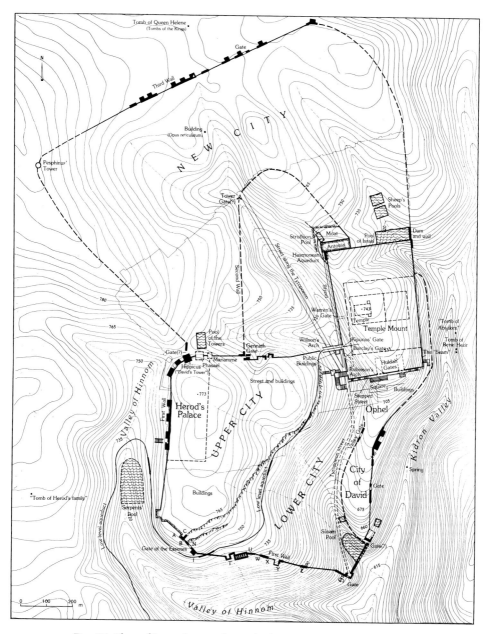

Fig. 27. Plan of Jerusalem at the end of the Second Temple period.

Fig. 28. The Herodian tower ("David's Tower) in the Citadel, Jerusalem.

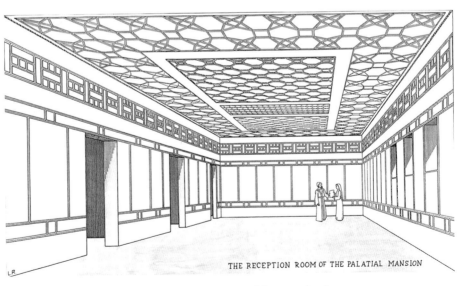

THE RECEPTION ROOM OF THE PALATIAL MANSION

Fig. 29. Stucco room in "the mansion."

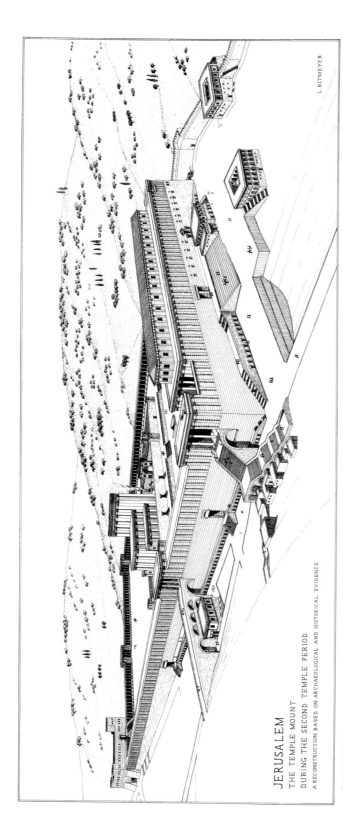

JERUSALEM
THE TEMPLE MOUNT
DURING THE SECOND TEMPLE PERIOD
A RECONSTRUCTION BASED ON ARCHAEOLOGICAL AND HISTORICAL EVIDENCE

© RITMEYER ARCHAEOLOGICAL DESIGN

L. RITMEYER

Fig. 30. Reconstruction of the Herodian Temple Mount.

Fig. 31. Reconstruction of the Temple in the Holyland Model on the grounds of the Israel Museum, Jerusalem.

Fig. 32. Soreg inscription from the Jerusalem temple in the Istanbul Archaeological Museum.

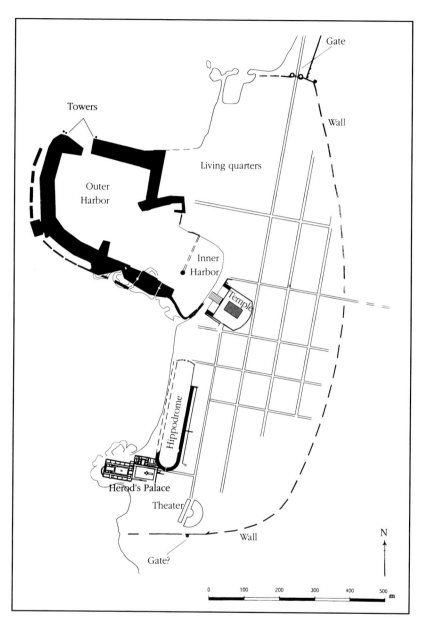

Fig. 33. Plan of Caesarea.

Fig. 34. The Pontius Pilate inscription from Caesarea, now in the Israel Museum, Jerusalem.

Fig. 35. The high-level aqueduct at Caesarea.

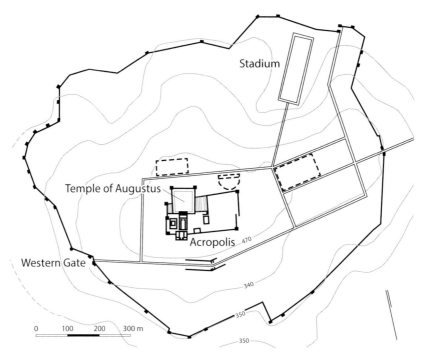

Fig. 36. Plan of Samaria-Sebaste.

Fig. 37. View of the Hasmonean and Herodian palaces at Jericho on the north
bank of Wadi Qelt.

Fig. 38. The western peristyle courtyard of the north wing of Herod's third palace at Jericho, showing *opus reticulatum* walls (mud bricks laid in a net pattern characteristic of Roman architecture).

Fig. 39. Isometric reconstruction of Greater Herodium showing Herod's tomb.

Fig. 40. View of Gamla looking west.

Fig. 41. The Arch of Titus at Rome.

Fig. 42. A "transit camp" at Masada.

Fig. 43. A stove from the time of the revolt at Masada.

Fig. 44. Yigael Yadin showing David Ben-Gurion around Masada.

Fig. 45. A braid of human hair found in Yadin's excavations at Masada.

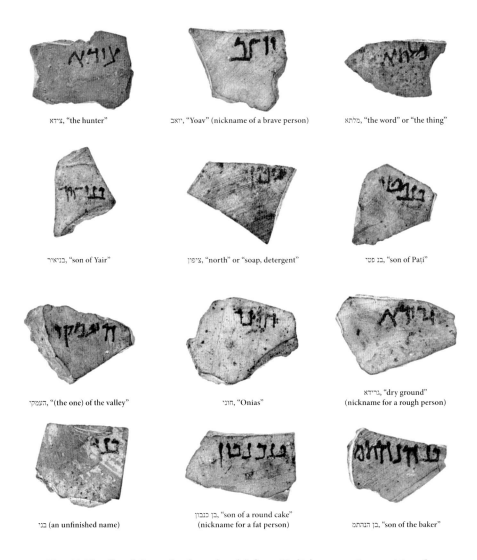

צידא, "the hunter"

יואב, "Yoav" (nickname of a brave person)

מלתא, "the word" or "the thing"

בניאיר, "son of Yair"

ציפון, "north" or "soap, detergent"

בן פטי, "son of Paṭi"

העמקי, "(the one) of the valley"

חוני, "Onias"

גרידא, "dry ground" (nickname for a rough person)

בני (an unfinished name)

בן כנבון, "son of a round cake" (nickname for a fat person)

בן הנהתם, "son of the baker"

Fig. 46. The "lots" (inscribed potsherds) from Yadin's excavations at Masada.

The Synagogue

In some cases, the rebels modified Herod's buildings and added installations that attest to their continued observance of Judaism, even under harsh conditions. For example, they converted one of the rooms in the casemate wall for use as a synagogue (fig. 24; see chapter 4). This was done by removing the dividing wall between the porch or anteroom and the main room, thereby enlarging the interior space, and adding tiers of plastered benches along the walls. Because this is one of the earliest examples of a synagogue building, it lacks the features we expect to see today, such as a Torah Shrine, Jewish symbols used as decoration, and orientation toward Jerusalem (the direction of prayer). These features did not appear in synagogue buildings until centuries after the destruction of the second temple, when liturgy and prayer services developed. Instead, the Masada building is a synagogue in the most basic sense of the word.

Originally, the term synagogue denoted a congregation or assembly of Jews (a meaning it still retains). At some point, Jews began to erect purpose-built buildings to house these assemblies, although synagogue congregations still can (and do) meet anywhere, even in churches. Because the Masada building dates to a period when the mountain was occupied only by Jews and has benches to accommodate an assembly, it is a Jewish house of assembly—a synagogue. Had this same type of building been discovered in a non-Jewish or mixed (Jewish and gentile) context, we would not be able to identify it positively as a synagogue. The earliest synagogues were assemblies for the public reading of the Torah—usually on the Sabbath and festivals—which was necessary because most Jews were entirely or functionally illiterate. Remember that, by definition, ancient Jews worshiped the God of Israel as their national deity, and therefore lived according to his laws. The reading of the Torah portion still lies at the heart of synagogue services today.

A handful of other synagogue buildings dating to the first century CE have been discovered around Israel, including at Gamla (which is probably the earliest example, and unlike Masada, was built as a synagogue right from the start), Herodium (where, as at Masada, a synagogue was installed by the Jewish rebels in a Herodian structure), and Migdal/

Magdala, the hometown of Mary Magdalene (where a very small, recently discovered synagogue is equipped with an enigmatic stone table carved with symbols alluding to the Jerusalem temple). All of these synagogues are similar to Masada's in consisting of a rectangular hall with pillars to support the roof and one or more tiers of benches lining the walls. The Masada synagogue, however, differs in having a room added to the back of the hall by the rebels, which apparently served as a *genizah*—that is, a repository in a synagogue where damaged sacred writings are buried (although not every synagogue has such a repository). The Masada *genizah* consists of two pits dug into the dirt floor of the back room, one containing buried scroll fragments belonging to Deuteronomy (the last of the Five Books of Moses), and the other fragments of Ezekiel.[26]

Miqva'ot (Jewish Ritual Baths)

Miqva'ot (singular *miqveh*) are baths used by Jews for ritual purification. Ancient *miqva'ot* typically were plastered pools dug into the ground, with a broad set of steps running along the width of the pool, from top to bottom, which facilitated immersion in the water. Many ritual baths have other features, such as low partitions running down the steps (to separate pure from impure), staggered broad and narrow steps (with the broad steps being used as bathing platforms depending on the level of the water), and a deep basin at the bottom to enable immersion when the water reached its lowest level.

The concept of ritual purity, which was central to the lifestyle of many ancient Jews including the refugees at Masada, is poorly understood by many modern Westerners. According to the Torah, impurity is caused by coming into physical contact with certain things or experiencing certain natural processes. The sources of impurity appear random to us, ranging, for example, from touching mildew on the walls of a house to touching a lizard to touching a corpse, or having a menstrual period (for a woman) or a nocturnal emission (for a man). Ritual impurity in Judaism is a mechanical category, meaning it does not make a person bad or sinful (in the Christian sense of the word) or dirty or unhygienic. Every human being becomes impure at various times. The method of purification varies depending on the status of the affected person (layperson versus priest) and the nature of the impurity (corpse impurity is the worst and requires a complicated purification procedure). But in most cases, purification is accomplished by immersion in a pool of undrawn water and waiting for the passage of a certain amount of time (usually until sundown). Undrawn water means that the pool cannot be filled by mechanical means, such as a hose or bucket (although the pool can be filled by allowing water to flow by gravity from a natural source through a channel). Natural bodies of water, such as lakes, rivers, streams, and pools of rainwater, are permissible sources.

The need to observe biblical purity laws was limited to certain times or situations—mostly when entering the presence of the God of Israel. The purity laws apply only to Israelites/Jews, as gentiles were prohibited from entering the presence of the God of Israel at all. Many religions in the Mediterranean world and Near East had similar purity laws. In ancient Judaism, the focal point for entering the presence of God was the Jerusalem temple. Therefore, everyone—including Jesus and Paul—took for granted that ritual purification was required first. For example, Acts 21:26 says that Paul entered the temple after "having purified himself." But most of the time, most ancient Jews were ritually impure. Only priests had to be concerned with a more regular observance of the ritual purity laws, due to their service in God's presence in the Jerusalem temple. Judaism was distinguished from other ancient religions in that some groups or sects (such as the Essenes and Pharisees) in the late Second Temple period extended the observance of ritual purity beyond the boundaries of the temple cult, reflecting their belief that God's presence was not limited to the Jerusalem temple.

When Yadin conducted his excavations at Masada in the mid-1960s, no ancient *miqva'ot* had ever been identified (although numerous *miqva'ot* had been discovered more than a decade earlier at Qumran, which Roland de Vaux identified as pools or cisterns; see fig. 17).[27] Yadin vividly describes how the identification of the first *miqveh*, which was installed by the rebels in a room in the southeast casemate wall, was confirmed by two rabbis:

one hot day, during the hottest hour of the afternoon, the two Rabbis arrived on the summit. They had climbed the tough "snake path" on the east face under the broiling sun, wearing their characteristic heavy garments, and accompanied by a group of their Hassidic followers. Though they are no longer young, neither agreed to rest when they finally reached the top; nor did they wish to see any of the handsome structures of King Herod. They wanted one thing only: to be led directly to the *mikve*. We took them there, and the aged Rabbi Muntzberg immediately went into one of the pools . . . When he completed his meticulous study, he announced with beaming face and to the delight of us all, that this *mikve* was indeed a ritual bath.[28]

Yadin's expedition discovered a second *miqveh*, also installed by the rebels, in the northern palace complex.[29] Since then, hundreds of *miqva'ot*, dating to the first century BCE and first century CE, have been identified at sites around the country, including additional examples at Masada. Some of the Masada *miqva'ot* were added by the rebels, while others date to the time of Herod, as for example a narrow, stepped pool in the bathhouse of the western palace.[30] All of the *miqva'ot* at Masada were filled with rainwater (surface runoff) channeled from the surrounding buildings and open spaces.

Since Yadin's time, when *miqva'ot* were unknown in the archaeological record, the pendulum has swung in the opposite direction, with a tendency among many archaeologists nowadays to identify every stepped and plastered pool as a *miqveh*. The problem is that it is not always clear that a stepped and plastered pool functioned as a *miqveh*. Furthermore, *miqva'ot* could be (and were) used for purposes other than ritual purification, including drinking, washing, and laundering. Although this might seem like an obscure academic debate—after all, who cares if a pool was a *miqveh* or not?—it has important ramifications, as *miqva'ot* reflect the presence of Jews concerned with the observance of biblical purity laws. Therefore, the discovery of *miqva'ot* dating to the time of Herod would indicate that Herod and members of his family observed these biblical laws while at Masada or provided these facilities for guests. Similarly, larger numbers of *miqva'ot* added at the time of the revolt would indicate a concern on the part of the rebels to observe purity laws under harsh conditions, even after the temple's destruction. Therefore, it is significant that since Yadin identified the first two examples at Masada, the number of claimed *miqva'ot* at Masada has risen to between sixteen and twenty-one.[31] The different numbers reflect the uncertain identification of some of the pools as *miqva'ot*.

In chapter 4 we encountered one such questionable *miqveh*: a large, wide, and deep, stepped and plastered pool that was installed in a quarry to the south of the western palace complex and next to Building 11 (fig. 25). It is enclosed by stone walls containing rows of square niches. The date of this pool—from the time of Herod or the revolt—and its function—as a swimming pool or *miqveh*—are debated. Yadin, followed by Eshel, dated the pool to the time of Herod and identified it as a swimming pool.[32] However, Netzer and Ronny Reich (followed by Asher Grossberg and Yonatan Adler) identify it as a *miqveh* from the time of the revolt and speculate that it might have been used by Essenes or other sectarians who may have occupied the western palace and/or Building 11.[33] Arguments can be made in support of both positions. On the one hand, the niches forming a cabana suggest a swimming pool, which Eshel proposed was located in a spot that served the royal residents of the western palace as well as distinguished guests who ascended the mountain from the west. In addition, the scanty rainfall at Masada hardly could have filled a pool this size (even with surface runoff), but water brought by mechanical means would have invalidated it for use as a *miqveh*. On the other hand, as Netzer and Grossberg note, Herodian swimming pools typically are rectilinear with above-ground walls (like the large pool at the southern end of the mountain). Furthermore, the plastered steps with a deep basin at the bottom (which facilitate immersion as the water level drops) are characteristic features of *miqva'ot*. Therefore, the date and function of this pool remain uncertain.

Stone and Dung Vessels

Other artifacts discovered in connection with the rebel occupation attest to a concern with the observance of biblical purity laws. Among these are vessels made of soft Jerusalem chalk, which presumably were brought to Masada at the time of the revolt.[34] Similar to *miqva'ot*, vessels made of soft chalk or limestone are typical of Jewish sites around the country in the first century BCE and first century CE. By far the most common type are the so-called mugs, which are cylindrical in shape and have vertically pared walls, flat bases, one or two pierced handles, and sometimes a spout. The mugs were carved by hand using a knife or chisel. A small number of stone vessels are much finer (and were more expensive) as they were manufactured on a lathe. The lathe-turned vessels mostly comprise table wares, that is, dining dishes such as plates, cups, and bowls.[35]

Stone vessels appear to have become common because many Jews considered stone insusceptible to ritual impurity, whereas vessels made of processed or fired materials such as pottery, metal, and glass are susceptible to impurity.[36] According to biblical law, once a ceramic vessel becomes impure, it must be broken as it cannot be purified: "And if any of them falls into any earthen vessel, all that is in it shall be unclean, and you shall break the vessel" (Lv 11:33). Therefore, although stone vessels were more expensive than pottery because they cost more to manufacture, the investment paid off for those who were careful about observing the purity laws and could afford to acquire them. For this reason, most scholars attribute the popularity of stone vessels to the observance of purity laws among broad sectors of the Jewish population in the late Second Temple period.

Thirty-one complete mugs and 110 fragments of mugs were discovered in Yadin's excavations together with a small number of lathe-turned vessels, similar to the proportions of stone vessels found at other sites around the country, where mugs predominate. Although they resemble measuring cups (as they are sometimes called), Reich has demonstrated that mugs could not have served this purpose due to variations in their capacities.[37] According to another suggestion, mugs might have been used for ritual handwashing.[38]

Yadin also found a small number of vessels made of unfired clay and animal dung at Masada. Vessels made of these materials were not uncommon in the ancient world (and are still used in some parts of the world today), especially in arid regions.[39] However, they are rarely discovered in archaeological excavations because they were unfired (but sun-dried). The unfired clay and dung vessels from Masada come from rebel contexts and are represented by large bowls and basins which presumably were used to hold and serve dry foodstuffs such as grain and dried fruit. Because they are not processed materials, ancient Jews considered unfired clay and dung vessels—like stone—insusceptible to impurity, as expressed in later rabbinic legislation:[40]

> Clay vessels—from what time do they receive uncleanness? When they are fired in the furnace. And that is the completion of their manufacture. (m. Kelim 4:5)

> These vessels afford protection [from impurity] with a tightly stopped-up cover: Vessels made of dung, vessels of stone, vessels of unfired earth, vessels of [fired] clay, and vessels of alum crystal. (m. Kelim 10:1)

Despite their insusceptibility to impurity, the presence of unfired clay and dung vessels does not necessarily indicate a concern for purity observance among the Jewish rebels at Masada, as they were in widespread use among the Jewish population (and probably non-Jews as well). The examples from Masada were preserved due to the arid conditions and the circumstances surrounding the site's destruction. Because these crude, handmade vessels were manufactured from materials that were readily available to all sectors of the population, it is not surprising to find them in a siege context where they could have been made on the spot. It is likely that some ancient Jews used unfired clay and dung vessels without any connection to purity concerns because they were cheap and easy to manufacture.

Scrolls and Sectarians at Masada

Many finds associated with the rebel occupation come from post-revolt contexts such as dumps and fills that apparently were deposited by the Roman soldiers during looting after the end of the siege, or, in some cases (but less likely), by Byzantine monks as part of clearing activities. For example, the casemate tower with the possible tannery (discussed above) was filled to the top with 4–5 meters (13–16.5 feet) of debris that included straw, painted plaster fragments, pieces of leather, pottery, a papyrus fragment with names in Greek and Latin, and thirty-four coins.[41]

One particularly rich deposit was discovered in a casemate room (L1039) near the synagogue which the excavators dubbed the "Casemate of the Scrolls." During the revolt the occupants of this room installed a stove, a silo, a pool, and two small cells. On and just above the floor level, the excavators discovered hundreds of ballista stones (see chapter 1). The stones were covered by a thick layer of debris containing reed baskets and pieces of fabric, seventy-one coins including nineteen silver sheqels from the time of the revolt, seven fragments of biblical and extra-biblical scrolls, eighteen Latin papyri, and four Greek papyri.[42]

The silver sheqels, which were scattered along the room's south wall, apparently represent a hoard and might have been hidden in the wall.[43] In antiquity, just as today, the issuing of currency was controlled by the central ruling authority. This is true even in the United States, where currency is issued by the federal government, not individual states. It is illegal for individuals or entities to issue currency without the consent of the ruler or central government. When the revolt broke out in 66 CE and the Jews established a government, they began to mint their own coins, which from the Roman point of view was illegal and therefore an act of rebellion. The Jews called their coins a *sheqel*—a biblical term denoting a measure of weight, as was common in many periods (similar to the idea of the British pound). The sheqels were emblazoned with symbols and slogans alluding to the Jerusalem temple and Jewish independence, including depictions of pomegranates and cups used in the temple ritual, and inscriptions reading "Holy Jerusalem" and "freedom of Jerusalem." The Jews marked their independence from Rome with a new calendar that began with the first year of the revolt, indicated on the coins by the letters A (Hebrew *aleph*) for "Year One," B (Hebrew *bet*) for "Year Two," and so on. Of the seventeen silver sheqels found in the Casemate of the Scrolls, ten were minted in year two of the revolt; two in year three; two in year four, and three in year five. Because the fifth year of the revolt was short, beginning in April (the Hebrew month Nisan) and ending on the ninth of Av (August) in 70, sheqels of year five are very rare.[44]

The biblical scrolls from the Casemate of the Scrolls include fragments of Genesis, Leviticus, and Psalms. Among the extra-biblical scrolls is a work called the Songs of the Sabbath Sacrifice, nine more copies of which were found among the Dead Sea Scrolls at Qumran. The work includes thirteen hymns describing angels extolling God in his heavenly temple, and probably was recited on certain Sabbaths and festivals as a means of mystical communion with angels in the act of praising God. Although nine copies were found at Qumran, it is not clear whether the Songs of the Sabbath Sacrifice represents a sectarian work or was composed by other Jews who shared a similar outlook.[45] The discovery of a copy at Masada led Yadin to suggest that small numbers of Essenes might have fled south and joined the rebels when the Romans destroyed Qumran in 68. Eshel disagrees, arguing that as the work is not necessarily a sectarian composition and probably circulated in other Jewish circles, it does not provide evidence of Essene presence at Masada.[46]

However, other evidence supports Yadin's position. For example, the Casemate of the Scrolls also yielded fragments of the Joshua Apocryphon. This genre—in which the author retells and reshapes the story in a biblical book—is well-represented at Qumran, where five other fragments of the Joshua Apocryphon were found. Furthermore, there are indications that the Joshua Apocryphon might be a sectarian composition.[47] The debris filling the casemate tower with the possible tannery contained a fragment of the book of Jubilees, which, like the Joshua Apocryphon, is a retelling and reshaping of biblical stories, specifically Genesis and the first part of Exodus. Although Jubilees is not generally considered a sectarian composition, the presence of at least fourteen copies among the Dead Sea Scrolls attests to its popularity and authority at Qumran.[48] Not only are the works just described represented among the Dead Sea Scrolls, but they are compatible with the distinctive beliefs and outlook of the Qumran sect, such as their apparent preference for a solar calendar. In fact, Emanuel Tov, who as editor-in-chief oversaw the publication of the Dead Sea Scrolls, believes it is likely that the Songs of the Sabbath Sacrifice, Jubilees, and the Joshua Apocryphon were brought to Masada from Qumran.[49]

Another piece of evidence for sectarian presence at Masada consists of three fragments of ovoid and cylindrical ceramic jars found in rebel contexts—types represented by the dozens at Qumran and in the surrounding caves, but virtually nowhere else.[50] Some of the scrolls from Cave 1 at Qumran reportedly had been stored in cylindrical jars. The discovery at Masada of these jars—which are one of the hallmarks of the Qumran caves and settlement—is significant.

Based on the distribution of spindle whorls, Ronny Reich has proposed that not only were sectarians among the refugees at Masada, but it is possible to pinpoint their living quarters.[51] Spindle whorls are small, perforated discs with one flat side that resemble a button (with which they are sometimes confused) made of stone, glass, bone, or wood. A hooked wooden or bone rod called a distaff was inserted through a hole in the center of the whorl. Raw wool or linen was tied to the distaff and then teased out by hand, using the weighted stick (the spindle) to twist the raw material into thread or yarn. In antiquity spinning was done exclusively by women, and the portable nature of spindles meant the activity could be performed inside and outside the house. In other words, spindle whorls are an indicator of women's presence in the archaeological record.

Three hundred and eighty-four spindle whorls were discovered at Masada, mostly from rebel contexts, representing the largest number from any site in Israel. Reich noticed that certain buildings used as dwellings by the rebels contained large numbers of spindle whorls—specifically, some of the rooms in the casemate wall (which yielded almost half of the spindle whorls) and Building 9 (which yielded approximately one-third of the total).[52] The latter is a large building between the northern palace and western palace that may have served as a hostel for visitors in Herod's time and that displays evidence of intensive occupation at the time of the revolt. This suggests that the casemate wall rooms and Building 9 housed families of men, women, and perhaps children. In contrast, Buildings 7, 11, 12, and 13, which also show evidence of rebel occupation, yielded no spindle whorls. In fact, Building 13 has the most intensive signs of rebel use of any structure at Masada.[53] Building 7, located next to the storerooms in the northern palace complex, is one of the earliest Herodian buildings on Masada, while Buildings 11, 12, and 13 are three small Herodian palaces to the southeast of the western palace. The absence of spindle whorls from these buildings might indicate that the rebel occupants were single men. Furthermore, Reich observed that whereas large numbers of coins were found in Buildings 7 and 13, Buildings 11 and 12 yielded few coins. Because ancient authors tell us that the Essenes pooled their possessions, Reich proposes that Buildings 11 and 12 were inhabited by Essene men, who used the large pool nearby as a *miqveh* (the same pool discussed above which has been identified either as a swimming pool or a *miqveh*).[54]

While there is reasonably compelling evidence of sectarian presence at Masada, Reich's proposal is much more speculative, for several reasons. First, Reich assumes that Essene men were celibate, following the descriptions of Philo, Josephus, and Pliny. However, nowhere in the sectarian scrolls from Qumran is celibacy mandated; to the contrary, the scrolls suggest that many male members were married and had families. Second, although ancient authors and the scrolls inform us that the sectarians pooled their possessions, the hundreds of coins found at Qumran indicate they did use currency. Third, spindle whorls and coins are small (even tiny) portable objects, which were easily carried, moved, transported, and dropped or lost. Therefore, although the pattern of distribution noted by Reich is interesting, it is hazardous to draw firm conclusions about the original provenience or context of these objects, especially in light of the looting activities of the Romans and other later disturbances at Masada.[55]

One papyrus fragment from the Casemate of the Scrolls, which is inscribed on both sides, is unique as it is the only papyrus from Masada written in Hebrew (the other Hebrew documents, specifically the biblical and extra-biblical scrolls, are written on parchment, which is processed animal hide). Furthermore, whereas the other Hebrew documents are written in Aramaic script (the same alphabet used to write Hebrew today), this papyrus is written in Paleo-Hebrew script—the ancient biblical Hebrew alphabet that was replaced largely by the Aramaic alphabet in the Second Temple period (the Aramaic alphabet is still used to write Hebrew today). Most interesting of all, one of the few words preserved on this papyrus fragment reads "Mount Gerizim" [*Hargerizim*], which was the sacred mountain of the Samaritans. Therefore, Shemaryahu Talmon, who published the papyrus, proposed that it was brought to Masada by a Samaritan and therefore indicates that Samaritans were among the refugees. Eshel disagrees, arguing that the Hebrew phrase "Come, let us sing joyously" [*leranana*], which appears twice in lines above the reference to Mount Gerizim, suggests that this was an anti-Samaritan hymn recited by Jews to commemorate the destruction of the Samaritan temple. The most recent study concluded that this papyrus is too fragmentary to provide definite evidence of Samaritan presence at Masada.[56]

Clothing

Like spinning, in antiquity weaving was carried out exclusively by women. However, whereas spinning could be done anywhere, weaving required fixed looms, which usually were located inside houses. In the first century BCE and first century CE, looms had vertical wooden frames ("warp-weighted looms") to hold wool threads, the ends of which were tied to perforated weights to hold them down. Because they were vertical, warp-weighted looms required the weaver to stand and walk from side to side while working. Approximately 110 loom weights—all of unfired clay—were found at Masada.[57] Nearly all of them come from rooms in the casemate wall, and five of these rooms yielded groups of between five and forty-five loom weights. Orit Shamir, who published the loom weights, remarked, "In the Roman period, loom weights throughout the Roman Empire were customarily fired, so as to increase their durability . . . To date, unfired loom weights dating to the Roman period have been found in Israel only at Masada. The use of unfired clay suggests that the loom weights at Masada were not manufactured by experts skilled in such work, but rather by the inhabitants, perhaps even the weavers themselves, laboring hastily under difficult conditions."[58]

Approximately two thousand textile fragments were discovered at Masada, only 122 of which have been published. Most come from the casemate wall rooms and the dumps and fills left from the Roman looting.[59] In the Roman world, everyone—men, women, children, members of the elite, soldiers, and slaves—wore the same two basic articles of clothing: a tunic and a mantle (cloak). The tunic was similar to a dress or a shift, usually worn with no undergarments. A sleeveless tunic was made by folding a large rectangular sheet and sewing it along the sides, with holes provided for the head and arms. Jewish tunics sometimes were made of two rectangular sheets sewn together at the shoulders, so that if one side became ritually impure it could be removed and replaced without discarding the entire garment. Two parallel narrow stripes descended from the shoulders along the length of the tunic. The stripes, called *clavi* in Latin, were usually purple in color and indicated the wearer's status (broader stripes indicated higher status). The length of the tunic varied depending on the wearer's circumstances, status, and gender. For example, slaves and soldiers wore short tunics (just above the knee) for greater mobility, while women and priests wore long tunics for the purposes of modesty. The tunic's length could be adjusted by hitching up the cloth over a belt made of cloth, rope, or leather. The cloak or mantle worn over the tunic typically consisted of a large rectangular sheet (Greek *himation*), although Roman citizens wore a cloak with a curved hem called a toga. Dark notched bands and gamma-shaped designs were sometimes woven into the corners of mantles worn by both men and women, including Jews. Although color was not confined to women's clothes, women's clothing was more likely than men's to be colored (dyed). Most of the clothing worn by Jews in Roman Judea was made of wool, although according to our sources, priests serving in the Jerusalem temple and Essene men wore linen garments.

In many cases it is impossible to determine with certainty the original date or owners of the textiles at Masada: Herod's time, the period of the revolt, the Roman garrison that occupied the fortress after the siege, or Byzantine monks. However, it is likely that some fragments of linen clothing and wool tunics with *clavi* and mantles with notched bands belonged to the rebels. Although overall the textiles are of relatively high quality, they display evidence of repeated mending and patching.[60] There are also fragments of a linen sock with a division for the big toe to accommodate a sandal, and a drawstring around the top. The small size suggests that it belonged to a child. The sock comes from the dump in the casemate tower with the possible tannery.[61] Leather sandals with a strap between the big toe and the second toe—a timeless design still common today—were also found at Masada.[62]

Women at Masada

As we have seen, spindle whorls and loom weights indicate that women were among the refugees at Masada, and the sock might have belonged to a child. Women are also named or referred to in some of the inscribed potsherds (ostraca; see below), for example, "the wife of [Ze]beida," "the wife of Jacob," "the daughter of Domli," and "Shalom (or Salome) the Gali[lean."[63] In describing the final moments before the fall of the mountain, Josephus refers repeatedly to wives and children, as for example in these passages:

> and setting before his [Eleazar ben Yair's] eyes what the Romans, if victorious, would inflict on them [the rebels], their children, and their wives, he deliberated on the death of all. (*War* 7.321)

> let us have pity on ourselves, our children and our wives. (*War* 7.380)

Some of the other artifacts found in rebel contexts are associated exclusively with women. Among the most distinctive are four hair-nets—a rare find. Hair-nets typically were worn with Greek-style (eastern) attire but not with Roman (western) dress and seem to have been standard for Jewish women. All four of the hair-nets are made of wool, and two still had human hairs stuck in them which indicate that the nets matched the wearer's hair color: light-colored nets for fair-haired women, and darker nets for dark-haired women. The nets were edged with a braided or woven ribbon sewn along one side of the opening and had a draw-string on the other side that was knotted to the ends of the ribbon. The net was worn by placing the ribbon across the brow, pulling the ends of the draw-string at the base of the nape, and then tying the draw-string around the top of the head.[64]

The casemate wall rooms yielded jewelry and women's cosmetic items including a stone palette with two circular depressions on top and a mother-of-pearl shell for holding eye color; bronze eye shadow sticks; a bronze mirror case; and tiny ceramic bottles for perfume and kohl (eye liner).[65] Among the toiletry items are wooden combs, which were used also by men and children. Like many ancient combs, the Masada examples have fine, closely spaced teeth designed not only to detangle hair but to remove lice and their eggs. This is confirmed by analyses which identified hair lice and eggs still adhering to the teeth of the combs.[66] In addition, a body louse was found in a textile fragment from one of Herod's storerooms that was occupied at the time of the revolt.[67] Apparently the crowded and unsanitary living conditions bred lice which infested the rebels' hair and clothing.

One more piece of evidence for women at Masada comes from a different location along the Dead Sea: a rugged canyon to the south of Qumran called Wadi Murabbaʿat. During the First Jewish Revolt and the Bar Kokhba Revolt (the Second Jewish Revolt against the Romans; 132–135 CE), Jews took refuge in caves in this canyon. After the discovery of the first Dead Sea Scrolls, the exploration of these caves yielded finds associated with these refugees, including documents. One of these is a bill of divorce (Hebrew *get*), in which "Yehoseph [Joseph] son of Naqsan from . . . residing in Masada" divorces his wife, Miriam, daughter of Yehonathan [Jonathan] from the Nablata, residing in Masada. The *get* is dated "On the First of Marḥeshvan in the Year Six, at Masada," that is, 71 CE. This shows that the rebels at Masada continued to count calendrical years from the beginning of the revolt even after year five, when Jerusalem fell (70 CE). For this document to have ended up in Wadi Murabbaʿat, Miriam must have left Masada before the Roman siege began in 72 or 73.[68] Even under these dire circumstances, after the fall of Jerusalem and on the run, this Jewish woman apparently sought and was granted a divorce from her husband. The discovery of this *get* in Wadi Murabbaʿat indicates that the population at Masada fluctuated, with refugees coming and going until the beginning of the siege. When Miriam departed Masada for Wadi Murabbaʿat, she took the *get* with her.

Administration

Seven hundred and one inscriptions on ceramic jars and on broken pieces of pottery were discovered in Yadin's excavations. In antiquity, broken pieces of pottery were often used as writing material, similar to today's "Post-It" notes. They are called ostraca (plural; singular ostracon). The vast majority of the inscribed jars and ostraca from Masada are in the Aramaic or Hebrew language and date to the time of the revolt.[69] Although Aramaic appears to have been the dominant language spoken at Masada (as it was more generally among the Jewish population in the late Second Temple period), Hebrew and Greek were also spoken, and some of the refugees must have been bilingual or even trilingual. Furthermore, most of the inscriptions relating to priestly tithes are written in Hebrew.[70]

The inscriptions generally relate to matters of internal administration, particularly the ownership or distribution of food supplies. These include "tags" (the excavators' term) consisting of one to five letters, many of which were written by the same hand; tags inscribed with names; and lists of names followed by a number indicating a quantity (presumably of food items). Forty-nine of the tags with names are inscribed Yehohanan (John) with two Hebrew letters below, another twenty-one are inscribed Shimeon (Simon) with two Hebrew letters below, and nine are inscribed Yehuda (Judah) with a Hebrew letter and a Greek letter below. This group—designated "tags with specific names" by the excavators—comes from a dump near the storerooms and large bathhouse in the northern palace complex. Based on references in rabbinic literature to a similar system in the Jerusalem temple, Yadin suggested that the names on these tags refer to the issuing authority, and the individual letters denote ritually pure products such as flour, wine, and oil which were allocated to priests and Levites. Other tags inscribed with random names or individual letters might have been used as food-rationing tokens without any connection to priestly tithes.[71]

A jar fragment found in the synagogue inscribed "priest's tithe" provides additional evidence that the rebels at Masada observed biblical laws requiring the tithing of produce to priests and Levites. Other jars were inscribed with the Hebrew letters *tav* and *tet*, which Yadin identified as abbreviations for *terumah* (heave offering) and *tebel* (produce from which tithes and *terumah* have not been separated). Four ostraca (all inscribed in the same hand) bear the inscription "fit for the purity of hallowed things," with "fit" apparently referring to the storage jars or the storerooms in which the jars were found. There are also inscriptions that read "clean for hallowed things" or "for hallowed things." Some storage jars bear inscriptions indicating that their contents (wine or oil) were either suited or not suited "for the purity of hallowed things." These jars had been smashed after being emptied, apparently to prevent re-use. Some inscriptions indicate that other jars had been disqualified, presumably as containers of hallowed things.

Finally, a high priest is named in an ostracon found in a casemate room: "A[nani]as the High Priest, 'Aqavia his son." Yadin identified this high priest as Ananias son of Nedebaus, who is mentioned by Josephus and whose son Eleazar was the "captain of the temple" and a leader of the revolutionary party at the time the revolt broke out. Yadin and Joseph Naveh suggest that Ananias had another (otherwise unknown) son named 'Aqavia, who was present at Masada and certified the jar's contents as ritually pure. These inscriptions shed light on the internal administration at Masada and indicate that the rebels continued to collect and set aside priestly tithes and consecrated food.[72]

CHAPTER 9

"Masada Shall Not Fall Again"

YIGAEL YADIN, THE MASS SUICIDE,
AND THE MASADA MYTH

Nowadays multitudes of visitors make their way to the top of Masada to see the place where, two thousand years ago, a group of Jews
holding out against the mighty Roman Empire chose suicide over surrender. This narrative—the Masada myth—is inextricably bound with
the site's excavator, Yigael Yadin. In this chapter we examine Yadin's life,
consider the evidence for the mass suicide, and explore the creation of
the Masada myth.

YIGAEL YADIN (1917–1984)

The 1963–1965 excavations at Masada were conducted by Yigael Yadin,
arguably Israel's most famous archaeologist (fig. 44).[1] Yadin lived through
the British Mandate of Palestine and played a significant role in the establishment and formative years of the modern State of Israel. His archaeological accomplishments are intertwined with a career in public
service that was devoted to the Zionist enterprise.

Yadin was born and raised in Jerusalem as Yigael Sukenik. His father,
Eleazar Lipa Sukenik, was an archaeologist who specialized in ancient
synagogues. While a young student of archaeology in Jerusalem,
Yadin became involved with the Haganah, a Zionist paramilitary army
that was active in Palestine during the British Mandate. The name

Haganah—Hebrew for "defense"—reflects the original intention to protect Jewish settlements from Arab riots. After the State of Israel was established in 1948, the Haganah was transformed into the national army and renamed the Israel Defense Forces (IDF).[2] In 1939, the twenty-three-year-old Yadin became the personal aide to Yaacov "Dan" Dostrovsky, the Haganah's chief of staff. Because the Haganah was outlawed by the British, its members used code names. Yadin chose a code name that alludes to Genesis 49:16: "Dan will judge (Hebrew: *yadin*) his people."[3] When the State of Israel was established, David Ben-Gurion, the first prime minister, required his officers to adopt Hebrew names. From that point on, Yigael Sukenik became known as Yigael Yadin.

In 1945, Yadin resigned from the Haganah and returned to his studies. He wrote a master's thesis on ancient and medieval Arabic inscriptions and began work on a PhD dissertation about ancient warfare in biblical lands.[4] But only a couple of years later, David Ben-Gurion recalled Yadin to service as an operations officer for the Haganah. It was at this time—as the British Mandate of Palestine was ending and all-out war was about to erupt—that Yadin's father purchased the three Dead Sea Scrolls from Cave 1 at Qumran. These scrolls—together with the other four scrolls from Cave 1, which were later acquired by Yadin—are displayed in the Shrine of the Book in the Israel Museum in Jerusalem. In the meantime, Yadin had drafted a master plan ("Plan D") for the Haganah to secure control of Jewish settlements and territories in Palestine upon the withdrawal of British forces.[5] In 1949, Ben-Gurion appointed Yadin chief of staff of the IDF. After resigning the post in 1952, Yadin resumed his academic career, completing his long-delayed PhD dissertation on the War Scroll from Qumran, which, like his later publication of the Temple Scroll, is still a basic reference. In 1955, Yadin was appointed lecturer in archaeology at the Hebrew University of Jerusalem, and undertook the first of four seasons of excavations at Hazor, a large biblical tel (mound) in Galilee. He eventually became the head of Hebrew University's Institute of Archaeology.

Yadin was a brilliant scholar and a gifted public speaker. However, great archaeological discoveries usually involve some degree of luck, and Yadin was a very lucky archaeologist. In the wake of the discovery of the Dead Sea Scrolls, the Israel Exploration Society mounted a campaign in the early 1960s to explore caves in canyons along the southwest shore of the Dead Sea, from Ein Gedi to Masasda (see chapter 2). The canyons were divided among teams led by different archaeologists. Although Yadin got the leftovers after everyone else chose their canyons, Nahal Hever, which he was assigned, yielded the most spectacular finds. There Yadin excavated caves occupied by Jewish refugees from Ein Gedi at the time of the Bar-Kohkba Revolt (132–135 CE). The caves had been discovered by Roman troops, and the besieged refugees, trapped and unable to escape, starved to death. Their physical remains and personal belongings including documents remained inside the caves until their discovery by Yadin. Among the documents are letters written by the leader of the revolt himself, Bar-Kohkba (see chapter 3).

Yadin's crowning archaeological achievement was the excavations at Masada, which he directed for eleven months during the years 1963–1965.[6] Today's easy access to the site—less than a two-hour drive from Jerusalem along the western shore of the Dead Sea, followed by a short cable car ride to the top—makes it easy to forget the logistical challenges Yadin faced. Between 1948 and 1967, the only way to reach Masada was from the west or the south, as the western shore of the Dead Sea from Ein Gedi northward was in the West Bank under Jordanian control. The shortest route from Jerusalem to Masada was by way of the southern development town of Arad, from which point a narrow road winds through the desert to the foot of the Roman assault ramp. Yadin established the excavation camp with tents at this spot, close to Flavius Silva's position in Camp F two thousand years earlier. Thousands of volunteers from Israel and around the world cycled through the excavations in two-week rotations, supervised by Yadin's graduate students at the Hebrew University of Jerusalem. Many of these students became highly regarded archaeologists, among them Dan Bahat, Amnon Ben-Tor, Gideon Foerster, Ehud Netzer, and Yoram Tsafrir. Yadin maintained a strict, military-like schedule with reveille at 5:00 am every morning, and everyone was expected to report for work on the summit by 6:00 am. He even employed IDF officers in the camp administration. One year after the excavations ended, Yadin published a popular book on Masada, which was translated into different languages and became a best seller.[7]

Within a year of the publication of the book on Masada, Yadin was recalled to public service as tensions escalated between Israel and her Arab neighbors. Shortly before the outbreak of the Six-Day War in June

1967, Yadin accepted an appointment as Prime Minister Levi Eshkol's special advisor on security affairs. He played a central role in planning a military offensive which led to Israel's stunning victory and annexation of East Jerusalem and the West Bank, the Gaza Strip, and the Golan Heights.[8] As the fighting raged, Yadin ensured that Israeli forces secured the Rockefeller Museum in East Jerusalem, where most of the Dead Sea Scrolls were stored. A couple of days later, still in the midst of war, Yadin used the military to appropriate the Temple Scroll from Qumran, which was in the possession of an antiquities dealer in Bethlehem named Khalil Iskander Shahin (Kando).[9]

After the war ended, Yadin returned to academic life, teaching and working on the publication of the Temple Scroll, and resumed excavations at Hazor. His position as the foremost archaeologist in Israel was enshrined in James Michener's 1965 novel, *The Source*, which is inspired by the biblical tels of Hazor and Megiddo. The pipe-smoking Israeli archaeologist, Ilan Eliav, was modeled after Yadin.[10] However, the Yom Kippur War in 1973 prompted Yadin's return to public service, this time as the member of a commission charged with investigating the Israeli government's failure to anticipate the war's outbreak. The report issued by the Agranat Commission, so-called after Israeli Supreme Court chief justice Simon Agranat, led to the resignation of Prime Minister Golda Meir as well as Moshe Dayan's ouster from military leadership.[11]

In 1974–1976, I had the privilege of studying with Yadin after he again returned to academic life. As an eighteen-year-old, first-year undergraduate student majoring in archaeology at the Hebrew University of Jerusalem, I was required to take Yadin's course, "Introduction to the Archaeology of the Land of Israel." The experience was both terrifying and exhilarating because Yadin was as formidable as he was charismatic. In contrast to the other faculty members, with whom we were on a first-name basis, he was always "Professor Yadin." He would stride into the classroom, walk to the front, and begin to talk, sometimes writing on the chalkboard. Until today, Yadin was the most mesmerizing speaker I ever heard. During each class, I literally sat perched on the edge of my seat, waiting to hear what happened next. Yadin once wrote the name of a site in Arabic on the chalkboard and made us copy it in our notebooks. I remember struggling to reproduce the unfamiliar Arabic letters. As much as I enjoyed Yadin's lectures, I was too intimidated to speak to him, and I doubt he knew who I was. Nevertheless, I have always considered Yadin to be an inspirational teacher and scholar.

In the 1970s, the curriculum at the Hebrew University of Jerusalem followed a European, and specifically German, model. As a consequence, course grades were based on a single exam—the final—sometimes combined with a term paper. There were no makeups or "do-overs." Because the "Introduction to the Archaeology of the Land of Israel" was spread over two academic years, our final exam was scheduled at the end of the spring 1976 semester—specifically on July 4, 1976. In honor of the American bicentennial, the city of Jerusalem dedicated a new public park with a facsimile of the Liberty Bell. But the bicentennial was overshadowed by an unexpected event: on the night of July 3, Israel successfully conducted a daring raid in Uganda. Israeli commandos flew to the Entebbe airport and freed about one hundred hostages, most of them Israelis, who had been hijacked on an Air France flight from Tel Aviv to Paris by way of Athens. The only commando who lost his life in the raid was the unit's leader, Yonatan (Yoni) Netanyahu, the older brother of Benjamin Netanyahu, Israel's current prime minister. Operation Entebbe restored some of the confidence in its military ability that Israel had lost after the Yom Kippur War three years earlier.

Like my classmates, I spent the days before July 4 frantically preparing for Yadin's final exam, on which the entire course grade was based as there had been no term paper assignment. That morning, on my way to the Institute of Archaeology I heard the news about Entebbe. Never have I experienced such a sense of national euphoria. Everyone—on the streets, on buses, in shops—was smiling uncontrollably, almost in a daze. As my classmates and I entered the classroom to take the final exam, we too had grins plastered across our faces. It was then that Yadin entered the room and strode (as always) to the front. Sternly he asked, "What happened? Why are you all smiling?"—and then broke into a big grin himself. It is the only time I remember seeing Yadin smile like that.

Just a few months later, in November 1976, Yadin returned to public life, this time as the head of a new political party called *Dash* (pronounced "dosh," an acronym for the Democratic Movement for Change), which advertised itself as an alternative to the long dominant Labor Zionist party. However, the fifteen seats that Dash won in the 1977 elections came at the expense of the Labor party and enabled the right-wing Likud party led by Menachem Begin to obtain the largest number of seats in the Knesset (Israeli parliament). Dash ended up joining Begin's coalition government and Yadin was appointed deputy prime minister, selling out the principles on which the party had been founded. In 1981, Dash was disbanded and Yadin's political career ended in disgrace.[12]

Yadin spent his final years engaged again in archaeology and academic life. He died suddenly of a heart attack on June 28, 1984, at the age of sixty-seven. Neil Asher Silberman concludes his biography by observing, "Yigael Yadin's true legacy was in the study of the past, not in the reform of the present."[13]

THE MASS SUICIDE

Yadin closely followed Josephus's account in his interpretation of the remains at Masada and attempted to reconcile apparent inconsistencies. For example, he discovered that many of the excavated storerooms showed signs of burning and contained broken jars—contrary to Josephus's testimony that the rebels left their provisions intact. Yadin reasoned that "in order to achieve their purpose, the Zealots did not need to leave all their stores of food to the Romans. It was enough for them to leave one or two rooms with untouched victuals to show that they had not died through lack of food."[14] Similarly, Yadin interpreted an iron arrowhead workshop in the western palace as a pile of weapons set on fire by the rebels to prevent them from falling into Roman hands (see chapter 8).[15]

The mass suicide story is the reason for Masada's popularity as a tourist attraction today.[16] According to Josephus, after a pair of lengthy speeches, Eleazar ben Yair, the leader of the Jewish rebels at Masada, persuaded the men to commit mass suicide as the fortress was about to fall to the Romans. First, each man put his wife and children to death. Then the men drew lots, and ten of them killed the others. The remaining ten men drew lots again, and the one who drew the last lot slew the other nine:

> Finally, then, the nine bared their throats, and the last solitary survivor, after surveying the prostrate multitude, to see whether haply amid

the shambles there were yet one left who needed his hand, and finding that all were slain, set the palace ablaze, and then collecting his strength drove his sword clean through his body and fell beside his family. (*War* 7.397–98)

If the rebels committed suicide, what is the source of this information? In a slight twist to the story, Josephus adds that upon hearing the plans, two elderly women hid in a cistern with five children and surrendered to the Romans (*War* 7.399). Presumably Josephus would have learned of the mass suicide firsthand from these survivors or secondhand from a Roman witness. Notice that according to Josephus, the last victim was technically the only suicide at Masada, as everyone else died at the hands of others. This is significant because Jewish law prohibits taking one's own life.

On the lower terrace of the northern palace, Yadin discovered remains which he suggested might belong to the last victim and his family (fig. 45):

When, however, we came to clear the formidable pile of debris which covered the chambers of the small bath-house, we were arrested by a find which it is difficult to consider in archaeological terms, for such an experience is not normal in archaeological excavations. Even the veterans and the more cynical among us stood frozen, gazing in awe at what had been uncovered; for as we gazed, we relived the final and most tragic moments of the drama of Masada. Upon the steps leading to the cold-water pool and on the ground nearby were the remains of three skeletons. One was that of a man of about twenty—perhaps one of the commanders of Masada. Next to it we found hundreds of silvered scales of armor, scores of arrows, fragments of a prayer shawl (*talith*), and also an ostracon (an inscribed potsherd) with Hebrew letters. Not far off, also on the steps, was the skeleton of a young woman, with her scalp preserved intact because of the extreme dryness of the atmosphere. Her dark hair, beautifully plaited, looked as if it had just been freshly coiffeured. Next to it the plaster was stained with what looked like blood. By her side were delicately fashioned lady's sandals, styled in the traditional pattern of the period. The third skeleton was that of a child. There could be no doubt that what our eyes beheld were the remains of some of the defenders of Masada.[17]

Yadin's moving account shows that he interpreted these remains in light of Josephus's testimony. However, in recent years some scholars have questioned Josephus's account of the mass suicide at Masada on both archaeological and literary grounds. For example, Joe Zias claims that the remains on the lower terrace of the northern palace do not belong to one family but instead are random bones brought to this spot by hyenas.[18]

Because Josephus is the only ancient author who describes the siege and fall of Masada, his testimony cannot be verified independently. Is it possible that Josephus fabricated the mass suicide as a literary device to make the story of Masada—which concludes his seven-volume account of *The Jewish War*—more gripping? For example, some scholars have noted that mass suicides are a common literary motif in stories told by ancient historians including Josephus, who reports similar episodes at the sieges of Gamla in the Golan and Jotapata (Yodefat) in Galilee.[19] In addition, ancient Greek and Roman authors frequently invented long, emotional speeches and put them into the mouths of protagonists, like the speeches Eleazar ben Yair supposedly delivered to the rebels at Masada.[20] Shaye Cohen, who published a seminal article decades ago questioning the Masada mass suicide, writes, "Josephus the rhetorical historian realized that the murder-suicide of some of the Sicarii at Masada would be far more dramatic and compelling if it became the murder-suicide of all the Sicarii . . . Out of these strands—historical truth, a fertile imagination, a flair for drama and exaggeration, polemic against the Sicarii, and literary borrowings from other instances of collective suicide—Josephus created his Masada story."[21]

At this point, readers might be wondering: wouldn't the Romans—and among them Josephus's patrons, the Flavian family—have objected to an invented ending to the siege of Masada? After all, the Roman army was there, so they knew what happened. However, this objection reflects a modern expectation of "objective" history, a view not shared by the Greeks and Romans. Instead, ancient histories are more like stories, often focusing on the exotic (hence Josephus's long description of the Essenes), and typically were intended to convey messages or morals to the audience.[22] Readers might also be wondering if the Romans would not have objected to Josephus fabricating an ending to the siege of Masada that makes the defenders appear noble by choosing to die at their own hands instead of surrendering to the Romans. But portraying the Jewish rebels as brave elevated the Roman victory over them. After all, there is much greater glory in defeating a strong enemy than a weak one!

Even archaeology cannot verify whether the mass suicide took place because the archaeological remains can be interpreted differently, depending on how one evaluates Josephus's testimony. For example, today visitors to Masada are shown the spot where the "lots" were found, in a space to the west of the large bathhouse in the northern palace complex.[23] This area displayed signs of a violent conflagration, and more than 250 ostraca were found dumped here among and on top of heaps of ashes. They include "tags" inscribed with names which might be connected to the distribution of food among the rebels (see chapter 8). Yadin identified twelve of the ostraca as lots because they were written by the same hand and are inscribed with Hebrew names, including "ben Yair" (fig. 46). However, Joseph Naveh, who published these ostraca, was unable to identify them conclusively as the lots mentioned by Josephus. One problem is that there are twelve ostraca in the group, not ten. Yadin argued that one ostracon had never been completed, which leaves eleven ostraca. He then suggested that Josephus did not include Eleazar ben Yair among the final ten men who drew lots, based on the assumption that the ostracon inscribed ben Yair refers to the rebel leader. Another problem noted by Naveh is that the lots resemble the tags inscribed with names. Therefore, whether these ostraca are lots or simply tags used for other purposes remains an open question.

What about the physical remains of the rebels? Aside from the skeletons found on the lower terrace of the northern palace (discussed above), the only human remains Yadin discovered were in a cave on the southeastern side of the mountain. Here Yadin reportedly found about twenty-five skeletons, which he identified as Jewish rebels who had been disposed of by the Romans. However, Zias claims that there is documentary evidence of only five skeletons, and their association with pig bones found in the cave suggests they are Romans (or perhaps Byzantine monks), not Jewish rebels.[24] After Yadin's excavations, all these remains, which were assumed to be Jewish, were given an official burial by the State of Israel in a small mound at the foot of the Roman ramp.

The fact that Yadin found no other human remains atop Masada neither proves nor disproves Josephus's mass suicide story. On the one hand, had all the rebels committed suicide, presumably the Romans—who left a garrison on the mountain after the siege—would have disposed of the corpses by cremating them or burying them in a mass grave somewhere. Similarly, had only some of the rebels died, either at their own hand or in battle, with the rest taken captive, the result would have been the same: the Romans would have disposed of the corpses rather than leaving them to rot.

As we have seen, the archaeological remains have been interpreted as either supporting or disproving Josephus's testimony. For example, if Netzer is correct, the lack of evidence of burning in many rooms would support Josephus's account of the rebels' construction of a second wall of wood and earth. On the other hand, Hillel Geva has put forward an interpretation of one feature at Masada which, if true, would disprove the mass suicide story.[25] Piled against the outer (south) face of the white-plastered stone wall that separated the northern palace from the rest of the mountain (see chapter 4) was a massive mound of earth mixed with architectural fragments and artifacts. This debris has been attributed to cleaning and plundering activities by Roman soldiers or Byzantine monks or interpreted as a foundation for an observation tower established by the rebels during the siege. Geva points to difficulties with these explanations and instead interprets the debris as a Roman assault ramp. According to Geva, there was no mass suicide at Masada. Perhaps some of the rebels took their own lives but fighting continued after the Romans entered the fortress. Some of the rebels took refuge inside the northern palace, which was protected by the massive wall. The Romans piled the debris to create a ramp that enabled them to scale the wall and enter the northern palace. Geva's interpretation accords with Cohen's suggestion that Josephus embellished the story of the fall of Masada by reporting that all the defenders, not just some of them, committed suicide.

I am often asked if I believe there was a mass suicide at Masada, to which I respond that this is not a question archaeology is equipped to answer. The archaeological remains can be interpreted differently as supporting or disproving Josephus's account. Whether or not the mass suicide story is true depends on how one evaluates Josephus's reliability as an historian—a matter that I prefer to leave to Josephus specialists to resolve.

The Masada Myth

How did the site of a reported mass suicide of a band of Jewish rebels who terrorized other Jews become a symbol of the modern State of Israel? The creation of the Masada myth—in which these Jewish terrorists are transformed into freedom fighters and the mass suicide becomes a heroic last stand—has been explored by a number of scholars.[26] While archaeology has been used in many countries to advance political or nationalistic agendas, Masada perhaps best exemplifies this phenomenon. Although Masada's eventual fame is largely a result of Yadin's excavations, the site had become a symbol of the modern State of Israel long before the 1960s. It is the late Israeli archaeologist Shmaryahu Gutman who deserves much of the credit for the creation of the Masada myth. Beginning in the 1930s and through the next couple of decades, Gutman organized treks to Masada for youth movements and groups of guides which established the site as an emblem of Zionist aspirations.[27] With the creation of Israel in 1948, Masada became a symbol of the new state. Gutman continued to make a case for Masada's importance through the 1950s and was involved in the first archaeological explorations of the site (see chapter 2). It was because of Gutman's persistence that Yadin later undertook excavations at Masada.

Nachman Ben-Yehuda, an Israeli sociologist, notes that the Masada myth is based on a whitewashing of Josephus's account. For example, instead of referring to sicarii, the Jews atop Masada are typically described as Zealots, as for example by Yadin, or as defenders or rebels—neutral terms that mask the group's violent activities. Their terrorism of other Jews, including the massacre of innocent villagers at Ein Gedi, is overlooked in the Masada myth (see chapters 7 and 8).

A constellation of interrelated events in the twentieth century made possible Masada's transformation into a symbol of Jewish heroism and the modern State of Israel.[28] First, the European Jews who immigrated to Palestine in the first half of the twentieth century sought to establish a physical connection to the Zionist homeland. Treks like those organized by Gutman to Masada were intended to forge this bond. Even today, hikes around the country remain an integral part of Israeli life.[29] Second, archaeology proved a useful tool in establishing Zionist claims to a land that had not been under Jewish rule for two thousand years.

Third, the notion that heroic Jewish freedom fighters held out against the mighty Roman Empire to the bitter end countered the image of millions of passive European Jews starving to death or being gassed in Nazi concentration camps. In fact, the defenders of Masada have been compared explicitly to the Jewish resistance in the Warsaw Ghetto uprising.[30] Fourth, after 1948, Masada became a metaphor for the State of Israel: isolated, besieged, and surrounded by enemies on all sides, as expressed by the popular slogan, "Masada shall not fall again." This phrase was coined in 1927 by a poet named Yitzhak Lamdan in reference to persecuted European Jews returning to Zion. From the early 1950s on, the IDF's armored units climbed to the top of Masada for induction ceremonies.[31]

After Yadin's excavations, the archaeological remains underwent restoration and Masada became a national park. Yadin's 1966 book introduced the story of Masada to an international audience. The first cable car, which began operating in 1971 but fell short of the summit, was replaced in 1999 by a newer model that goes all the way to the top. The cable car not only greatly increased the number of visitors by facilitating access but has made it possible to hold bar and bat mitzvah ceremonies and other events on top of the mountain.

In a remarkable conflation of archaeology and nationalism, Masada's image as a symbol of Jewish heroism, the Zionist enterprise, and the State of Israel was elevated through its association with Yadin.[32] Yadin promoted this association in various ways, as reflected in the subtitle of his 1966 book: *Herod's Fortress and the Zealots' Last Stand*. The book cover reads: *The Momentous Archaeological Discovery Revealing the Heroic Life and Struggle of the Jewish Zealots*. The subtitle emphasizes the Jewish resistance at Masada and deemphasizes or omits the rest of the site's history. The title of the Hebrew version is *Masada: In Those Days—At This Time*, a phrase taken from a Hanukkah prayer and used here to relate Masada to modern Israel.[33] Yadin's book is peppered with similar analogies, as for example his description of the excavation camp at the foot of the Roman siege ramp:

> The sight of the adjoining camps, Silva's and our own, was not without its symbolism, and it expressed far more pungently than scores of statements something of the miracle of Israel's renewed sovereignty.

Here, cheek by jowl with the ruins of the camp belonging to the destroyers of Masada, a new camp had been established by the revivers of Masada.[34]

Ben-Yehuda concludes that Yadin's interpretation of the archaeological remains at Masada may have been impacted by his Zionist-nationalistic perspective, but it did not affect the quality of the fieldwork, as I can confirm from personal experience.[35] For example, every evening during the excavations, Yadin convened all his area supervisors for a meeting to review the day's findings. The meetings were recorded and later transcribed. I used the transcripts as a source of information when I prepared the publication of the military equipment from Yadin's excavations. Two rooms in the western palace contained hearths with large numbers of iron arrowheads and shafts. According to the transcripts, Yadin decided immediately that these must be stockpiles of weapons destroyed by the Jewish rebels to prevent them from falling into Roman hands, following Josephus's account. However, Ben-Tor, the area supervisor, correctly interpreted these rooms as iron arrowhead workshops dating to the time of the revolt (see chapter 8).

Ironically, within a couple of years of Yadin's excavations, Masada began to decline as a symbol of the State of Israel. First, the 1967 Six-Day War transformed Israel from an underdog nation into a conquering military power.[36] Second, a 1971 *Newsweek* article by Stewart Alsop described Israel's diplomatic inflexibility in negotiating with Egypt as a "Masada complex," suggesting an unhealthy national preference for mass suicide rather than survival. Third, the Yom Kippur War in 1973 undermined Israel's confidence in its military ability and created the feeling that Masada could fall again.[37] Fourth, by the late 1980s a new movement—post-Zionism—began to spread among Israeli Jews (and especially intellectuals), who felt that Zionist ideology was obsolete. In the meantime, Israel was transitioning from the collective socialist ideal of its Zionist founders to a free market, capitalist society.[38] It is no coincidence that by the late 1980s the IDF ceased to hold its induction ceremonies at Masada.[39]

Nevertheless, Masada remains the second-most-visited archaeological site in Israel. In 2001, Masada became Israel's first UNESCO World Heritage site.[40] It is an especially popular destination for the busloads of tourists who ascend the mountain each day by way of the Snake Path, the cable car, or the Roman assault ramp. Although Masada has lost much of its relevance to Israelis as a national symbol, it still resonates with Diaspora Jews who make the pilgrimage to the top of the mountain, where their guides relate the story of a small band of freedom fighters who made a heroic last stand against Rome. Silberman notes that Masada tells us as much about modern Israel as it does about ancient Jewish history: "the visible archaeological remains on the summit of Masada were not so much tangible proof of the story's historical accuracy as they were elaborate and persuasive stage scenery for a modern passion play of national rebirth."[41]

Even in today's post-Zionist era, Masada retains some of its potency as a symbol of the State of Israel. On May 22, 2017, US President Donald Trump made an historic, twenty-two-hour-long trip to Israel. In the weeks and days leading up to Trump's visit, Israelis agonized over what to pack into his brief itinerary—Jerusalem's Western Wall? the Holocaust memorial at Yad Vashem? To my astonishment, Masada was chosen as the site that Trump must visit above all others. Apparently, Trump too liked the idea of giving a speech at a site associated with underdogs.[42] Ultimately, however, the plans were scrapped when he was informed that helicopters could not land on Masada's summit because of the potential damage to the archaeological remains. Trump refused to take the cable car and ended up staying in Jerusalem.

Pinned to a corkboard in my office is a newspaper clipping with a photo of Bill and Hillary Clinton on a tour of Masada in 1998, three years after I co-directed excavations in the Roman siege works. Both Clinton and George W. Bush visited Masada during their presidencies, but neither gave a speech there out of a concern to appear neutral to the Palestinians. In the eyes of the world, Masada remains a symbol of the State of Israel and the Zionist enterprise.

EPILOGUE

A TOUR OF MASADA

I have led hundreds of tours around Masada, most of them from 1977 to 1980, when I worked as a guide and naturalist at the Ein Gedi Field School. Because nearly every group's itinerary included Masada, I usually visited the site once a week and sometimes more. Since then the site has changed, with the replacement of the cable car, the expansion of the visitor's center, and establishment of a museum at the base of the mountain, and the restoration of additional buildings and remains on the summit. However, my recommended itinerary has remained the same, and here I share it with you. For the visit, you should wear comfortable walking shoes, a hat, sunglasses, and sunscreen, and bring a large water bottle. Refer to the plan in figure 18 for the places mentioned in this tour.

THE NORTHERN PALACE COMPLEX

Ascending the east side of the mountain via the cable car or Snake Path, enter through a guardroom with stuccoed walls and benches in the casemate wall. Once through the gate, follow the path upward and toward the right, but instead of taking a hard right go west across the barren mountaintop. Some of Herod's buildings and a quarry will be visible to your right. Once across the mountain follow the path to the right to the northern palace complex. In this area you will find the northern palace, the large bathhouse (with a restored roof), and the room where the "lots" were found (now a covered rest area outside the large bathhouse).

   Enter the living rooms of the northern palace by walking around the tall, sloping, white-plastered wall and through the small guardroom, where a bored guard scratched graffiti on the wall two thousand years ago. Admire the amazing view from the semicircular upper terrace of the palace, including the badlands at the foot of Masada (created by the erosion of the white marl deposits); Roman siege camps A–C (to the right or east; notice the reconstructed outer wall of Camp A), D (straight ahead), and E–F (to the left or west); the circumvallation wall; and the runner's path. Ein Gedi is visible as a dark patch straight ahead (due north) at the foot of a mountain in the distance. The bedrooms behind the semicircular porch of the upper terrace are paved with simple black and white geometric mosaics.

Exit the upper terrace via the same small guardroom and visit the large bathhouse, walking through a peristyle courtyard that was decorated with mosaic floors and wall paintings and traversing the bathhouse rooms: the apodyterium (dressing room), which was paved with black and white *opus sectile* tiles and decorated with Second Style wall paintings, and notice the bin and bench made of pieces of columns installed by the rebels; the tepidarium with a small cold-water plunge bath on the right; and to the left, the caldarium (steam room), with the small pillars (suspensura) that supported a tiled floor. An arched opening for the furnace is visible in the opposite wall of the caldarium, with pipes along the walls which carried the hot air to heat the room.

The exit from the bathhouse takes you through the storerooms of the northern palace complex and ends up at the room where the "lots" were found. From this point, wooden steps descend the northwestern side of the mountain to the middle and lower terraces of the northern palace. If you can make the trek back up, I recommend going all the way down, passing the circular middle terrace along the way, as the lowest terrace is decorated with colorful wall paintings (some are modern copies) arranged to give an illusion of depth. Toward the bottom, notice that the modern steps incorporate the original Herodian staircase which wound around a central pier (square pillar). Below the eastern edge of this terrace, you will see a small bathhouse with a cold-water pool where Yadin found human remains which he identified as belonging to the family of the last rebel to commit suicide, including braided human hair, fragments of a prayer shawl (*talith*), an ostracon inscribed in Hebrew, and arrowheads and scales of armor. From the western side of the lowest terrace Camps E and F, the circumvallation wall, and the runner's path are clearly visible directly opposite. To the left the assault ramp climbs the side of the mountain, and at its base is a pointy small brown hill with a concavity in the side where the human remains found in Yadin's excavations were buried by the State of Israel.

The Synagogue, Assault Ramp, and Western Palace Complex

From the top of the steps proceed southward, stopping to refill water at the water container and using the restroom facilities nearby if needed. The next stop is the synagogue, located in one of the northwest rooms of the casemate wall. Notice the rows of benches to accommodate an assembly, and the back room, which was the *genizah*. Exiting right from the synagogue brings you to the top of the assault ramp, where the casemate wall was broken through. Nearby is a pile of large rolling stones— boulders collected by the rebels to roll down on to the Romans.

From the ramp continue a short distance to the south, entering the western palace complex by way of a stuccoed guardroom with benches and an elongated corridor that takes you to the area of the throne room. Go up the steps for a view over the western palace's bathhouse, with its mosaic floors, bathtub, and narrow stepped pool. Notice the small bin that the rebels added, cutting through a beautiful Herodian mosaic. Admire another Herodian mosaic in a nearby room—the most elaborate one found at Masada, which incorporates the seven species as decorative motifs. The lines that the artisan drew in the plaster underneath are clearly visible where the mosaic is gone. This was an antechamber or waiting room for the throne room beyond, and it is the room that the rebels converted into an iron arrowhead workshop. Return to the ground level by way of the original Herodian staircase which, like the one in the northern palace complex, consists of steps winding around a central pier.

The Southern Part of the Mountain

Most visitors to Masada never continue beyond this point, but the southern part of the mountain should not be missed. Upon exiting the western palace complex, notice how barren and brown and empty the area to the south appears. Two thousand years ago it was green with gardens, and the brown stone walls gleamed with white plaster. Immediately ahead (to the south) is the large stepped pool with niches in the enclosing wall which is the debated swimming pool or *miqveh*. A structure with irregular rooms built of small stones directly ahead (to the south) is easily identifiable as a rebel addition. To its left (east) a circular structure with small niches in the walls and no doorways is a columbarium (dovecote). Continuing southward will bring you to the only large cistern on Masada's summit (the others of comparable size are on the mountain's sides, mostly the northwest). It is not easy to climb the tall, steep, rock-cut steps, but the impressive size of the cistern's interior makes the effort worthwhile. Notice the thick layers of plaster coating the cistern's walls to prevent water seepage, and the horizontal lines on the plaster indicating different water levels over time. The cistern was hewn by hand out of bedrock, and the bottom is covered by a thick layer of silt. This cistern, unlike those on the northwest side, was filled mostly by hand (supplemented by rain water), not by aqueduct.

Depending on your interest, you could proceed from here to the southeastern side of the mountain, where the *miqveh* that Yadin identified with the aid of rabbis is installed in one of the casemate rooms. But do not miss visiting the southern tip, which is protected by a small fort. From here admire the breathtaking view, encompassing Camps G (on the hillside to the right or west), H (atop Mount Eleazar directly ahead or to the south), and A (to the far left or east, near the cable car station), and the circumvallation wall and runner's path. Before leaving, listen to the amazing echo created by the sheer cliff of Mount Eleazer opposite by shouting as loudly as possible across the chasm.

NOTES

PROLOGUE. THE FALL OF MASADA

1. Unless otherwise indicated, all translations of Josephus's works are from the relevant volume of the Loeb edition (Feldman 1965; Marcus 1943; Thackeray 1927–1928).

CHAPTER 1. THE SIEGE OF MASADA (72–73 OR 73–74 CE)

1. See Josephus, *War* 7.553–65; Kennedy and Riley 1990: 99–100; Vörös 2015: 228–33. For the Roman siege works at Masada, see Richmond 1962; Davies 2011.
2. *War* 7.252. For Flavius Silva's life and career, see McDermott 1973.
3. For the date of the siege and fall of Masada, see Campbell 1988; Cotton and Geiger 1989: 21–23; Ben-Tor 2009: 253–54; Davies 2011: 65–66 n.1; Mason 2016: 561–63.
4. See Roth 1995; Mason 2016: 563–65. Ben-Tor 2009: 238, writes, "Some 40,000 cu. m of stone were required to build the camps and the siege wall (which was 4,500 m long, an average of 1.6 m wide and approximately 3 m tall). According to a calculation based on contemporary sources, one person could build about one cubic meter a day. Thus, 8,000 soldiers would need no more than a week to complete the work."
5. For the Roman army, see Webster 1998; Le Bohec 1994; Parker 1985.
6. At the time of the outbreak of the First Revolt, there were twenty-seven legions, and in 70 CE there were thirty-one legions; see Parker 1985: 98, 106.
7. Yadin 1966: 223, estimated that "the built camps alone could house almost 9,000 troops, including the legion. But there is no doubt that the entire besieging force was very much larger, probably reaching 15,000 men." Davies 2011: 81 n.15 argues that the number was closer 8,000.
8. Davies 2011: 68, 81. Also see Davies 2018, who discusses the blurring of boundaries between civilians and combatants in antiquity in the context of the First Revolt.
9. For the distribution of troops among the different camps, see Cotton and Geiger 1989: 15.
10. For the 1995 excavations, see Magness 1996; Arubas and Goldfus 2008; Magness 2009b. Davies 2011: 68 argues that as the siege of Masada was a specialist operation, it is not "a generally applicable model for all Roman siege actions."
11. Davies 2011: 68.
12. Ben-Tor 2009: 237, states that, "A cautious calculation shows that about 16 tons of food and 26,000 liters of water would have to be brought to Masada every day." Aside

from a small spring in Nahal Se'elim (Wadi Seiyal) a short distance to the north of Masada, the closest fresh-water sources are at Ein Boqeq to the south and Ein Gedi to the north, some 12–16 km (ca. 7–10 miles) away.

13. See Stiebel and Magness 2007. For Roman military equipment in general, see Bishop and Coulston 1993.
14. Stiebel and Magness 2007: 26.
15. The ramp fell 13 meters (ca. 42 feet) short of the Masada summit; see Davies 2011: 76–77.
16. See Magness 2011a: 352–56.
17. Holley 1994: 359; Ben-Tor 2009: 240.
18. Holley 1994: 360–63. Davies 2011: 81, associates the stone shot in L1039 and L1045 with artillery from the time of Herod or the post-Herodian garrison.
19. Stiebel and Magness 2007: 16–19.
20. Stiebel and Magness 2007: 31.
21. Email communication, July 29, 2010.
22. See Magness 2011a: 352–56.
23. Cotton and Geiger 1989: 16–17; Netzer 1991a: 422. For coins associated with the post-siege occupation, see Meshorer 1989.
24. For the Latin papyri, see Cotton and Geiger 1989: 27–79; Ben-Tor 2009: 171–77.
25. Cotton and Geiger 1989: 103–4; Ben-Tor 2009: 180.
26. For an analysis of the wood used in the ramp, see Lev-Yadun et al. 2010, who propose that it was brought from more humid and cooler areas to the east of the Dead Sea (responding to an earlier claim by other scholars that in the Roman period the climate at Masada was less arid than today). For a discussion of the ramp's construction, see Davies 2011: 77–78.
27. See Gill 1993; Gill et al. 2000. For a geomorphological analysis of the ramp, see Goldfus et al. 2016. For responses to Goldfus and Arubas's claim (endorsed by Mason) that the ramp was never completed or operational, see Davies and Magness 2017; Magness 2011a: 352–58; Davies 2011: 78–79.
28. Netzer 1991b.
29. For Josephus's life and works, see Rajak 1983, 2016; Cohen 2002; Mason 2001; Edmonson et al. 2005; Atkinson 2016: 4–22; Klawans 2012.
30. For Josephus's sources and other lost works on the First Revolt, see Cohen 2002: 24–66, 248–52. For Josephus's use of the writings of Nicolaus of Damascus, who was Herod the Great's historian and minister, see Wacholder 1989; Atkinson 2016: 17, 51.
31. For *Life* see Mason 2001; Cohen 2002: 17–23, 101–80; Rajak 1983: 12–14, 152–54; Atkinson 2016: 15–16. Josephus devotes much of *Life* to defending his reputation from attacks by a detractor named Justus of Tiberias.
32. See Cohen 2002: 105; Mason 2001: xxxv.
33. See Rajak 1983: 32–38; Cohen 2002: 106–7.
34. For Josephus's claim to be a Pharisee, see Cohen 2002: 144–51.
35. See Rajak 1983: 39–43, 65; see pp. 43–44 for Josephus's shipwreck on the way to Rome (*Life* 14–15).
36. See the discussion in Rajak 1983: 72.

37. Later in life, Josephus's patron was a man named Epaphroditus; see Rajak 1983: 223.
38. See Cohen 2002: 89; Edmonson 2005: 4.
39. See Rajak 1983: 175–76.
40. For the relationship between Josephus's writings and Greek historiography, see Tomson 2017 (focusing on Josephus's account of the 50s CE in *War* compared with Thucydides's *Peloponnesian War*); Cohen 2002: 25–33; Eshel 1999: 229; Rajak 1983: 155.
41. Rajak 1983: 79; also see p. 102; Rajak 2016: 229–30.
42. All translations of *The Peloponnesian War* are from Warner 1972. Cohen 2002: 91, remarks, "In true Thucydidean fashion the proem to BJ claims that the Jewish war was the greatest of all time."
43. See Eshel 2009: 128–29; Mason et al. 2012: 296. For ancient historians' realism, see Mason 2016: 231.
44. Atkinson 2016: 4, 166–68.
45. See Cohen 2002: 234–36.
46. Chapman 2007: 88; also see Atkinson 2007: 366.
47. Atkinson 2016: 4. Also see Rajak 2016: 228, who refers to "Josephus's divided self."
48. For the dating of *Antiquities* and *Life*, see Mason 2001: xv–xix; Cohen 2002: 170–80; Edmonson 2005: 6–7; Atkinson 2016: 6–7.
49. For a comparison of the accounts, see Cohen 2002: 1ff. For example, *Life* 145 reports that Josephus's house was surrounded by 600 soldiers, whereas *War* places the number at 2,000 (see Cohen 2002: 7). Cohen notes that *Life* and *War* "contradict each other in many other details, large and small" (p. 7); for differences between *War* and *Antiquities*, see pp. 48–66. Atkinson 2016: 14, says that the two works should not be harmonized.
50. See Cohen 2002: 236–42.
51. See Rajak 1983: 228. Eshel 1999: 232–33, says that *Antiquities* "has a much more optimistic view" than *War*, as by the time the latter was written, it had become clear that Judaism could survive the temple's destruction.
52. From Stern 1980: 101 (vol. 2).
53. See Schwartz 2005: 73–74.
54. See Cohen 2002: 240; Edmonson 2005: 7.
55. For Josephus's aims, see Cohen 2002: 91–100, 114–41; also see Atkinson 2016: 4, 18–19; for intended audience(s), see Rajak 2016: 224–25.
56. See, for example, Barnes 2005, who applies postcolonial theory to a passage in *Against Apion*; also see Atkinson 2016: 171.
57. Cohen 2002: 181 (originally published in 1979 and reprinted in 2002), who, however, qualified this by stating, "Josephus does exaggerate but he does not normally engage in large scale invention" (p. 204 n.44). Mason (2016) has a more skeptical attitude about reconstructing history based on Josephus's accounts. For a response to Mason's approach, see Eliav 2017.
58. See Hata 2014.
59. For a discussion, see the footnote accompanying this passage in the Loeb edition.
60. The writings of Josephus's contemporary and nemesis, Justus of Tiberias, have not survived; see Klawans 2012: 185–86.

61. For Josephus's revival in Jewish circles from the late eighteenth century on, see Rajak 2016: 221–22.
62. See Netzer 1991a: 527–29 (Tower Room L1156); Cotton and Geiger 1989: 211 (misattributed to L1139). For a possible Latin inscription on a jar from Qumran, see Lemaire 2003: 354–55 (KhQ 1401).

CHAPTER 2. THE SEARCH FOR MASADA

1. For the history of exploration of Masada, see Netzer 1993: 974; Yadin 1966: 238–59; Schulten 1933: 30–52. For the exploration of the Dead Sea region in the nineteenth century, see Kreiger 1988: 29–112 (and her recommended bibliography); also see Silberman 1982: 37–88.
2. For Masada, see Robinson et al. 1856: 525–26; Robinson 1843: 42–68 (reporting on Wolcott and Tipping's visit).
3. For accounts of Costigan's expedition, see Masterman 1911: 13–19; O'Loughlin 2011; Jampoler 2005: 156–65; Kreiger 1988: 35–42; Silberman 1982: 53.
4. From Masterman 1911: 15. I have not been able to find the name of the Maltese sailor in any of the accounts of Costigan's expedition.
5. From Jampoler 2005: 159–60.
6. Jampoler 2005: 160.
7. From Masterman 1911: 16.
8. Masterman 1911: 19.
9. The stone was marked on October 8, 1900 by Robert Alexander Stewart Macalister, accompanied by Masterman, on behalf of the Palestine Exploration Fund; see Macalister 1901; Masterman 1902; Underhill 1967: 45. In 1964 the stone was relocated and the incised letters were painted yellow; see Klein 1973: 42–43; Underhill 1967: 46.
10. Ilan 1973; also see Kreiger 1988: 41–42.
11. For accounts of Molyneux's expedition, see Masterman 1911: 19–26; Jampoler 2005: 165–72; Kreiger 1988: 52–57; Silberman 1982: 53.
12. From Masterman 1911: 24.
13. From Masterman 1911: 25.
14. From Masterman 1911: 24.
15. From Masterman 1911: 26.
16. We possess a great deal of information about Lynch's expedition, as it was much better-documented than Costigan's and Molyneux's; see Lynch 1850. For a recent book-length study, see Jampoler 2005. Also see Kreiger 1988: 58–75; Silberman 1982: 53–62.
17. From Lynch 1850: 205–6.
18. From Lynch 1849: 333.
19. See de Saulcy 1853; Delessert 1853; Silberman 1982: 63–72.
20. de Saulcy 1853: 165 (vol. 2).
21. de Saulcy 1853: 199–229 (vol. 1); Delessert 1853: 53–69.
22. See Yadin 1966: 244–45.
23. See Tristram 1866; Kreiger 1988: 78–106; Yadin 1966: 247.
24. Tristram 1866: vi.
25. Tristram 1866: 316.

26. For Judea (including Masada), see Conder and Kitchener 1883. For the history of the survey, see Silberman 1982: 113–27. For their exploration of Masada, see Yadin 1966: 250–52.
27. See Conder and Kitchener 1883: 417; Yadin 1966: 250.
28. Silberman 1982: 115.
29. Silberman 1982: 123.
30. Brünnow and von Domaszewski 1909: 217, 220–44.
31. Yadin 1966: 252.
32. For Schulten's expedition, see Schulten 1933; Yadin 1966: 253–54 (who incorrectly states that Schulten lived at Masada for eleven months; see Schulten 1933: 4; Netzer 1993: 974).
33. See Yadin 1966: 254; Netzer 1993: 974.
34. The results of this expedition are published in Avi-Yonah et al. 1957. Also see Yadin 1966: 254–55. For the background to this expedition, see Kletter 2014: 216–18.
35. See Yadin 1966: 6, 12–13.
36. See Yadin 1966: 13–14, 19–26.
37. The popular book: Yadin 1966. The preliminary report: Yadin 1965. The final reports: Yadin and Naveh 1989; Meshorer 1989; Cotton and Geiger 1989; Netzer 1993; Barag and Hershkovitz 1994; Sheffer and Granger-Taylor 1994; Koren 1994; Shamir 1994; Bernick 1994; Liphschitz 1994; Holley 1994; Zias et al. 1994; Foerster 1995; Talmon 1999; Yadin 1999; Qimron 1999; Martínez 1999; Bar-Nathan 2006; Stiebel and Magness 2007; Grossberg 2007; Shimron 2007; Kislev and Simhoni 2007; Reich 2007a, 2007b, 2007c; Hershkovitz and Amorai-Stark 2007. For a popular summary of the final reports, see Ben-Tor 2009.
38. See Netzer and Stiebel 2008.
39. See Arubas and Goldfus 2008. The Roman siege works had not been excavated previously, aside from a very limited excavation by Yadin in one of the camps that was never published; see Yadin 1966: 209.
40. The results are not yet published, but for media coverage, visit https://forward.com/news/382132/exclusive-new-archaeology-shows-refugee-camp-not-just-rebels-atop-masada/.

CHAPTER 3. MASADA IN CONTEXT

1. Ilan 1973 is a valuable source of information on the Dead Sea region.
2. See Freund 1973.
3. See Gadot 1973: 5.
4. See Gadot 1973: 1.
5. See Gadot 1973: 5–6; Kolton 1973.
6. See Gadot 1973: 3; Yaffe 1973.
7. See Halevy 1973; Danin 1973.
8. For an overview of the fauna, see Fishelzon 1973.
9. See Niv and Omri 1973: 29–31, 35.
10. See Orland 1973: 56.
11. See Kreiger 1988: 183.
12. See Orland 1973.

13. For the history of the Dead Sea Works and its counterpart in Jordan, see Kreiger 1988: 142–70, 195–98 (including her bibliography).
14. See Niv and Omri 1973: 28.
15. See Klein 1973 for the fluctuations in level up to that time.
16. http://wikitravel.org/en/Dead_Sea_(Israel) (accessed July 30, 2016).
17. The idea of a Med-Dead or Red-Dead canal originated in the mid-nineteenth century. For an overview, see Kreiger 1988: 176–80; also see Underhill 1967: 45.
18. "Israel, Jordan Advance $800m. Red-Dead Canal, Water Swapping Project" (December 1, 2015); http://www.jpost.com/Business-and-Innovation/Environment/Israel-Jordan-advance-800m-Red-Dead-canal-water-swapping-project-435984 (accessed July 30, 2016).
19. Unless otherwise indicated, all biblical passages are from the NRSV.
20. For Herodian Jericho, see chapter 4.
21. For the expedition to the Judean Desert, see Aviram 1993; Patrich 1993b. The preliminary reports were published in the *Israel Exploration Journal* 11 (1961) and 12 (1962).
22. See Bar-Adon 1980, 1993.
23. Mazar 1993.
24. de Vaux 1973: 1–3; Magness 2002: 48–49.
25. Bar-Adon 1989: 18–29; Patrich 2000; Netzer 2001: 77–78.
26. For the sectarian settlement at Qumran, see de Vaux 1973; Humbert and Chambon 1994; Magness 2002.
27. For Ein Feshkha, see de Vaux 1973: 60–87; Magness 2002: 210–16.
28. For Ein el-Ghuweir, see Bar-Adon 1977; Magness 2002: 216–23.
29. Netzer 2006: 213–13; Netzer 2001: 75; Patrich 1993a; Tzafrir 1982.
30. Clamer 1999, 1997. For a reconstruction of the Herodian-period buildings, see Netzer 2006: 234–36, who proposes that the main structure included two large colonnaded halls flanked by rooms and separated by a garden.
31. See Vörös 2013, 2015.
32. Netzer 2006: 216, suggests that the "double triclinium" was a two-story wing with accommodations for the garrison on the ground floor and the royal living quarters above.
33. Netzer 2006: 213–17; Netzer 2001: 75–76; Piccirillo 1997; Tzafrir 1982.
34. Fischer and Tal 2000; Gichon 1993a, 1993b.
35. http://www.haaretz.com/israel-news/science/.premium-1.633460 (accessed August 2, 2016).
36. Avigad 1962: 169–81; Avigad 1993b: 832.
37. For the Cave of Horror, see Aharoni 1962, 1993. For a popular account of the Bar Kokhba Revolt and the discoveries in Nahal Hever, see Yadin 1971. For scientific reports, see Yadin 1963; Lewis 1989; Yadin et al. 2002; also see Yadin 1993.
38. For the Judean Desert monasteries, see Hirschfeld 1992; Chitty 1966.

CHAPTER 4. MASADA AND HEROD'S OTHER BUILDING PROJECTS

1. For the sites discussed in this chapter aside from Masada, see the relevant entries in Stern 1993 and 2008; Netzer 2001, 2006. For a map of Herod's building projects in Palestine, see Marshak 2015: 263. For Herod's building projects inside and

outside Palestine, see Rocca 2008: 42–52, 96–122, 153–90, 325–47; Richardson 1999: 174–215; Roller 1998: 85–238 (who emphasizes the influence of the rebuilding of late Republican and Augustan Rome on Herod's building program). For Herod's building projects outside of Palestine, see also Marshak 2015: 232–47.

2. For a discussion, see Roller 1998: 119–24.

3. For the information in this chapter, see the Masada final report volumes (*Masada I–VIII*); Ben-Tor 2009; Eshel 2009; and Yadin 1966.

4. For a summary of the Herodian construction phases, see Ben-Tor 2009: 124–28. These are technical phases represented mostly by abutting walls and different orientations of rooms or buildings, reflecting additions or changes during the course of Herod's reign. Richardson 1999: 198, dates Herod's construction of Masada to 37–10 BCE. Eshel 1999: 24–25, notes that the fact that Herod did not take Marcus Agrippa to visit Masada in 15 BCE suggests that construction had not been completed by then. He proposes (pp. 104–5) that wine amphorae with inscriptions dated to 27/26 and 19 BCE were brought to Masada before construction was completed, or after 15 BCE when their contents were considered old vintage.

5. Eshel 2009: 22.

6. For the graffiti, see Eshel 2009:114–15; Ben-Tor 2009: 48–49; Netzer 1993: 116, 120; Yadin 1965: 28. Greek and Latin abecedaries were written in charcoal over the graffito of a ship on the wall of the storeroom (L120), perhaps by a Jewish rebel or a Roman soldier stationed atop Masada after the siege; see Cotton and Geiger 1989: 213–14.

7. See Eshel 2009: 119–20.

8. See Eshel 2009: 26, 33, 122–24; Eshel 1999: 231–32.

9. See Cotton and Geiger 1989: 140–67; Cotton et al. 1996; Finkielsztejn 2006; Berdowski 2008; Ben-Tor 2009: 182–84.

10. For the pool surrounded by niches (L625), see Netzer 1991a: 329–34; Grossberg 2007: 101–6; Ben-Tor 2009: 117–18; Eshel 2009: 49–50 (also see chapter 8). For the large swimming pool at the southern end of the mountain (L711), see Netzer 1991a: 482–83; Ben-Tor 2009: 88–89.

11. Eshel 2009: 93, suggests that in Herod's time, the lower row of cisterns was accessed by a path that went southward and joined the route ascending the west side of the mountain, which was later covered by the Roman ramp.

12. Ben-Tor 2009: 68–72, provides the following figures: the two rows of cisterns on the northwest side of the mountain contained approximately 36,000 cubic meters of water; the large cistern at the southern end of the top of the mountain contained 2,500 cubic meters of water; the total capacity of the cisterns and pools on top of the mountain is an estimated 10,000–15,000 cubic meters of water. According to Ben-Tor, there were "many other" cisterns on top of the mountain which are not well-known because their roofs have collapsed.

13. See Ben-Tor 2009: 27.

14. In addition to the references cited at the beginning of the section on Herod's building projects, see Bahat 1990.

15. For Herod's practice of naming his cities and monuments in honor of others, see Marshak 2015: 250–57. For Herod's friendship with Marcus Agrippa, see Richardson 1999: 232–33, 263–64; Roller 1998: 43–53.

16. For a recent publication of the remains in this area, see Re'em 2018.
17. For these urban villas, see Avigad 1993a; for the Burnt House, see Geva 2010.
18. In addition to the references cited at the beginning of the section on Herod's building projects, see Marshak 2015: 312–34; Grabar and Kedar 2009; Rocca 2008: 291–306; Mazar 1975.
19. The translation of the *soreg* inscription is from Cotton et al. 2010: 43.
20. For discussions, see Marshak 2015: 328–30; Rocca 2008: 297–302.
21. This is the only known building that Herod named after Mark Antony; see Marshak 2015: 106–8.
22. Caesarea Maritima is a modern name for the site. Its ancient name was Caesarea (and the harbor was Sebastos). In antiquity, to distinguish the city from others named Caesarea, it was sometimes referred to as Caesarea near Sebastos, Caesarea of Straton, or Caesarea of Palestine; see Stern 1993: 270, s.v. "Caesarea." In addition to the references cited at the beginning of the section on Herod's building projects, see Holum et al. 1988. For a discussion, see Marshak 2015: 149, 151–53.
23. See Marshak 2015: 218–20.
24. For an overview of Herod's temples outside of Jerusalem, see Marshak 2015: 209–17, 272–75; for his motives, see pp. 284–311.
25. I agree with Netzer 2006: 102 (*pace* Yosef Porath) that the high-level aqueduct was built by Herod rather than dating to later in the first century CE.
26. For a discussion, see Marshak 2015: 150.
27. See Marshak 2015: 221–24; Netzer 2006: 55–58.
28. See Marshak 2015: 258–64; Netzer et al. 2013. The location of a Herodium "towards Arabia" mentioned by Josephus is unknown; Vörös 2013: 153–55 proposes it is Machaerus.
29. See Porat et al. 2016; Porat et al. 2015; Netzer et al. 2013. Marshak 2015: 261, erroneously places the tomb's location in Lower Herodium.
30. I am unpersuaded by the argument to the contrary by Patrich and Arubas 2015.

CHAPTER 5. JUDEA BEFORE HEROD

1. Only a small part of the vast corpus of secondary literature on Second Temple period Judaism and Jewish history is cited in this chapter. For general overviews and basic studies, see Schalit 1972; Schürer 1973–1986; Hengel 1981; Jagersma 1986; Cohen 1989; Bickerman 1988; Lieberman 1994; Tcherikover 1999; Smallwood 2001; VanderKam 2001; Collins and Harlow 2012. For a recent study of the Hasmonean state, see Atkinson 2016, who dates as follows the reigns of the Hasmoneans: John Hyrcanus I, 135–105; Aristobulus I, 105–104; Alexander Jannaeus, 104–76 (p. 106). My discussion focuses on Palestine and therefore largely excludes the Jewish Diaspora communities.
2. See Barton 2010: 191–92, although he focuses on Israelite religion (pre-exilic).
3. See Stavrakopoulou and Barton 2010, and the other papers in that volume.
4. See Niehr 2010: 30–31. In contrast, Friedman 2017: 149–66, argues that some Israelites and all early Jews were monotheistic. In my opinion, sources such as Daniel 2:47 and 3:26, Mark 5:7 and Luke 2:32, 35 (which refer to the Most High God) attest to a monolatrous attitude well into the Second Temple period.

5. See Niehr 2010: 29. In some cultures kings also served as intermediaries with the divine.

6. For this development, see Niehr 2010: 32. In the first temple (Solomon's temple), God's presence was thought to be enthroned on the Ark of the Covenant.

7. See Stavrakopoulou and Barton 2010: 4; Edelman 2010; Grabbe 2010. Deities (including the God of Israel) were also worshiped at other types of cultic sites such as shrines.

8. See Pucci Ben Zeev 2012: 368; Jagersma 1986: 20; Tcherikover 1972: 67–68.

9. Some scholars feel that Judean is a more accurate rendering of *Ioudaios*, whereas others argue that this translation is problematic because it obscures and even eliminates the religious dimension of ancient Judaism. For discussions, see Mason 2016: 90–91; Schwartz 2014 (especially pp. 91–112); Schwartz 2005; Mason 2007; Cohen 1999: 69–106. Here I use the term Jew.

10. See Pucci Ben Zeev 2012: 368; Tcherikover 1972: 67–68, 84.

11. The complex relationship between Judaism and Hellenization or Hellenism, and even the definition of these terms, are much debated. See, e.g., Hengel 1981; Bickerman 1988; Lieberman 1994; Tcherikover 1999. For overviews, see Cohen 1989: 35–45; Pucci Ben Zeev 2012: 370–73 (who focuses on the Diaspora). For a recent discussion relating to 1–2 Maccabees, see Honigman 2014: 26–28, 141–46, 197–228; also see Nickelsburg 2005: 102–10.

12. See Honigman 2014: 64, 92, 210–12.

13. See, for example, the prohibition against public nudity in the pseudepigraphic book of Jubilees 3:31 and 7:20, whose author presents the violation of this prohibition as one of the reasons God wiped out humankind with the great flood; Charlesworth 1985: 60, 70; Mendels 1987: 84. For an overview of Jubilees, see Nickelsburg 2005: 69–74, who dates its composition to the early 160s.

14. For the Jewish priesthood, see VanderKam 2001: 176–83.

15. See Tcherikover 1972: 124–25. For a different view, see Honigman 2014: 359–61.

16. Although this is the dominant view, not all scholars understand Jason's actions as meaning that Jerusalem became a *polis*. For discussions see Honigman 2014: 19; Seeman and Marshak 2012: 39; Jagersma 1986: 45; Schürer 1973: 148–49 (vol. 1); Tcherikover 1972: 125–27.

17. See Tcherikover 1972: 125–29; VanderKam 2004: 202; Honigman 2014: 375–77.

18. See Atkinson 2016: 24; VanderKam 2004: 18–19, 203–22; Jagersma 1986: 47–50; Tcherikover 1972: 129–35. For the Oniad temple at Leontopolis/Heliopolis, see Grabbe 2010: 183; Rocca 2008: 294–96, including n.44; Bohak 1996; Barclay 1996: 36. For Zadok, see Kugler 2000.

19. See VanderKam 2004: 204–22; Jagersma 1986: 47–50; Schürer 1973: 151–54 (vol. 1); Tcherikover 1972: 131–35; Seeman and Marshak 2012: 40. For the date of the outbreak of the revolt, see Honigman 2014: 381–82.

20. See Stern 1980: 47; Cohen 1989: 46–49; Schäfer 1997.

21. The motivation behind Antiochus IV's decree is debated. For different views, see Honigman 2014: 20; Seeman and Marshak 2012: 40–41; Jagersma 1986: 49–53; Tcherikover 1972: 137–44.

22. For a recent reevaluation of the causes, circumstances, and events surrounding the revolt based on the information in 1–2 Maccabees, see Honigman 2014: 38, 259–86,

who argues that the opposition of Jewish Hellenizers and conservatives (or "pious" Jews) is based on a misreading of 1–2 Maccabees. For earlier studies, see Jagersma 1986: 57–61; Schürer 1973: 155–63 (vol. 1); Avi-Yonah 1972: 147–71.

23. See Schürer 1973: 162–63 (vol. 1); Jagersma 1986: 61.

24. For an overview of the Jewish holidays, see VanderKam 2001: 204–8.

25. For the history of the celebration of Hanukkah, see Rocca 2008: 288–90.

26. See Jagersma 1986: 61–67, 79–82; Schürer 1973: 164–99 (vol. 1); Avi-Yonah 1972: 171–82; Klausner 1972a. For John Hyrcanus I's renewal of treaties with Rome, see Atkinson 2016: 59–62; VanderKam 2004: 293–95.

27. This is the dominant view; see, e.g., Jagersma 1986: 66; Klausner 1972a: 188. However, some scholars argue that although the Hasmoneans were not Oniads, they were Zadokites; see Schofield and VanderKam 2005; Collins 2010: 97–98. Atkinson 2016: 24 n.3, and Eshel 2008: 55 n.71, reject this claim.

28. See Marshak 2015: 57. VanderKam 2004: 319, 336, notes that none of our sources mentions Jewish opposition to the Hasmoneans due to incurring corpse impurity (which is forbidden to high priests) during the many wars they waged.

29. For these sects, see Baumgarten 1997; Saldarini 2001. For the Essenes, see below.

30. See Cohen 1989: 124–37; Saldarini 2001: 123–27.

31. For Josephus's treatment of these sects, see Klawans 2012, with an overview on pp. 9–13.

32. See Cohen 1989: 60–62, 146; Honigman 2014: 52–58.

33. See Honigman 2014: 38–39, 51–64.

34. See Saldarini 2001: 79–123; Atkinson 2016: 135–38; Cohen 1989: 145; Main 2000: 813–14.

35. For the Sadducees, in addition to the references on the Jewish sects cited above, see Stemberger 2010; Meier 2008: 389–487; Regev 2005; Main 2000; Schürer 1979: 404–14 (vol. 2).

36. See Davies 2000: 1007. For the origin of the term Sadducee, see Schürer 1979: 405–7 (vol. 2); Main 2000: 812–13; Kugler 2000: 1005; VanderKam 2001: 189.

37. For the Pharisees, in addition to the sources cited above, see Deines 2010; Meier 2008: 289–388; Baumgarten 2000; Schürer 1979: 381–403 (vol. 2).

38. See Heszer 1997: 64.

39. See Baumgarten 2000: 658; Saldarini 2001: 134; Meier 2001: 300–3. For Josephus's Pharisaic views, see Klawans 2012.

40. See Heszer 1997: 59–61.

41. The Pharisees might have been a sub-elite or retainer class; see Saldarini 2001: 48, 106; Meier 2001: 297.

42. For a discussion, see Klawans 2012 (ch. 2 and 3).

43. Translation from Danby 2013: 452.

44. For a discussion, see Meier 2001: 295–96, 332–40, 353 n. 33; for scribes see 549–60.

45. See Meier 2001: 339.

46. For a discussion of this episode with references, see Magness 2011b: 18.

47. For the Qumran sect/Essenes and the Dead Sea Scrolls in general, see Vermes 2011; VanderKam 2010; VanderKam and Flint 2002; Davies et al. 2002; Magness 2002; Schiffman and VanderKam 2000; Martínez and Tigchelaar 2000; Abegg et al. 1999; Stegemann 1998; Schiffman 1994; Cross 1980.

48. This is the traditional view, as expressed for example by Eshel 2008: 33. Some scholars now question the authority of Zadokite priests within the sect (including as its founders) and argue that the sobriquet "Teacher of Righteousness" does not refer to Zadok or Zadokites but derives from a phrase in Joel 2:23 which means "for he has given you the early rain for your vindication." See, e.g., Kugler 1999: 97–100; Davies 2000; Knibb 2000: 918; Collins 2010: 9, 46–48, 64, 95–97; Klawans 2012: 19–23. Assuming the sobriquet derives from Joel, I do not see why it cannot also be a pun on Zadok/Zadokite.

49. For a discussion of Jesus's relationship to the Essenes, see Meier 2001: 492–532.

50. See Yadin 1966: 173–74; Bar-Nathan 2006: 67–72; Reich 2007a: 188; Crawford 2012. For a dissenting view, see Eshel 2009: 76–79.

51. For John Hyrcanus I, see Atkinson 2016: 47–79; VanderKam 2004: 285–312; Schürer 1973: 200–15 (vol. 1); Klausner 1972b.

52. For a similar view but expressed differently, see VanderKam 2004: 292. For the possibility that the Idumaeans might have adopted some Jewish (Judean) customs even before John Hyrcanus I's conquest, see Marshak 2015: 56 n.13. For the Idumaeans, see Richardson 1999: 54–62.

53. For the Samaritans, see Knoppers 2013; Pummer 2016, 1987; Meier 2001: 533–49. For the Samaritan temple on Mount Gerizim, see Rocca 2008: 294–96 n.45. Relations between the two peoples were complex and not always hostile, including intermarriage at the highest levels of the Judean and Samarian priesthoods.

54. See Atkinson 2016: 69–78.

55. See Barclay 1996: 38, 40, 64, 401 n.3.

56. For Aristobulus I, see Atkinson 2016: 80–99; VanderKam 2004: 312–18; Schürer 1973: 216–18 (vol. 1); Klausner 1972c.

57. See Marshak 2015: 64–72.

58. See Atkinson 2016: 81, 83; VanderKam 2004: 313–15.

59. Aristobulus I's conquest and Judaization of Galilee are not explicitly mentioned in our sources, but are inferred by modern scholars; see Schürer 1973: 217–18. For the possibility that the Hasmoneans did not forcibly convert the Idumaeans and Ituraeans to Judaism but instead forged a political alliance with them, see VanderKam 2004: 317. Atkinson 2016: 86–97, doubts that the Ituraeans were ever under Hasmonean rule, and suggests that Jewish expansion into Ituraean territory was a gradual process. For the Ituraeans, see Richardson 1999: 68–72.

60. For a discussion of the Gospels' birth narratives, see Meier 1991: 208–19.

61. For the possibility that Herod sought to associate himself with the house of David, including by rebuilding the Jerusalem temple, see Marshak 2015: 279–84; Rocca 2008: 22–29, 63. For the tradition of a Davidic messiah, see Pomykala 1995.

62. For this passage, see Meier 1991: 214–16.

63. See Reed 2000: 39–55; Aviam 2004: 41–50.

64. For Alexander Jannaeus, see Atkinson 2016: 100–33; VanderKam 2004: 318–36; Schürer 1973: 219–28 (vol. 1); Klausner 1972c.

65. For the identity of Alexander Jannaeus's wife and the relevant biblical laws, see VanderKam 2004: 318 n.210; Klausner 1972c: 225–26. Atkinson 2016: 85–86, questions that Salome Alexandra was married to Aristobulus I, noting that early Christian copyists emended Salina Alexandra, which occurs in Josephus's manuscripts, to Salome Alexandra.

66. Wassen 2005: 169.
67. For the law of levirate marriage in Deuteronomy, see Pressler 1993: 63–73.
68. For a discussion of this episode, see Atkinson 2016: 123–24; VanderKam 2004: 320–23.
69. For discussions of this episode in the Pesher Nahum, see Eshel 2008: 117–31; Berrin 2004: 87–125, 165–92; VanderKam 2004: 323–32.
70. See Berrin 2000.
71. Unless otherwise indicated, all translations of the Dead Sea Scrolls are from Martínez and Tigchelaar 2000.
72. See VanderKam 2001: 189.
73. Berrin 2004: 188–89 argues that the reference to an atrocity as restored by modern scholars is incorrect, and that the point of this sentence was not to condemn Alexander Jannaeus's actions but to witness the fulfillment of God's punishment of the Pharisees. In contrast, Eshel 2008: 126–29 understands this passage as condemning Alexander Jannaeus for transgressing biblical law by hanging men alive. For recent studies of crucifixion in antiquity, see Chapman 2008; Samuelsson 2011.
74. See Netzer 1993: 973.
75. See Avi-Yonah et al. 1957: 2–3.
76. Meshorer 1989: 71; Eshel 2009: 13–15, who notes that an ostracon from Wadi Murabbat dated to the first quarter of the first century BCE includes a line that reads, "And I went up from there to Masada," indicating that Masada was inhabited by then.
77. See Netzer 1991a: xv, 573, 615, 647–49. For remains that might be Hasmonean or date early in Herod's reign, see Netzer 1991a: 124–33 (the "Abandoned Bathhouse"); 542–43 (cistern L1907); Ben-Tor 2009: 9–11.
78. For Salome Alexandra (whose Hebrew name was Shelamzion), see Atkinson 2016: 134–45; Schürer 1973: 229–32 (vol. 1); Klausner 1972d.
79. Atkinson 2016: 135–38, contrasts Josephus's positive account of Salome Alexandra in *War* with the negative portrayal in *Antiquities*.
80. For the events covered in this section, see Atkinson 2016: 146–65. Although Atkinson says the death of Salome Alexandra marks the "true end" of the Hasmonean kingdom (p. 145), he believes it continued until 31 BCE, when, according to Josephus, Herod captured Hyrcania from Mattathias Antigonus's sister Alexandra. Atkinson notes that "this desert queen had kept Herod from participating in the Battle of Actium" (p. 165). Also see VanderKam 2004: 337–85; Smallwood 2001: 16–51; Richardson 1999: 95–130; Schürer 1973: 233–80 (vol. 1).
81. See Marshak 2015: 75; Kokkinos 1998: 94–95; Roller 1998: 1 including n.1.
82. From Stern 1980: 28; see Smallwood 2001: 26–27. From the Roman point of view, the absence of a physical representation of the deity meant there was no god in the inner sanctum, as statues provided the means by which humans interacted with the divine. See Honigman 2014: 99.
83. For the Roman reorganization, see Smallwood 2001: 28–29.
84. For the titles see VanderKam 2004: 354–55, including n.301; Richardson 1999: 105–6.
85. For the events in this section, see Marshak 2015: 92–104; VanderKam 2004: 367–69; Smallwood 1981: 51–56; Schürer 1973: 281–86 (vol. 1).

86. For different versions of these events, see Marshak 2015: 99 including n.13; VanderKam 2004: 369.
87. For an overview of this episode, see Avi-Yonah et al. 1957: 3–4.
88. On his father's side, Herod was an Idumaean Jew while his mother was Nabataean (perhaps the daughter of the Nabataean king). For ancient slurs about Herod's ancestry, see Marshak 2015: 110–11 n.1; Kokkinos 1998: 96 n. 41. On the question of Herod's Jewish identity, see Cohen 1999: 13–24, 268–73, who shows that the principle of matrilineal descent was not yet established in the Second Temple period; also see Marshak 2015: 292–93.

CHAPTER 6. FROM HEROD TO THE FIRST JEWISH REVOLT AGAINST ROME (40 BCE–66 CE)

1. For the events covered in this chapter, see Schürer 1973: 330–483 (vol. 1); Jagersma 1986: 115–37; Smallwood 2001: 105–19, 144–200, 256–92; Goodman 2007: 379–403.
2. Goodman 2007: 390–99 (quote from p. 390).
3. See Mason 2016: 199–280 (with a summary of other scholars' views), who explicitly does not base his interpretation on Josephus's narrative (p. 217). The local conditions he cites include the long-term consequences of Hasmonean expansion into non-Jewish territories (p. 224) and the Romans' deployment of Sebastene and Caesarean (gentile) auxiliaries in Judea. For a critique of Mason's approach, see Eliav 2017.
4. For popular books about Herod, see Grant 1971; Gelb 2013; Rozenberg and Mevorah 2013. For a semi-popular study, see Richardson 1999 (see pp. xv–xx for a timeline of Herod's life; for Herod's family tree, see pp. 46–51). For specialist books about Herod, see Schalit 1978 (available only in German and Hebrew); Roller 1998 (for Herod's family tree, see pp. 278–90); Rocca 2008; Marshak 2015. Also see Schürer 1973: 287–329 (see pp. 287–94 for a timeline of Herod's reign) (vol. 1); Smallwood 2001: 56–104. Although Herod is now commonly referred to as "the Great," Josephus uses this epithet only once (*Ant.* 17.130) (Schürer 1973: 329 n.167; Richardson 1999: 12). Here I refer to Herod as "the Great" because it is common usage, and to differentiate him from his successors with the same name.
5. See Richardson 1999: 160 n.32, who says that beheading a king was not unprecedented, but doing so without the approval of the Roman Senate was unusual.
6. Schürer 1973: 296 (vol. 1), divides Herod's reign into the following periods: (1) 37–25 BCE (consolidation of authority); (2) 25–13 BCE (era of prosperity and great buildings); (3) 13–4 BCE (domestic miseries). Some scholars have suggested different dates for Herod's reign, questioning especially its end in 4 BCE, although a majority continue to cite Schürer's dates. For example, for a recent proposal to date Herod's reign from late 39 BCE to early 1 BCE, see Steinmann 2009.
7. For Herod's wives, see Josephus, *War* 1.562–63; Thackeray 1927: 266–67; Kokkinos 1998: 206–45; Richardson 1999: 235; Rocca 2008: 75–77; Marshak 2015: 292. By marrying Mariamme, Herod sought to associate himself with the Hasmoneans; see Marshak 2015: 110–11, 116–36 (on Herod's use of art and architecture [including coins] to connect himself to the Hasmoneans), 278; Rocca 2008: 29–35;

Richardson 1999: 121–22. For intermarriage between Jews and gentiles, especially among the elite, see Goodman 2007: 112–14.

8. See Rocca 2008: 282–83.

9. Aristobulus III was probably too young anyway to be appointed initially as high priest. For Hananel (who might have been a Zadokite), see VanderKam 2004: 394–98, 405–6; for Aristobulus III see pp. 398–405. Herod reinstalled Hananel after Aristobulus III's death.

10. For the high priests during Herod's reign, see VanderKam 2004: 394–416.

11. For the reasons behind Herod's execution of Hyrcanus II, see Marshak 2015: 115 including n.5; 140 including n.1; Richardson 1999: 169–71; Schürer 1973: 301 (vol. 1).

12. See Richardson 1999: 131, 173; Schürer 1973: 319 (vol. 1).

13. See Eshel 2009: 20–21.

14. Marshak 2015: 112, notes that Herod did not have Mariamme put to death until after Octavian reconfirmed him as king, suggesting that by then she had outlived her political usefulness to him.

15. According to Richardson 1999: 220, the Antonia and "whatever fortifications existed on the site of the present citadel." For these fortresses, see below.

16. As in the case of the term "Hellenization," there is much scholarly debate concerning the definition of "Romanization" and the nature of Rome's relationship with native peoples around the Empire. See, e.g., Lee 2003; Keay and Terrenato 2001; Woolf 1998. For the impact of Romanization on Herod and his circle, see Marshak 2015: 174–229 (chapter 8: "Bringing Judaea into the Roman Sphere: Herod and Romanization"); for the education of Herod's sons in Rome, see pp. 174–77. Josephus (*Ant.* 15:342–43) relates that upon arriving in Rome, Alexander and Aristobulus stayed "in the house of Pollio"—probably the famous poet, orator, and historian Gaius Asinius Pollio—before moving into Augustus's house. For discussions, see Richardson 1999: 231 n.49; Roller 1998: 23–28.

17. For endogamy and exogamy (outside marriages arranged for political purposes) in Herod's time, see Richardson 1999: 43; Kokkinos 1998: 145, 216–17, 353–56.

18. See Marshak 2015: 111.

19. Herod produced a total of seven wills during his reign; see Richardson 1999: 33–38. For the different sons named by Herod as his heirs, see Rocca 2008: 80–83.

20. See Marshak 2015: 293.

21. See Richardson 1999: 288, 295–98, who notes that Herod's execution of Alexander and Aristobulus took place in 7 BCE, around the time of Jesus's birth; also see Roller 1998: 4.

22. See Thackeray 1927: 306–7.

23. See Magness 2011b: 10, 196–97 n. 71; also see Marshak 2015: 290.

24. As noted by Marshak 2015: 286–89, who proposes that the incident was motivated by opposition to Herod's reign instead of by religious sensitivities, although it is not clear why the eagle symbolized Herod (as opposed to focusing on another part of the temple complex or even another monument built by Herod). For a discussion of this incident, see Richardson 1999: 15–18.

25. For possible diagnoses, see Richardson 1999: 18 including n.10; Trivedi 2002.

26. For Herod's family members, offspring, and descendants, see Kokkinos 1998. For Herod's dynastic family tree, see Goodman 2007: frontmatter.

27. For the territories ruled by Philip, see Schürer 1973: 336 (vol. 1).

28. See Kokkinos 1998: 228–29; Schürer 1973: 354–57 (vol. 1); Smallwood 2001: 114–19; Jagersma 1986: 116–17.

29. See Kokkinos 1998: 236–40 ("Philip the Tetrarch"); Schürer 1973: 336–40 (vol. 1); Smallwood 2001: 181–82; Jagersma 1986: 117–18.

30. Our sources confuse Herodias and Salome; see Kokkinos 1998: 237, 265–71; Schürer 1973: 339, 344–45, 350–52 (vol. 1); Smallwood 2001: 182, 185. Here I follow Kokkinos.

31. See Kokkinos 1998: 233–35; Schürer 1973: 340–53 (vol. 1); Smallwood 2001: 183–87; Jagersma 1986: 118. Antipas established his capital at Sepphoris after Judea became a Roman province in 6 CE.

32. See Reed 2000: 100–138.

33. For Herodias and Salome, see Kokkinos 1998: 265–71, 310–11; Schürer 1973: 344–48 (vol. 1); Smallwood 2001: 185.

34. Schürer 1973: 346 (vol. 1), notes that these accounts are not incompatible; also see Smallwood 2001: 185.

35. The prefects and procurators of Judea usually were of equestrian rank (Marcus Antonius Felix, who was a freedman, was an exception). For these titles, see Schürer 1973: 357–60 (vol. 1); Smallwood 2001:145, 269 n.39 (on freedmen serving as provincial governors). For a discussion of Judea's status under the prefects and procurators, see Mason 2016: 240–45, 278 (who defines Judea as an "ethnic zone [surrounding Jerusalem] in Syria").

36. The main auxiliary force (around 3,000 troops) was stationed at Caesarea Maritima, with small garrisons posted elsewhere around the country. When the Roman governor was in residence in Herod's palace in Jerusalem, the Jerusalem cohort stayed there. See Schürer 1973: 361–66 (vol. 1); Smallwood 2001: 146–47; Mason 2016: 258–59.

37. Until 44 CE, when the privilege was given to Herod's descendants; see Schürer 1973: 379 (vol. 1).

38. See Schürer 1973: 383–87 (vol. 1); Smallwood 2001: 160–74; Mason 2016: 265–69 (see p. 265 for the dates of Pilate's administration). From Colson 1971: 151–53.

39. See Smallwood 2001: 167–70, who believes that Pilate acted out of weakness in consenting to Jewish demands to have Jesus put to death.

40. See Schürer 1973: 349–50 (vol. 1); Smallwood 2001: 169 n.87.

41. Kokkinos 1998: 264, 271–304; See Schürer 1973: 442–54 (vol. 1); Schwartz 1990; Smallwood 2001: 187–200; Goodman 2007: 76–85; Jagersma 1986: 130–31.

42. For the education of native princes in Rome, see Mason 2016: 261.

43. See Schürer 1973: 379 (vol. 1).

44. For the events in Alexandria and the delegation to Gaius, see Schürer 1973: 389–94, 444–45 (vol. 1); Smallwood 2001: 220–55; Goodman 2007: 400–2.

45. Josephus (*Ant.* 18.257–60) provides a brief account of the delegation, which he collapses into one meeting with the emperor instead of two meetings as reported by Philo. In addition, whereas Josephus says that Apion headed the gentile delegation, Philo names others. For discussions, see Sterling 2013: 110–11; Schürer 1973: 393–94.

46. See Schürer 1973: 394–96 (vol. 1); Smallwood 2001: 174–80.

47. See Kokkinos 1998: 291; Goodman 2007: 77, 79.

48. See Schürer 1973: 451–52 (vol. 1); Kokkinos 1998: 301; Goodman 2007: 77.

49. Smallwood 2001: 193 notes that Agrippa I preferred to downplay his Herodian ancestry, at least among the Jewish population. Josephus and Philo do not call him
Herod, and his coins are inscribed "King Agrippa."
50. According to Smallwood 2001: 199–200, Agrippa I was 54 years old at the time of
his death, and his son Agrippa II was 16.
51. For these procurators, see Schürer 1973: 455–70 (vol. 1); Smallwood 2001: 256–84;
Goodman 2007: 386–90.
52. See Kokkinos 1998: 294, 302. Berenice was only 15 when Marcus Julius Alexander died.
53. *Historia Romana* 66.15:3–4, *apud* Xiphilinus; from Stern 1980: 378–79 (vol. 2).
54. See Kokkinos 1998: 327–30.
55. For a recent analysis of this episode, see Mason 2016: 271–72, who sees it as prefig-
uring the causes for the outbreak of the revolt a decade later.
56. Felix and Drusilla's son Agrippa III and his wife, who lived in Campania, lost their
lives when Mount Vesuvius erupted in 79; see Josephus, *Ant.* 20.144; Kokkinos
1998: 321.
57. For a discussion of the sicarii, see Mason 2016: 254–57, who argues that the term
denotes the mode of killing rather than a distinct terrorist group.
58. See Goodman 2007: 390; Schürer 1973: 464 (vol. 1). The Egyptian is mentioned in
Acts 21:38 and in Josephus.
59. See Goodman 2007: 73.
60. See Kokkinos 1998: 317–40; Schürer 1973: 471–83 (vol. 1); Smallwood 2001: 272–84.
61. For the chronology, see Smallwood 2001: 262 n.22.
62. From Stern 1980: 99–100 (vol. 2).
63. See Schürer 1973: 481 (vol. 1); Edmonson 2005: 6–7.
64. See Goodman 2007: 391–92.

CHAPTER 7. THE FIRST JEWISH REVOLT AGAINST ROME (66–70 CE)

1. For the revolt, see Schürer 1973: 484–508, Smallwood 2001: 293–330, who provide
summaries of Josephus's account in *War* with references to the relevant passages.
Josephus has a longer version in *Vita* (his autobiography), which was written a couple of decades after *War* and for clearly apologetic purposes; see Smallwood 2001:
302 n.30; also see Cohen 2002: ch. 1. For a literary analysis of Josephus's description of the siege of Jerusalem, see Mason 2016: 402–43.
2. Josephus, *War* 2.285–92.
3. Josephus, *War* 2.409–21.
4. Josephus, *War* 2.422–40.
5. Josephus, *War* 2.447–48. Smallwood 2001: 299 n.22, notes that Josephus's use of
Zealot to describe Menahem's followers in *War* 2.444 (and only here) has caused
scholars to confuse the sicarii at Masada with Zealots. For a discussion see chapter 8.
6. Josephus, *War* 2.457–60, 499–516.
7. Josephus, *War* 2.517–55. Mason 2016: 281–334, suggests that the disastrous outcome
was not necessarily due to incompetence on Cestius's part.
8. Josephus, *War* 2.556–654. For John and Simon, see Mason 2016: 450–59. Simon was
from Gerasa, probably modern Jerash in Jordan (ancient Peraea). His patronym

"Giora" perhaps derives from the Hebrew word *ger* (stranger, alien, or foreigner), which might indicate his father was a proselyte.

9. Josephus, *War* 3.1–4, 64–69.

10. Mason 2016: 335–95, argues that there was no "war" in Galilee, and Vespasian instead aimed to suppress the rampant banditry in the region.

11. Josephus, *War* 3.115–282, 316–39. For the excavations, see Adan-Bayewitz and Aviam 1997.

12. Josephus, *War* 3.540.

13. For the sieges of Gamla and Jotapata, see Aviam 2007, who believes that the archaeological remains support Josephus's narrative of the battles. Atkinson 2007: 358–65, suggests that Gamla's downfall was due to internal infighting.

14. For archaeological remains associated with the siege, see Yavor 2010; Holley 2014; Stiebel 2014; Magness 2014.

15. See Schürer 1973: 498 (vol. 1). Smallwood 2001: 298 n.18, believes it is more likely that members of the community fled the city individually over time, instead of at once en masse.

16. Josephus, *War* 4.399–405.

17. For the chronology of Vespasian's visit to Jericho and Qumran, see de Vaux 1973: 38–39; Mason 2016: 412–13.

18. Josephus, *War* 4.491–99.

19. Josephus, *War* 4.505; it is not clear to which part of Masada Josephus is referring.

20. Josephus, *War* 4.504, 517.

21. Josephus, *War* 4.440–86.

22. Translation from Stern 1980: 30 (vol. 2). Also see Josephus, *War* 5.5–13. Eleazar's designation as "the son of Simon bar Giora" in some manuscripts of Josephus's works apparently is an error; see Smallwood 2001: 312 n.81. Josephus describes the faction led by Eleazar as "Zealots," the meaning of which is debated; see Smallwood 2001: 299; Mason 2016: 444–50; also see the discussion in chapter 8.

23. Josephus, *War* 5.40–46.

24. Josephus, *War* 5.57–97, 258–359.

25. Later in the siege, Josephus reports being knocked out by a stone flung at him by one of the defenders (*War* 5.541).

26. Josephus, *War* 5.424–41.

27. Josephus, *War* 5.550–52.

28. Josephus, *War* 5.466–510.

29. Josephus, *War* 6.201–13.

30. Schürer 1973: 504 (vol. 1).

31. Josephus, *War* 6.9–93.

32. The Loeb edition corrects Josephus's text from lack of men to lack of lambs (*War* 6.94) (p. 205); Schürer 1973: 505 (vol. 1) prefers lack of men.

33. Translation from Danby 2013: 200.

34. Josephus, *War* 6.96–156, 220–66.

35. From Stern 1980: 64–67 (vol. 2), including a consideration of the differences between this account of the temple's destruction and Josephus's. For a discussion, see Mason 2016: 487–513.

36. Mason 2016: 494, argues that Sulpicius's source was Josephus, not Tacitus. He concludes that Titus destroyed Jerusalem and the temple "without evident regret" (p. 501), and that, whether or not he ordered the temple destroyed, this was not a matter of policy on Titus's part (p. 513). Also see the discussions in Barnes 2005; Smallwood 2001: 325–26; Rajak 1983: 206–12.

37. Josephus, *War* 6.316; see other sources in Schürer 1973: 507 n.116 (vol. 1), who notes that this acclamation led to suspicions that Titus intended to make himself independent ruler of the East.

38. For the book of Daniel, see Nickelsburg 2005: 17–22, 77–83.

39. See the NRSV notes to these passages. For the date of Mark and Matthew, see Meier 1991: 43; Ehrman 2016: 242–43.

40. See Smallwood 2001: 325.

41. Josephus, *War* 6.363–400.

42. See http://www.haaretz.com/israel-news/jerusalem-s-time-tunnels-1.357872 (accessed January 1, 2017), which describes the political and archaeological controversies surrounding these excavations.

43. Josephus, *War* 6.433; 7.26–33.

44. See Avigad 1993a: 120–39. For the final report on the Burnt House, see Geva 2010.

45. For much lower and more reasonable estimates, see Mason 2016: 439.

46. For this section, see Magness 2008, 2009a.

47. Josephus, *War* 7.1–5.

48. See Schürer 1973: 514 (vol. 1); the governor of Judea was now of senatorial instead of equestrian rank, and therefore no longer was subordinate to the Syrian legate. Also see Mason 2016: 280, who adds that to reduce ethnic tensions, local (Sebastene and Ascalonite) auxiliary units were moved out of the region.

49. Josephus, *War* 7.22–25, 37–40, 96–119.

50. See Mason 2016: 9–12, 17–19.

51. See Magness 2009a, 2008; Mason 2016: 19–33.

52. Mason 2016: 279, notes that Vespasian punished only those Jewish leaders (John and Simon) who had continued to defy Rome during the revolt, and says that although Simon satisfied the Roman need to sacrifice a "scapegoat," the choice was ironic as Simon was hated by most Jews, who would not have mourned his loss (p. 32). In my opinion, the singling out of Simon indicates that he was considered the more senior of the two leaders, as Smallwood 2001: 319 n.111, suggests on other grounds.

53. From Stern 1980: 31.

54. See Magness 2008: 215.

55. See Magness 2008: 217. For the theological significance of the tearing of the veil, see Ehrman 2016: 173–76.

56. See Magness 2008: 206.

57. See Magness 2008: 207–8.

58. See Magness 2009a: 37–38; Magness 2008: 212–15; Mason 2016: 13–17, 33: "By diverting the residual anxiety from Rome's crippling civil war to an alleged foreign threat, the [Flavian] regime could hope to consolidate loyalties orphaned by the civil war. The Judaean conflict was not ideal for this purpose, but since it was the foreignish conflict they had on hand, they pressed it into service" (p. 33).

59. See Magness 2009a: 37–38; Magness 2008: 212–15; Mason 2016: 39.

60. See Magness 2008: 214–15; Magness 2009a: 39; Mason 2016: 8.
61. Mason 2016: 3.
62. See Mason 2016: 6, 42.
63. See Magness 2009a: 38. Mason 2016: 35, is skeptical that Jerusalem and Judea could have yielded enough money to fund these projects, concluding that "the perception of an infusion of Judaean wealth counted more than any reality" (p. 36). For Flavian building projects in Rome, see Mason 2016: 33–41.
64. See Magness 2009a: 36; Magness 2008: 201; Mason 2016: 4–5.
65. See Magness 2008: 202–3.
66. See Magness 2008: 209–10.
67. See Magness 2008: 209–10.
68. See Magness 2008: 217.

CHAPTER 8. THE REBEL OCCUPATION OF MASADA (66–73/74 CE)

1. Eshel 2009: 28–29, 132, and Eshel 1999: 231 suggest that Josephus's description of the fall of Masada on Passover Eve in 73 or 74 CE is intended to present this event as divine retribution for the Passover massacre by the sicarii at Ein Gedi a few years earlier. He finds the episode "difficult to accept" and says Josephus's goal was to present himself as one of the moderate rebels.
2. Ben-Tor 2009: 23, 96.
3. Ben-Tor 2009: 283.
4. See Mason 2016: 254–57, 444–50, who describes the Zealots as "Disciples." Also see Rajak 1983: 85–89.
5. See Ben-Tor 2009: 3–4, 282. In *Masada III*, Netzer (1991a) follows Yadin in referring to the rebels as Zealots.
6. Mason 2016: 257.
7. Eshel 2009: 27. Also see Atkinson 2016: 10–11, who says that Josephus changed his attitude toward the Sicarii over time, as reflected in *War* and *Antiquities*.
8. For this section, see Ben-Tor 2009; Eshel 2009; Yadin 1966; and the Masada final report volumes (*Masada* I–VIII).
9. Yadin 1966: 154.
10. See Ben-Tor 2009: 23, 95; Yadin 1966: 155–56, who describes the dwellings as "mud huts."
11. See Ben-Tor 2009: 95–96. Approximately ninety dwelling units were found in the casemate wall (p. 79).
12. Ben-Tor 2009: 79.
13. Yadin 1966: 156–61.
14. Netzer 1991a: 449 (L1264). Another possible bakery was found in Tower L1196 in the southeastern casemate wall; see Netzer 1991a: 514–16, 640.
15. The rooms are L497 and L542; see Netzer 1991a: 304–5; 316–17, 634. Also see Ben-Tor 2009: 112, 140–41.
16. Eshel 2009: 56–57.
17. Netzer 1991a: 440–45 (L1276); Ben-Tor 2009: 86–87. For the process of tanning in the Roman world, see Bond 2016: 97–125; Ermatinger 2015: 110–12. Aside from the vats and plastering, the basis for the identification of L1276 as a tannery is unclear,

as the process was malodorous, required a lot of fresh water, and involved the use of urine and possibly animal dung (see Bond 2016: 113).

18. See Stiebel and Magness 2007: 24–25.

19. See Stiebel and Magness 2007: 31.

20. See Ben-Tor 2009: 129–47; Bar-Nathan 2006.

21. Ben-Tor 2009: 33, 162; Netzer 1991a: 40–42 (L135). There are also inscriptions in Greek.

22. See Ben-Tor 2009: 162–65.

23. Yadin 1966: 55 top photo; Ben-Tor 2009: 35–36. See for example Netzer 1991a: 164 (food remains buried in the collapse of the bathhouse on the lower terrace of the northern palace [L16]).

24. See Kislev and Simhoni 2007. Ben-Tor 2009: 36, writes, "more than 300 food items of different kinds (wheat, barley, dates and nuts) were damaged by 25 different kinds of pests. Most of the food (more than 85%) was hit by four kinds of pests and the rest by minor pests."

25. Yadin 1966: 97.

26. Eshel 2009: 89–90, suggests that the Deuteronomy fragments were once part of a complete Torah scroll, which would show that by this time, the Five Books of Moses were compiled and read together. However, Tov 2004: 300, says that had either Deuteronomy or Ezekiel been part of larger scrolls, fragments of other books in those scrolls should have been deposited with them in the pits.

27. See Magness 2002: 134.

28. Yadin 1966: 166; see Netzer 1991a: 507–10 (L1197). For the publication of the Masada *miqva'ot*, see Grossberg 2007.

29. L151 in Building 7; see Netzer 1991a: 13–17. Yadin identified small pools associated with both *miqva'ot* as an *otsar*—that is, a reservoir of undrawn water that could purify drawn water according to rabbinic law. Grossberg 2007: 109–18 identifies other *miqva'ot* with an *otsar* at Masada. However, this identification (and whether the concept of an *otsar* even existed at this time) have been challenged by Adler 2014.

30. Netzer 1991a: 259–60 (L546); Grossberg 2007 (who suggests that some plastered basins at Masada were used for handwashing). For studies of *miqva'ot*, see Reich 2013; Adler 2011: 9–160.

31. For lists of the Masada *miqva'ot*, see Grossberg 2007: 103, 108, 113 (totaling 21); Adler 2011: 343 (totaling 16). Both are maximal estimates that include some questionable examples, such as the "swimming pool" next to Building 11.

32. Yadin 1966: 134; Eshel 2009: 50.

33. See Netzer 1991a: 333–34; Grossberg 2007: 101–4.

34. For the mugs from Masada, see Reich 2007b, who does not mention whether any of them might have originated in pre-revolt contexts at Masada. Presumably most (if not all) were found in rebel contexts, but that does not rule out the possibility that some were brought to Masada during Herod's time.

35. For stone vessels in general, see Magness 2011b: 70–74 (with references); Adler 2011: 161–220; Gibson 2003.

36. Although most of our evidence for the susceptibility of processed or manufactured materials to impurity (especially glass) and the insusceptibility of stone comes from later rabbinic legislation, the popularity of stone vessels suggests that most Jews

before 70 CE shared this view. For a discussion, see Magness 2011b: 66–74, with references.

37. Reich 2007b; Ben-Tor 2009: 221–22. Reich publishes only the stone mugs, although he refers to other chalk stone vessels (p. 195) and Yadin 1966: 152–153 illustrates one lathe-turned dish with a group of mugs.

38. Proposed by Andrea Berlin; for reference and a discussion, see Magness 2011b: 71.

39. For the unfired clay and dung vessels from Masada, see Bar-Nathan 2006: 238–43, who cites modern examples from Palestinian villages and Kurdistan (p. 239).

40. For a discussion of whether vessels made of unfired clay and dung were considered insusceptible to impurity before 70 CE, see Magness 2011b: 75–76.

41. Netzer 1991a: 445 (L1276); Ben-Tor 2009: 86.

42. See Netzer 1991a: 416–22; Ben-Tor 2009: 82; Eshel 2009: 70–82.

43. Meshorer 1989: 74; Netzer 1991a: 418.

44. Eshel 2009: 74–75, who notes that at the time his book was published, only twenty sheqels of year five—three of which come from this room at Masada—had been found.

45. See Newsom 2000.

46. See Yadin 1966: 172–74; Eshel 2009: 76–79.

47. See Tov 2008: 89–90; Dimant 2003: 181.

48. See VanderKam 2000.

49. Tov 2004: 300–2.

50. See Magness 2016: 187.

51. See Reich 2007a: 188–89.

52. See Ben-Tor 2009: 97–100, 224–25; Reich 2007.

53. Ben-Tor 2009: 120.

54. Reich 2007a: 188; Reich 2001; Ben-Tor 2009: 225–26. Reich does not make explicit the reason why he attributes buildings with low numbers of coins to Essenes (2001: 162, states only that the men who inhabited these buildings "handled coins far less frequently than was usually common at the fort").

55. In fact, Reich 2007a: 188, notes in discussing spindle whorls that "their minute weight and portability allowed the Masada refugees to bring them with them to Masada."

56. See Pummer 2016: 53–54; Talmon 1997; Eshel 2009: 79–80; Ben-Tor 2009: 206–8.

57. See Shamir 1994; Ben-Tor 2009: 226–27.

58. Shamir 1994: 275; also see Reich 2007a: 188.

59. Ben-Tor 2009: 227; for the textiles from Masada, see Sheffer and Granger-Taylor 1994.

60. See Sheffer and Granger-Taylor 1994: 172–77.

61. Sheffer and Granger-Taylor 1994: 221–22; Ben-Tor 2009: 232.

62. See Yadin 1966: 57, upper photo (from the lower terrace of the northern palace); the leather sandals have not been published yet in the Masada final reports.

63. Yadin and Naveh 1989: 21–22; Ben-Tor 2009: 156.

64. Sheffer and Granger-Taylor 1994: 216–20; Ben-Tor 2009: 231–32.

65. See Yadin 1966: 146, 149; Bar-Nathan 2006: 205–6 (the "Judean Kohl Bottle"); Hurwitz 2014: 48–49. The non-ceramic cosmetic items have not been published yet in the Masada final reports.

66. See Hurwitz 2014: 52 (top); Mumcuoglu and Zias 1988; King and Stager 2001: 74.
67. Mumcuoglu et al. 2003.
68. For the *get*, see Yadin and Naveh 1989: 9–11; Yadin 1965: 119 n.112; Eshel 2003: 94; Eshel 1999: 233–34.
69. See Yadin and Naveh 1989: 6.
70. Yadin and Naveh 1989: 8–9; Ben-Tor 2009: 149.
71. Yadin and Naveh 1989: 17–18; Ben-Tor 2009: 152–54. For the dump, see chapter 9.
72. See Yadin and Naveh 1989: 32–39; Ben-Tor 159–62; Magness 2011b: 19–20; Eshel 2009: 105–6. Other scholars have suggested that these ostraca indicate that among the rebels at Masada were individuals who ate ordinary food (*hullin*) in accordance with the purity laws governing the consumption of hallowed (holy) things (*qodesh*), with the *tet* inscribed on some jars being an abbreviation for *tahor* (pure). According to Asher Grossberg, the numerous water basins at Masada were used by these individuals for immersing their hands before eating *hullin*; see Magness 2011b: 20. According to Atkinson 2007: 358, the role of priests as leaders atop Masada might have been obscured by Josephus as he himself was a priest living in Rome.

CHAPTER 9. "MASADA SHALL NOT FALL AGAIN": YIGAEL YADIN, THE MASS SUICIDE, AND THE MASADA MYTH

1. For Yadin's biography, see Silberman 1993.
2. For the Haganah, see Ben-Yehuda 1995: 318–20.
3. See Silberman 1993: 73.
4. See Silberman 1993: 84–85.
5. See Silberman 1993: 102–3.
6. For Yadin's expedition to Masada, see Silberman 1993: 270–93. The two excavation seasons were conducted from October 1963 to May 1964, and November 1964 to April 1965.
7. Yadin 1966; see Silberman 1993: 291.
8. See Silberman 1993: 295–302.
9. See Silberman 1993: 304–5.
10. See Silberman 1993: 314.
11. See Silberman 1993: 325–31.
12. See Silberman 1993: 343–59.
13. See Silberman 1993: 375.
14. Yadin 1966: 97.
15. See Stiebel and Magness 2007: 24 n.219.
16. See Chapman 2007.
17. Yadin 1966: 54.
18. Zias 1998: 66.
19. Atkinson 2007 concludes that, "There is no archaeological evidence to support Josephus' accounts of the mass suicides at Masada and Gamla"; Josephus presents these stories as fictional literary devices. Aviam 2007 believes that the archaeological remains support Josephus's account of the sieges of Jotapata and Gamla.
20. See Klawans 2012: 118–19; Eshel 2009: 129; Eshel 1999: 229; Rajak 1983: 80–81, 89.

21. Cohen 1982: 404. For a recent and more radically revisionist reading of Josephus's account, see Mason 2016. For responses to Mason's approach in general, see Klawans 2012; Eliav 2017; for his analysis of Josephus's account of the mass suicide at Masada (which he calls "murderology" and understands as conveying a negative message), see pp. 129–35. For a defense of Josephus's credibility, see Broshi 1982; for his credibility relating to Masada, see Rajak 1983: 219–22.
22. See Atkinson 2016: 18.
23. For the "lots," see Yadin 1966: 197, 201; Yadin and Naveh 1989: 28–31; Netzer 1991a: 64–65; Ben-Tor 2009: 67, 157–59; 297–99; Eshel 2009: 128–32.
24. See Yadin 1966: 193, 197; Zias 1998, 2000; Ben-Tor 2009: 299–307.
25. See Geva 1996; Ben-Tor 2009: 48; Yadin 1965: 25–26; Netzer 1991a: 624; Eshel 2009: 133–34. The debris consists of 600–750 cubic meters of earth and measures 20 meters long × 15 meters wide.
26. For archaeology, politics, and nationalism in general, see Silberman 1989; Trigger 2006. For Masada, see Silberman 1989: 87–101; Ben-Yehuda 1995; Zerubavel 1995: 60–76; Shavit 2013: 79–97; Rajak 2016.
27. See Shavit 2013: 79–97; Ben-Yehuda 1995: 232–36; Zerubavel 1995: 64.
28. See Ben-Yehuda 1995: 190; Zerubavel 1995: 63–64; Rajak 2016: 222–23, 230–33.
29. See Ben-Yehuda 1995: 296.
30. See Ben-Yehuda 1995: 130–31, 303. For the Holocaust and Masada, see Zerubavel 1995: 70–76.
31. See Ben-Yehuda 1995: 147–59. The venue was moved from Masada to Latrun.
32. See Silberman 1993: 275, 289.
33. See Ben-Yehuda 1995: 161, 176; Zerubavel 1995: 66; Silberman 1993: 291.
34. Yadin 1966: 21–26; see Zerubavel 1995: 66.
35. See Ben-Yehuda 1995: 67–68; also see Silberman 1993: 285–86.
36. Silberman 1989: 99–100.
37. See Ben-Yehuda 1995: 112, 243–49. The phrase had been coined earlier and became most closely identified with the positions of Golda Meir and Moshe Dayan.
38. For post-Zionism, see Kaplan 2015; for its impact on the Masada myth, see Rajak 2016: 223.
39. See Ben-Yehuda 1995: 147–59; Chapman 2007: 86.
40. See Chapman 2007: 82–84.
41. Silberman 1989: 88.
42. https://www.theatlantic.com/international/archive/2017/05/why-does-trump-want-to-address-israel-from-masada/525531/.

BIBLIOGRAPHY

Abegg Jr., M., P. Flint, and E. Ulrich. 1999. *The Dead Sea Scrolls Bible. The Oldest Known Bible Translated for the First Time into English*. San Francisco: HarperCollins.

Adan-Bayewitz, D., and M. Aviam. 1997. Iotapata, Josephus, and the Siege of 67: Preliminary Report on the 1992–94 Seasons. *Journal of Roman Archaeology* 10: 131–65.

Adler, Y. 2011. *The Archaeology of Purity. Archaeological Evidence for the Observance of Ritual Purity in Ereẓ-Israel from the Hasmonean Period until the End of the Talmudic Era (164 CE—400 CE)*. Unpublished PhD dissertation; Ramat-Gan: Bar-Ilan University, Department of Land of Israel Studies and Archaeology [in Hebrew] (accessed on www.academia.edu).

Adler, Y. 2014. The Myth of the *ʿôṣār* in Second Temple-Period Ritual Baths: An Anachronistic Interpretation of a Modern-Era Innovation. *Journal of Jewish Studies* 65: 263–83.

Aharoni, Y. 1962. Expedition B—The Cave of Horror. *Israel Exploration Journal* 12: 186–99.

Aharoni, Y. 1993. Judean Desert Caves: The Naḥal Ḥever Caves. In *The New Encyclopedia of Archaeological Excavations in the Holy Land, Vol. 3*, ed. E. Stern, 827–29. New York: Simon & Schuster.

Arubas, B., and H. Goldfus. 2008. Masada: The Roman Siege Works. In *The New Encyclopedia of Archaeological Excavations in the Holy Land 5, Supplementary Volume*, ed. E. Stern, 1937–40. Jerusalem: Israel Exploration Society.

Atkinson, K. 2007. Noble Deaths at Gamla and Masada? A Critical Assessment of Josephus' Account of Jewish Resistance in Light of Archaeological Discoveries. In *Making History, Josephus and Historical Method*, ed. Z. Rodgers, 349–71. Leiden: Brill.

Atkinson, K. 2016. *A History of the Hasmonean State. Josephus and Beyond*. London: Bloomsbury.

Aviam, M. 2004. *Jews, Pagans and Christians in the Galilee. 25 Years of Archaeological Excavations and Surveys, Hellenistic to Byzantine Periods*. Rochester, NY: University of Rochester Press.

Aviam, M. 2007. The Archaeological Illumination of Josephus' Narrative of the Battles at Yodefat and Gamla. In *Making History, Josephus and Historical Method*, ed. Z. Rodgers, 372–84. Leiden: Brill.

Avigad, N. 1962. Expedition A. *Israel Exploration Journal* 12: 169–83.

Avigad, N. 1993a. *Discovering Jerusalem*. Nashville, TN: Thomas Nelson.

Avigad, N. 1993b. Judean Desert Caves: The Naḥal David Caves. In *The New Encyclopedia of Archaeological Excavations in the Holy Land, Vol. 3*, ed. E. Stern, 832–33. New York: Simon & Schuster.

Aviram, J. 1993. Judean Desert Caves: The "Judean Desert Expedition." In *The New Encyclopedia of Archaeological Excavations in the Holy Land, Vol. 3*, ed. E. Stern, 821. New York: Simon & Schuster.

Avi-Yonah, M. 1972. The Hasmonean Revolt and Judah Maccabee's War against the Syrians. In *The World History of the Jewish People, Volume Six: The Hellenistic Age. Political History of Jewish Palestine from 332 B.C.E. to 67 B.C.E.*, ed. A. Schalit, 147–82. New Brunswick, NJ: Rutgers University Press.

Avi-Yonah, M., N. Avigad, Y. Aharoni, I. Dunayevsky, and S. Gutman. 1957. The Archaeological Survey of Masada. *Israel Exploration Journal* 7: 1–60.

Bahat, D. 1990. *The Illustrated Atlas of Jerusalem*. Jerusalem: Carta.

Bar-Adon, P. 1977. Another Settlement of the Judean Desert Sect at 'En el-Ghuweir on the Shores of the Dead Sea. *Bulletin of the American Schools of Oriental Research* 227: 1–25.

Bar-Adon, P. 1980. *The Cave of the Treasure: The Finds from the Caves in Naḥal Mishmar*. Jerusalem: Israel Exploration Society.

Bar-Adon, P. 1989. *Excavations in the Judean Desert ('Atiqot Hebrew Series 9)*. Jerusalem: Israel Antiquities Authority (Hebrew with English summaries).

Bar-Adon, P. 1993. Judean Desert Caves: The Naḥal Mishmar Caves. In *The New Encyclopedia of Archaeological Excavations in the Holy Land, Vol. 3*, ed. E. Stern, 822–27. New York: Simon & Schuster.

Barag, D., and M. Hershkovitz. 1994. Lamps. In *Masada IV: The Yigael Yadin Excavations 1963–1965, Final Reports*, 1–106. Jerusalem: Israel Exploration Society.

Barclay, J.M.G. 1996. *Jews in the Mediterranean Diaspora, From Alexander to Trajan (323 BCE—117 CE)*. Berkeley: University of California Press.

Barclay, J.M.G. 2005. The Empire Writes Back: Josephan Rhetoric in Flavian Rome. In *Flavius Josephus and Flavian Rome*, ed. J. S. Edmonson, S. Mason, and J. Rives, 315–32. New York: Oxford University Press.

Bar-Nathan, R. 2006. *Masada VII: The Yigael Yadin Excavations 1963–1965, Final Reports. The Pottery of Masada*. Jerusalem: Israel Exploration Society.

Barnes, T. D. 2005. The Sack of the Temple in Josephus and Tacitus. In *Flavius Josephus and Flavian Rome*, ed. J. S. Edmonson, S. Mason, and J. Rives, 129–44. New York: Oxford University Press.

Barton, J. 2010. Reflecting on Religious Diversity. In *Religious Diversity in Ancient Israel and Judah*, ed. F. Stavrakopoulou and J. Barton, 191–93. London: T & T Clark.

Baumgarten, A. I. 1997. *The Flourishing of Jewish Sects in the Maccabean Era: An Interpretation*. Leiden: Brill.

Baumgarten, A. I. 2000. Pharisees. In *Encyclopedia of the Dead Sea Scrolls, Vol. 2*, ed. L. H. Schiffman and J. C. VanderKam, 657–63. New York: Oxford University Press.

Ben-Tor, A. 2009. *Back to Masada*. Jerusalem: Israel Exploration Society.

Ben-Yehuda, N. 1995. *The Masada Myth, Collective Memory and Mythmaking in Israel*. Madison: University of Wisconsin Press.

Berdowski, P. 2008. Garum of Herod the Great (Latin-Greek Inscription on the Amphora from Masada). *Qumran Chronicle* 16.3–4: 107–22.

Bernick, K. 1994. Basketry, Cordage and Related Artifacts. In *Masada IV: The Yigael Yadin Excavations 1963–1965, Final Reports*, 283–317. Jerusalem: Israel Exploration Society.

Berrin, S. L. 2000. Pesharim. In *Encyclopedia of the Dead Sea Scrolls, Vol. 2*, ed. L. H. Schiffman and J. C. VanderKam, 644–47. New York: Oxford University Press.

Berrin, S. L. 2004. *Pesher Nahum Scroll from Qumran: An Exegetical Study of 4Q169*. Leiden: Brill.

Bickerman, E. J. 1988. *The Jews in the Greek Age*. Cambridge, MA: Harvard University Press.

Bishop, M. C., and J.C.N. Coulston. 1993. *Roman Military Equipment: From the Punic War to The Fall of Rome*. London: B. T. Batsford.

Bohak, G. 1996. *Joseph and Aseneth and the Jewish Temple in Heliopolis*. Atlanta, GA: Scholars Press.

Bond, S. E. 2016. *Trade and Taboo, Disreputable Professions in the Roman Mediterranean*. Ann Arbor: University of Michigan Press.

Broshi, M. 1982. The Credibility of Josephus. *Journal of Jewish Studies* 33: 379–84.

Brünnow, R. E., and A. v. Domaszewski. 1909. *Die Provincia Arabia, auf Grund Zweier in den Jahren 1897 und 1898 Unternommenden Reisen under der Berichte Früherer Reisender, Dritter Band*. Strassburg: Karl J. Trübner.

Campbell, D. B. 1988. Dating the Siege of Masada. *Zeitschrift für Papyrologie und Epigraphik* 73: 156–58.

Chapman, D. 2008. *Ancient Jewish and Christian Perceptions of Crucifixion*. Tübingen: Mohr Siebeck.

Chapman, H. H. 2007. Masada in the 1st and 21st Centuries. In *Making History, Josephus and Historical Method*, ed. Z. Rodgers, 82–102. Leiden: Brill.

Charlesworth, J. H. (ed.). 1985. *The Old Testament Pseudepigrapha, Volume 2*. New Haven, CT: Yale University Press.

Chitty, D. J. 1966. *The Desert a City*. London: Mowbrays.

Clamer, C. 1997. *Fouilles archéologiques de ʿAïn ez-Zâra/Callirrhoé, villégiature hérodienne*. Beirut: Institut Français d'archéologie du Proche-Orient.

Clamer, C. 1999. The Hot Springs of Kallirrhoe and Baarou. In *The Madaba Map Centenary 1897–1997, Travelling Through the Byzantine Umayyad Period*, ed. M. Piccirillo and E. Alliata, 221–25. Jerusalem: Studium Biblicum Franciscanum.

Cohen, S.J.D. 1982. Masada: Literary Tradition, Archaeological Remains, and the Credibility of Josephus. *Journal of Jewish Studies* 33: 385–405.

Cohen, S.J.D. 1989. *From the Maccabees to the Mishnah*. Philadelphia: Westminster Press.

Cohen, S.J.D. 1999. *The Beginnings of Jewishness. Boundaries, Varieties, Uncertainties*. Berkeley: University of California Press.

Cohen, S.J.D. 2002. *Josephus in Galilee and Rome*. Leiden: Brill.

Collins, J. J. 2010. *Beyond the Qumran Community, The Sectarian Movement of the Dead Sea Scrolls*. Grand Rapids, MI: Eerdmans.

Collins, J. J., and D. C. Harlow (eds.). 2012. *Early Judaism, A Comprehensive Overview*. Grand Rapids, MI: Eerdmans.

Colson, F. H. (transl.). 1971. *Philo in Ten Volumes. X: The Embassy to Gaius (Loeb Classical Library)*. Cambridge, MA: Harvard University.

Conder, C. R., and H. H. Kitchener. 1883. *The Survey of Western Palestine. Memoirs of the Topography, Orography, Hydrography, and Archaeology. Volume III. Sheets XVII–XXVI. Judea*. London: The Committee of the Palestine Exploration Fund (republished in 1998 by Archive Editions in association with the Palestine Exploration Fund).

Cotton, H. M., L. Di Segni, W. Eck, B. Isaac, A. Kushnir-Stein, H. Misgav, J. Price, I. Roll, and A. Yardeni (eds.). 2010. *Corpus Inscriptionum Iudaea/Palaestina, Volume I: Jerusalem. Part I: 1–704*. Berlin: Walter de Gruyter.

Cotton, H. M., and J. Geiger. 1989. *Masada II: The Yigael Yadin Excavations 1963–1965, Final Reports. The Latin and Greek Documents*. Jerusalem: Israel Exploration Society.

Cotton, H. M., O. Lernau, and Y. Goren. 1996. Fish Sauces from Masada. *Journal of Roman Archaeology* 9: 223–38.

Crawford, S. W. 2012. Scribe Links Qumran and Masada. *Biblical Archaeology Review* 38.6: 38–43, 72.

Cross Jr., F. M. 1980. *The Ancient Library of Qumran and Modern Biblical Studies*. Grand Rapids, MI: Baker.

Danby, H. 2013. *The Mishnah, Translated from the Hebrew with Introduction and Brief Explanatory Notes*. Peabody, MA: Hendrickson.

Danin, A. 1973. The Flora along the Dead Sea Shore. In *The Judean Desert and Dead Sea*, ed. Z. Ilan, 143–46. Ein Gedi Field School: The Society for the Protection of Nature in Israel (in Hebrew).

Davies, G. 2011. Under Siege: The Roman Field Works at Masada. *Bulletin of the American Schools of Oriental Research* 362: 65–83.

Davies, G. 2018. Prey or Participants? Civilian Siege Experiences during the First Jewish Revolt. In *Civilians and Warfare in World History*, ed. N. Foote and N. Williams, 67–79. London: Routledge.

Davies, G., and J. Magness. 2017. Recovering Josephus: Mason's *History of the Jewish War* and the Siege of Masada. *Scripta Classica Israelica* 36: 55–65.

Davies, P. R. 2000. Zadok, Sons of. In *Encyclopedia of the Dead Sea Scrolls, Vol. 2*, ed. L. H. Schiffman and J. C. VanderKam, 1005–7. New York: Oxford University Press.

Davies, P. R., G. J. Brooke, and P. R. Callaway. 2002. *The Complete World of the Dead Sea Scrolls*. London: Thames and Hudson.

Deines, R. 2010. Pharisees. In *The Eerdmans Dictionary of Early Judaism*, ed. J. J. Collins and D. C. Harlow, 1061–63. Grand Rapids, MI: Eerdmans.

Delessert, E. 1853. *Voyage aux Villes Maudites*. Paris: Victor Lecou.

Dimant, D. 2003. *The Apocryphon of Joshua*—4Q522 9 ii: A Reappraisal. In *Emanuel: Studies in Hebrew Bible, Septuagint, and Dead Sea Scrolls in Honor of Emanuel Tov*, ed. S. M. Paul, R. A. Kraft, L. H. Schiffman, and W. W. Fields, 179–204. Leiden: Brill.

Edelman, D. 2010. Cultic Sites and Complexes Beyond the Jerusalem Temple. In *Religious Diversity in Ancient Israel and Judah*, ed. F. Stavrakopoulou and J. Barton, 82–103. London: T & T Clark.

Edmonson, J. 2005. Introduction: Flavius Josephus and Flavian Rome. In *Flavius Josephus and Flavian Rome*, ed. J. S. Edmonson, S. Mason, and J. Rives, 1–33. New York: Oxford University Press.

Edmonson, J., S. Mason, and J. Rives (ed.). 2005. *Flavius Josephus and Flavian Rome*. New York: Oxford University Press.

Ehrman, B. D. 2016. *Jesus Before the Gospels. How the Earliest Christians Remembered, Changed, and Invented Their Stories of the Savior*. New York: HarperOne.

Eliav, Y. 2017. Review of S. Mason, *A History of the Jewish War, A.D. 66–74*, in *CJ Online* 2017.10.05: https://sites.lsa.umich.edu/yaroneliav/wp-content/uploads/sites/43/2014/02/EliavOnMason-JewishWar-1.pdf (accessed November 30, 2017).

Ermatinger, J. W. 2015. *The World of Ancient Rome: A Daily Life Encyclopedia, Vols. 1–2.* Santa Barbara, CA: ABC-CLIO, LLC.

Eshel, H. 1999. Josephus' View on Judaism without the Temple in Light of the Discoveries at Masada and Murabba'at. In *Gemeinde ohne Tempel, Community without Temple. Zur Substituierung und Transformation des Jerusalemer Tempels und seines Kults im Alten Testament, antiken Judentum und frühen Christentum*, ed. B. Ego, A. Lange, and P. Pilhofer, 229–38. Tübingen: Mohr Siebeck.

Eshel, H. 2003. The Dates Used during the Bar Kokhba Revolt. In *The Bar Kokhba War Reconsidered, New Perspectives on the Second Jewish Revolt against Rome*, ed. P. Schäfer, 93–105. Tübingen: Mohr Siebeck.

Eshel, H. 2008. *The Dead Sea Scrolls and the Hasmonean State.* Grand Rapids, MI: Eerdmans.

Eshel, H. 2009. *Masada, An Epic Story. A Carta Field Guide.* Jerusalem: Carta.

Feldman, L. 1965. *Josephus, Jewish Antiquities, Books XVIII–XIX (Loeb Classical Library).* Cambridge, MA: Harvard University Press.

Finkielsztejn, G. 2006. P. Vedius Pollio, producteur de vin à Chios et Cos et fournisseur d'Hérode le Grand. In *Grecs, Juifs, Polonais: A la recherché des racines de la civilization européenne. Acts du colloque organisé à Paris par l'Académie Polonaise des Sciences le 14 novembre 2003*, 123–39. Varsovie-Paris: Polish Academy of Sciences.

Fischer, M., and O. Tal. 2000. *'En Boqeq: Excavations in an Oasis on the Dead Sea. Vol. 2, The Officina, an Early Roman Building on the Dead Sea Shore.* Mainz: Philipp von Zabern.

Fishelzon, L. 1973. The World of Fauna in the Dead Sea Region. In *The Judean Desert and Dead Sea*, ed. Z. Ilan, 76–93. Ein Gedi Field School: Society for the Protection of Nature in Israel (in Hebrew).

Foerster, G. 1995. *Masada V: The Yigael Yadin Excavations 1963–1965, Final Reports. Art and Architecture.* Jerusalem: Israel Exploration Society.

Freund, R. 1973. The Geology of the Land of Israel against the Background of Continental Drift. In *The Judean Desert and Dead Sea*, ed. Z. Ilan, 23–26. Ein Gedi Field School: Society for the Protection of Nature in Israel (in Hebrew).

Friedman, R. E. 2017. *The Exodus.* New York: HarperOne.

Gadot, Y. 1973. The Judean Desert. In *The Judean Desert and Dead Sea*, ed. Z. Ilan, 1–7. Ein Gedi Field School: Society for the Protection of Nature in Israel (in Hebrew).

Gelb, N. 2013. *Herod the Great: Statesman, Visionary, Tyrant.* Lanham, MD: Rowman & Littlefield.

Geva, H. 1996. The Siege Ramp Laid by the Romans to Conquer the Northern Palace at Masada. In *Eretz-Israel* 25 (Aviram Volume), ed. A. Biran et al., 297–306. Jerusalem: Israel Exploration Society (Hebrew with English summary on 100*).

Geva, H. 2010. *Jewish Quarter Excavations in the Old City of Jerusalem conducted by Nahman Avigad, 1969–1982. Volume IV: The Burnt House of Area B and Other Studies, Final Report.* Jerusalem: Israel Exploration Society.

Gibson, S. 2003. Stone Vessels of the Early Roman Period from Jerusalem and Palestine. A Reassessment. In *One Land—Many Cultures, Archaeological Studies in*

Honour of Stansilao Loffreda, ed. G. C. Bottini, L. DiSegni, and L. D. Chrupucała, 287–308. Jerusalem: Franciscan Printing Press.

Gichon, M. 1993a. *En Boqeq: Ausgrabungen in einer Oase am Toten Meer. Band 1, Geographie und Geschichte der Oase das Spätrömisch-Byzantinische Kastell.* Mainz: Philipp von Zabern.

Gichon, M. 1993b. ʿEn Boqeq. In *The New Encyclopedia of Archaeological Excavations in the Holy Land, Vol. 2,* ed. E. Stern, 395–99. New York: Simon & Schuster.

Gill, D. 1993. A Natural Spur at Masada. *Nature* 364: 569–70.

Gill, D., V. Stivelman, and U. Basson. 2000. *Shallow Geophysical Surveys to Determine the Thickness of the Roman Assault Ramp at Masada.* Jerusalem: Geological Survey of Israel and the Geophysical Institute of Israel.

Goldfus, H., Y. Avni, R. Albag, and B. Arubas. 2016. The Significance of Geomorphological and Soil Formation Research for Understanding the Unfinished Roman Ramp at Masada. *Catena* 146: 73–87; http://dx.doi.org/10.1016/j.catena.2016.04.014.

Goodman, M. 2007. *Rome and Jerusalem, the Clash of Ancient Civilizations.* New York: Knopf.

Grabar, O., and B. Z. Kedar (eds.). 2009. *Where Heaven and Earth Meet: Jerusalem's Sacred Esplanade.* Austin: University of Texas Press.

Grabbe, L. L. 2010. "Many Nations Will Be Joined to YHWH in That Day": The Question of YHWH Outside Judah. In *Religious Diversity in Ancient Israel and Judah,* ed. F. Stavrakopoulou and J. Barton, 175–87. London: T & T Clark.

Grant, M. 1971. *Herod the Great.* New York: American Heritage Press.

Grossberg, A. 2007. The *Miqvaʾot* (Ritual Baths) at Masada. In *Masada VIII: The Yigael Yadin Excavations 1963–1965, Final Reports,* 95–126. Jerusalem: Israel Exploration Society.

Halevy, G. 1973. Acacias in the Negev and Sinai—a Sudanese Element in a Desert Region. In *The Judean Desert and Dead Sea,* ed. Z. Ilan, 137–43. Ein Gedi Field School: Society for the Protection of Nature in Israel (in Hebrew).

Hata, G. 2014. The Abuse and Misuse of Josephus in Eusebius' Ecclesiastical History, Books 2 and 3. In *Studies in Josephus and the Varieties of Ancient Judaism: Louis H. Feldman Jubilee Volume (1),* ed. S.J.D. Cohen and J. J. Schwartz, 91–102. Leiden: Brill.

Hengel, M. 1981. *Judaism and Hellenism, Vols. 1–2.* Philadelphia: Fortress.

Hershkovitz, M., and S. Amorai-Stark. 2007. The Gems from Masada. In *Masada VIII: The Yigael Yadin Excavations 1963–1965, Final Reports,* 217–32. Jerusalem: Israel Exploration Society.

Heszer, C. 1997. *The Social Structure of the Rabbinic Movement in Palestine.* Tübingen: Mohr Siebeck.

Hirschfeld, Y. 1992. *The Judean Desert Monasteries in the Byzantine Period.* New Haven, CT: Yale University Press.

Holley, A. E. 1994. The *Ballista* Balls from Masada. In *Masada IV: The Yigael Yadin Excavations 1963–1965, Final Reports,* 347–65. Jerusalem: Israel Exploration Society.

Holley, A. E. 2014. Stone Projectiles and the Use of Artillery in the Siege of Gamla. In *Gamla III: The Shmarya Gutmann Excavations 1976–1989, Finds and Studies, Part 1 (IAA Reports, No. 56),* ed. D. Syon, 35–55. Jerusalem: Israel Exploration Society.

Holum, K. G., R. L. Hohlfelder, R. J. Bull, and A. Raban. 1988. *King Herod's Dream, Caesarea on the Sea.* New York: W. W. Norton.

Honigman, S. 2014. *Tales of High Priests and Taxes. The Books of the Maccabees and the Judean Rebellion against Antiochos IV.* Berkeley: University of California Press.

Humbert, J.-B., and A. Chambon. 1994. *Fouilles de Khirbet Qumrân et de Aïn Feshkha I.* Fribourg: Éditions universitaires.

Hurwitz, G. 2014. *The Story of Masada. The Yigael Yadin Masada Museum, Gift of the Shuki Levy Foundation, Catalogue.* Jerusalem: Israel Exploration Society.

Ilan, Z. (ed.). 1973. *The Judean Desert and Dead Sea.* Ein Gedi Field School: Society for the Protection of Nature in Israel (in Hebrew).

Jagersma, H. 1986. *A History of Israel from Alexander the Great to Bar Kochba.* Philadelphia: Fortress.

Jampoler, A.C.A. 2005. *Sailors in the Holy Land. The 1848 American Expedition to the Dead Sea and the Search for Sodom and Gomorrah.* Annapolis, MD: Naval Institute Press.

Kaplan, E. 2015. *Beyond Post-Zionism.* New York: SUNY Press.

Keay, S., and N. Terrenato (eds.). 2001. *Italy and the West: Comparative Issues in Romanization.* Oxford: Oxbow.

Kennedy, D., and D. Riley. 1990. *Rome's Desert Frontier from the Air.* London: B. T. Batsford.

King, P. J., and L. E. Stager. 2001. *Life in Biblical Israel.* Louisville, KY: Westminster John Knox.

Kislev, M., and O. Simhoni. 2007. Hygiene and Insect Damage of Crops and Foods at Masada. In *Masada VIII: The Yigael Yadin Excavations 1963–1965, Final Reports*, 133–70. Jerusalem: Israel Exploration Society.

Klausner, J. 1972a. The First Hasmonean Rulers: Jonathan and Simeon. In *The World History of the Jewish People, Volume Six: The Hellenistic Age. Political History of Jewish Palestine from 332 B.C.E. to 67 B.C.E.*, ed. A. Schalit, 183–207. New Brunswick, NJ: Rutgers University Press.

Klausner, J. 1972b. John Hyrcanus I. In *The World History of the Jewish People, Volume Six: The Hellenistic Age. Political History of Jewish Palestine from 332 B.C.E. to 67 B.C.E.*, ed. A. Schalit, 211–21. New Brunswick, NJ: Rutgers University Press.

Klausner, J. 1972c. Judah Aristobulus and Jannaeus Alexander. In *The World History of the Jewish People, Volume Six: The Hellenistic Age. Political History of Jewish Palestine from 332 B.C.E. to 67 B.C.E.*, ed. A. Schalit, 222–41. New Brunswick, NJ: Rutgers University Press.

Klausner, J. 1972d. Queen Salome Alexandra. In *The World History of the Jewish People, Volume Six: The Hellenistic Age. Political History of Jewish Palestine from 332 B.C.E. to 67 B.C.E.*, ed. A. Schalit, 242–54. New Brunswick, NJ: Rutgers University Press.

Klawans, J. 2012. *Josephus and the Theologies of Ancient Judaism.* New York: Oxford University Press.

Klein, Z. 1973. Changes in the Level of the Dead Sea. In *The Judean Desert and Dead Sea*, ed. Z. Ilan, 38–43. Ein Gedi Field School: Society for the Protection of Nature in Israel (in Hebrew).

Kletter, R. 2014. *Just Past? The Making of Israeli Archaeology.* London: Routledge.

Knibb, M. A. 2000. Teacher of Righteousness. In *Encyclopedia of the Dead Sea Scrolls*, Vol. 2, ed. L. H. Schiffman and J. C. VanderKam, 918–21. New York: Oxford University Press.

Knoppers, G. N. 2013. *Jews and Samaritans: The Origins and History of Their Early Relations*. New York: Oxford University Press.

Kokkinos, N. 1998. *The Herodian Dynasty. Origins, Role in Society and Eclipse*. Sheffield: Sheffield Academic Press.

Kolton, Y. 1973. Springs along the Shores of the Dead Sea. In *The Judean Desert and Dead Sea*, ed. Z. Ilan, 61–67. Ein Gedi Field School: Society for the Protection of Nature in Israel (in Hebrew).

Koren, Z. C. 1994. Analysis of the Masada Textile Dyes. In *Masada IV: The Yigael Yadin Excavations 1963–1965, Final Reports*, 251–64. Jerusalem: Israel Exploration Society.

Kreiger, B. 1988. *The Dead Sea: Myth, History, and Politics*. Hanover, NH: Brandeis University Press.

Kugler, R. 1999. Priesthood at Qumran. In *The Dead Sea Scrolls after Fifty Years, A Comprehensive Assessment*, ed. P. W. Flint and J. C. VanderKam, 93–116. Leiden: Brill.

Kugler, R. 2000. Zadok. In *Encyclopedia of the Dead Sea Scrolls, Vol. 2*, ed. L. H. Schiffman and J. C. VanderKam, 1005. New York: Oxford University Press.

Le Bohec, Y. 1994. *The Imperial Roman Army*. London: B. T. Batsford.

Lee, R.Y.T. 2003. *Romanization in Palestine: A Study in Urban Development from Herod the Great to AD 70*. Oxford: Archaeopress.

Lemaire, A. 2003. Inscriptions du khirbeh, des grottes et de 'Aïn Feshkha. In *Khirbet Qumrân et 'Aïn Feshkha II, Études d'anthropologie, de physique et de chimie*, ed. J.-B. Humbert and J. Gunneweg, 241–88. Fribourg: Academic Press.

Lev-Yadun, S., D. S. Lucas, and M. Weinstein-Evron. 2010. Modeling the Demands for Wood by the Inhabitants of Masada and for the Roman Siege. *Journal of Arid Environments* 74: 777–85.

Lewis, N. (ed.). 1989. *The Documents from the Bar Kokhba Period in the Cave of Letters*. *Greek Papyri*. Jerusalem: Israel Exploration Society.

Lieberman, S. 1994. *Greek in Jewish Palestine, Hellenism in Jewish Palestine*. New York: Jewish Theological Seminary.

Liphschitz, N. 1994. Wood Remains from Masada. In *Masada IV: The Yigael Yadin Excavations 1963–1965, Final Reports*, 319–46. Jerusalem: Israel Exploration Society.

Lynch, W. F. 1849. *Narrative of the United States' Expedition to the River Jordan and the Dead Sea*. Philadelphia: Lea and Blanchard.

Lynch, W. F. 1850. *Narrative of the United States' Expedition to the River Jordan and the Dead Sea*. Philadelphia: Lea and Blanchard.

Macalister, R.A.S. 1901. Observation of Dead Sea Levels. *Palestine Exploration Fund Quarterly Statement*: 4–5.

Magness, J. 1996. Masada 1995: Discoveries at Camp F. *Biblical Archaeologist* 59.3: 181.

Magness, J. 2002. *The Archaeology of Qumran and the Dead Sea Scrolls*. Grand Rapids, MI: Eerdmans.

Magness, J. 2008. The Arch of Titus at Rome and the Fate of the God of Israel. *Journal of Jewish Studies* 59.2: 201–17.

Magness, J. 2009a. Some Observations on the Flavian Victory Monuments of Rome. In *Koine: Mediterranean Studies in Honor of R. Ross Holloway*, ed. D. B. Counts and A. S. Tuck, 35–40. Oxford: Oxbow.

Magness, J. 2009b. The Pottery from the 1995 Excavations in Camp F at Masada. *Bulletin of the American Schools of Oriental Research* 353: 75–107.

Magness, J. 2011a. A Reconsideration of Josephus' Testimony about Masada. In *The Jewish Revolt against Rome: Interdisciplinary Perspectives*, ed. M. Popović, 343–59. Leiden: Brill.

Magness, J. 2011b. *Stone and Dung, Oil and Spit: Jewish Daily Life in the Time of Jesus*. Grand Rapids, MI: Eerdmans.

Magness, J. 2014. Arrowheads and Projectile Points. In *Gamla III: The Shmarya Gutmann Excavations 1976–1989, Finds and Studies, Part 1 (IAA Reports, No. 56)*, ed. D. Syon, 21–33. Jerusalem: Israel Exploration Society.

Magness, J. 2016. The Connection between the Site of Qumran and the Scroll Caves in Light of the Ceramic Evidence. In *The Caves of Qumran, Proceedings of the International Conference, Lugano 2014 (STDJ 118)*, ed. M. Fidanzio, 184–94. Leiden: Brill.

Main, E. 2000. Sadducees. In *Encyclopedia of the Dead Sea Scrolls, Vol. 2*, ed. L. H. Schiffman and J. C. VanderKam, 812–16. New York: Oxford University Press.

Marcus, R. 1943. *Josephus, Jewish Antiquities, Books XII–XIII (Loeb Classical Library)*. Cambridge, MA: Harvard University Press.

Marshak, A. K. 2015. *The Many Faces of Herod the Great*. Grand Rapids, MI: Eerdmans.

Martínez, F. G. 1999. Ben-Sira: A Bibliography of Studies, 1965–1997. In *Masada VI: Yigael Yadin Excavations 1963–1965, Final Reports*, 233–52. Jerusalem: Israel Exploration Society.

Martínez, F. G., and E.J.C. Tigchelaar. 2000. *The Dead Sea Scrolls Study Edition, Vols. 1–2*. Leiden: Brill.

Mason, S. 2001. *Flavius Josephus: Volume 9, Life of Josephus: Translation and Commentary*. Leiden: Brill.

Mason, S. 2007. Jews, Judaeans, Judaizing, Judaism: Problems of Categorization in Ancient History. *Journal for the Study of Judaism* 38: 457–512.

Mason, S. 2016. *A History of the Jewish War, A.D. 66–74*. New York: Cambridge University Press.

Mason, S., J. S. McLaren, and J.M.G. Barclay. 2012. Josephus. In *Early Judaism, A Comprehensive Overview*, ed. J. J. Collins and D. C. Harlow, 290–321. Grand Rapids, MI: Eerdmans.

Masterman, E.W.G. 1902. Observations of the Dead Sea Levels. *Palestine Exploration Fund Quarterly Statement*: 155–60.

Masterman, E.W.G. 1911. Three Early Explorers in the Dead Sea Valley, Costigan-Molyneux–Lynch. *Palestine Exploration Fund Quarterly Statement* 43: 12–27.

Mazar, B. 1975. *The Mountain of the Lord, Excavating in Jerusalem*. Garden City, NY: Doubleday.

Mazar, B. 1993. En-Gedi: The Chalcolithic Enclosure. In *The New Encyclopedia of Archaeological Excavations in the Holy Land, Vol. 2*, ed. E. Stern, 405. New York: Simon & Schuster.

McDermott, W. C. 1973. Flavius Silva and Salvius Liberalis. *Classical World* 66.6: 335–51.

Meier, J. P. 1991. *A Marginal Jew, Rethinking the Historical Jesus. Volume 1: The Roots of the Problem and the Person*. New York: Doubleday.

Meier, J. P. 2001. *A Marginal Jew, Rethinking the Historical Jesus. Volume 3: Companions and Competitors*. New Haven, CT: Yale University Press.

Mendels, D. 1987. *The Land of Israel as a Political Concept in Hasmonean Literature. Recourse to History in Second Century B.C. Claims to the Holy Land.* Tübingen: J.C.B. Mohr.

Meshorer, Y. 1989. The Coins of Masada. In *Masada I: The Yigael Yadin Excavations 1963–1965 Final Reports*, 69–132. Jerusalem: Israel Exploration Society.

Mumcuoglu, Y. K., and J. Zias. 1988. Head Lice, Pediculus humanus capitis (Anoplura: Pediculidae) from Hair Combs Excavated in Israel and Dated from the First Century B.C. to the Eighth Century A.D. *Journal of Medical Entomology* 25(6): 545–47.

Mumcuoglu, Y. K., J. Zias, M. Tarshis, M. Lavi, and G. D. Stiebel. 2003. Body Louse Remains Found in Textiles Excavated at Masada, Israel. *Journal of Medical Entomology* 40(4): 585–87.

Netzer, E. 1991a. *Masada III: The Yigael Yadin Excavations 1963–1965, Final Reports. The Buildings: Stratigraphy and Architecture.* Jerusalem: Israel Exploration Society.

Netzer, E. 1991b. The Last Days and Hours at Masada. *Biblical Archaeology Review* 17.6: 20–32.

Netzer, E. 1993. Masada. In *The New Encyclopedia of Archaeological Excavations in the Holy Land, Vol. 3*, ed. E. Stern, 973–85. New York: Simon & Schuster.

Netzer, E. 2001. *The Palaces of the Hasmoneans and Herod the Great.* Jerusalem: Yad Ben-Zvi Press/Israel Exploration Society.

Netzer, E. 2006. *The Architecture of Herod, the Great Builder.* Tübingen: Mohr Siebeck.

Netzer, E., R. Porat, Y. Kalman, and R. Chachy. 2013. The Tomb Complex at Herodium. In *Herod the Great, The King's Final Journey*, ed. S. Rozenberg and D. Mevorah, 240–55. Jerusalem: Israel Museum.

Netzer, E., and G. Stiebel. 2008. Masada: Excavations on the Summit. In *The New Encyclopedia of Archaeological Excavations in the Holy Land 5, Supplementary Volume*, ed. E. Stern, 1935–37. Jerusalem: Israel Exploration Society.

Newsom, C. A. 2000. Songs of the Sabbath Sacrifice. In *Encyclopedia of the Dead Sea Scrolls, Vol. 2*, ed. L. H. Schiffman and J. C. VanderKam, 887–89. New York: Oxford University Press.

Nickelsburg, G.W.E. 2005. *Jewish Literature between the Bible and the Mishnah.* Minneapolis: Fortress Press.

Niehr, H. 2010. "Israelite" Religion and "Canaanite" Religion. In *Religious Diversity in Ancient Israel and Judah*, ed. F. Stavrakopoulou and J. Barton, 23–36. London: T & T Clark.

Niv, D., and K. A. Omri. 1973. The Dead Sea. In *The Judean Desert and Dead Sea*, ed. Z. Ilan, 27–37. Ein Gedi Field School: Society for the Protection of Nature in Israel (in Hebrew).

O'Loughlin, T. 2011. "The Unfortunate Costigan," First Surveyor of the Dead Sea. *History Ireland* 19, n.p., http://www.historyireland.com/18th-19th-century-history/the-unfortunate-costigan-first-surveyor-of-the-dead-sea/ (accessed August 7, 2016).

Orland, Y. 1973. The Dead Sea, Its Natural Resources and Their Exploitation. In *The Judean Desert and Dead Sea*, ed. Z. Ilan, 46–58. Ein Gedi Field School: Society for the Protection of Nature in Israel (in Hebrew).

Parker, H.M.D. 1985. *The Roman Legions.* Chicago: Ares.

Patrich, J. 1993a. Hyrcania. In *The New Encyclopedia of Archaeological Excavations in the Holy Land, Vol. 2*, ed. E. Stern, 639–41. New York: Simon & Schuster.

Patrich, J. 1993b. Judean Desert Caves: The Historical Periods. In *The New Encyclopedia of Archaeological Excavations in the Holy Land, Vol. 3*, ed. E. Stern, 820. New York: Simon & Schuster.

Patrich, J. 2000. Mazin, Khirbet. In *Encyclopedia of the Dead Sea Scrolls, Vol. 1*, ed. L. H. Schiffman and J. C. VanderKam, 529–30. New York: Oxford University Press.

Patrich, J., and B. Arubas. 2015. Revisiting the Mausoleum at Herodium: Is It Herod's Tomb? *Palestine Exploration Quarterly* 147.4: 299–315.

Piccirillo, M. 1997. Machaerus. In *The Oxford Encyclopedia of Archaeology in the Near East, Vol. 3*, ed. E. M. Meyers, 391–93. New York: Oxford University Press.

Pomykala, K. E. 1995. *The Davidic Dynasty Tradition in Early Judaism, Its History and Significance for Messianism*. Atlanta, GA: Scholars Press.

Porat, R., R. Chachy, and Y. Kalman. 2015. *Herodium, Final Reports of the 1972–2010 Excavations Directed by Ehud Netzer. Volume I: Herod's Tomb Precinct.* Jerusalem: Israel Exploration Society.

Porat, R., Y. Kalman, and R. Chachy. 2016. Excavation of the Approach to the Mountain Palace-Fortress at Herodium. *Journal of Roman Archaeology* 29: 142–64.

Pressler, C. 1993. *The View of Women Found in Deuteronomic Family Laws*. Berlin: Walter de Gruyter.

Pucci Ben Zeev, M. 2012. Jews among Greeks and Romans. In *Early Judaism, A Comprehensive Overview*, ed. J. J. Collins and D. C. Harlow, 367–90. Grand Rapids, MI: Eerdmans.

Pummer, R. 1987. *The Samaritans*. Leiden: Brill.

Pummer, R. 2016. *The Samaritans: A Profile*. Grand Rapids, MI: Eerdmans.

Qimron, E. 1999. The Ben Sira Scroll from Masada, Notes on the Reading. In *Masada VI: Yigael Yadin Excavations 1963–1965, Final Reports*, 227–31. Jerusalem: Israel Exploration Society.

Rajak, T. 1983. *Josephus, The Historian and His Society*. London: Duckworth.

Rajak, T. 2016. Josephus, Jewish Resistance and the Masada Myth. In *Revolt and Resistance in the Ancient Classical World and the Near East, in the Crucible of Empire*, ed. J. J. Collins and J. G. Manning, 219–33. Leiden: Brill.

Reed, J. L. 2000. *Archaeology and the Galilean Jesus, A Re-examination of the Evidence*. Harrisburg, PA: Trinity International.

Re'em, A. 2018. *The Qishle Excavation in the Old City of Jerusalem*. Jerusalem: Israel Exploration Society.

Regev, E. 2005. *The Sadducees and their Halakhah*. Jerusalem: Yad Ben-Zvi Press (in Hebrew).

Reich, R. 2001. Women and Men at Masada: Some Anthropological Observations Based on the Small Finds (Coins, Spindles). *Zeitschrift des Deutschen Palästina-Vereins* 117: 149–62.

Reich, R. 2007a. Spindle Whorls and Spinning at Masada. In *Masada VIII: The Yigael Yadin Excavations 1963–1965, Final Reports*, 171–94. Jerusalem: Israel Exploration Society.

Reich, R. 2007b. Stone Mugs from Masada. In *Masada VIII: The Yigael Yadin Excavations 1963–1965, Final Reports*, 195–206. Jerusalem: Israel Exploration Society.

Reich, R. 2007c. Stone Scale-Weights from Masada. In *Masada VIII: The Yigael Yadin Excavations 1963–1965, Final Reports*, 207–15. Jerusalem: Israel Exploration Society.

Reich, R. 2013. *Miqw'aot (Jewish Ritual Baths) in the Second Temple, Mishnaic, and Talmudic Periods*. Jerusalem: Yad Ben-Zvi (in Hebrew).

Richardson, P. 1999. *Herod, King of the Jews and Friend of the Romans*. Minneapolis, MN: Fortress Press.

Richmond, I. A. 1962. The Roman Siege Works of *Masàda, Israel. Journal of Roman Studies* 52: 142–55.

Robinson, E. (ed.). 1843. Researches in Palestine: V. Excursion to Hebron, Carmel, and Sebbeh or Masada, Return to Jerusalem. *Bibliotheca Sacra: or Tracts and Essays on Topics Connected with Biblical Literature and Theology* 1: 9–87.

Robinson, E., E. Smith, and others. 1856. *Biblical Researches in Palestine, and the Adjacent Regions: a Journal of Travels in the Years 1838 and 1852, Volume I*. London: John Murray.

Rocca, S. 2008. *Herod's Judaea. A Mediterranean State in the Classical World*. Tübingen: Mohr Siebeck.

Roller, D. W. 1998. *The Building Program of Herod the Great*. Berkeley: University of California Press.

Roth, J. 1995. The Length of the Siege of Masada. *Scripta Classica Israelica* 14: 87–110.

Rozenberg, S., and D. Mevorah (eds.). 2013. *Herod the Great, The King's Final Journey*. Jerusalem: Israel Museum.

Saldarini, A. J. 2001. *Pharisees, Scribes and Sadducees in Palestinian Society*. Grand Rapids, MI: Eerdmans.

Samuelsson, G. 2011. *Crucifixion in Antiquity, An Inquiry into the Background and Significance of the New Testament Terminology of Crucifixion*. Tübingen: Mohr Siebeck.

de Saulcy, L.F.J.C. 1853. *Voyage autour de la mer Morte et dans les terres bibliques: exécuté de décembre 1850 à avril 1851, Vols. 1–2*. Paris: Gide et J. Baudry.

Schäfer, P. 1997. *Judeophobia, Attitudes toward the Jews in the Ancient World*. Cambridge, MA: Harvard University Press.

Schalit, A. (ed.). 1972. *The World History of the Jewish People, Volume Six: The Hellenistic Age. Political History of Jewish Palestine from 332 B.C.E. to 67 B.C.E.* New Brunswick, NJ: Rutgers University Press.

Schalit, A. 1978. *King Herod, Portrait of a Ruler*. Jerusalem: Bialik Institute (in Hebrew).

Schiffman, L. H. 1994. *Reclaiming the Dead Sea Scrolls. The History of Judaism, the Background of Christianity, the Lost Library of Qumran*. Philadelphia: Jewish Publication Society.

Schiffman, L. H., and J. C. Vanderkam (ed.). 2000. *Encyclopedia of the Dead Sea Scrolls, Vols. 1–2*. New York: Oxford University Press.

Schofield, A., and J. C. VanderKam. 2005. Were the Hasmoneans Zadokites? *Journal of Biblical Literature* 124.1: 73–87.

Schulten, A. 1933. *Masada, Die Burg des Herodes und Die Römischen Lager mit einem Anhang: Beth-Ter*. Leipzig: J. C. Hinrichs'sche Buchhandlung.

Schürer, E. 1973–1986. *The History of the Jews in the Age of Jesus Christ, Vols. 1–3*, rev. and ed. G. Vermes, F. Millar, and M. Goodman) Edinburgh: T & T Clark.

Schwartz, D. R. 1990. *Agrippa I: The Last King of Judaea*. Mohr Siebeck: Tübingen.

Schwartz, D. R. 2005. Herodians and *Ioudaioi* in Flavian Rome. In *Flavius Josephus and Flavian Rome*, ed. J. S. Edmonson, S. Mason, and J. Rives, 63–78. New York: Oxford University Press.

Schwartz, D. R. 2014. *Judeans and Jews. Four Faces of Dichotomy in Jewish History.* Toronto: University of Toronto Press.

Seeman, C., and A. K. Marshak. 2012. In *Early Judaism, A Comprehensive Overview*, ed. Collins and D. C. Harlow, 30–69. Grand Rapids, MI: Eerdmans.

Shamir, O. 1994. Loomweights from Masada. In *Masada IV: The Yigael Yadin Excavations 1963–1965, Final Reports*, 265–82. Jerusalem: Israel Exploration Society.

Shavit, A. 2013. *My Promised Land: The Triumph and Tragedy of Israel.* New York: Spiegel & Grau.

Sheffer, A., and H. Granger-Taylor. 1994. Textiles. In *Masada IV: The Yigael Yadin Excavations 1963–1965, Final Reports*, 149–250. Jerusalem: Israel Exploration Society.

Shimron, A. E. 2007. Appendix: The Chemistry of Plasters and Carbonate Crusts from Some *Miqva'ot* and Another Water Installation at Masada. In *Masada VIII: The Yigael Yadin Excavations 1963–1965, Final Reports*, 127–31. Jerusalem: Israel Exploration Society.

Silberman, N. A. 1982. *Digging for God and Country: Exploration in the Holy Land, 1799–1917.* New York: Doubleday.

Silberman, N. A. 1989. *Between Past and Present. Archaeology, Ideology, and Nationalism in the Modern Middle East.* New York: Doubleday.

Silberman, N. A. 1993. *A Prophet from Amongst You. The Life of Yigael Yadin: Soldier, Scholar, and Mythmaker of Modern Israel.* Reading, MA: Addison-Wesley.

Smallwood, E. M. 2001. *The Jews under Roman Rule from Pompey to Diocletian.* Boston: Brill.

Stavrakopoulou, F., and J. Barton. 2010. Introduction: Religious Diversity in Ancient Israel and Judah. In *Religious Diversity in Ancient Israel and Judah*, ed. F. Stavrakopoulou and J. Barton, 1–8. London: T & T Clark.

Stegemann, H. 1998. *The Library of Qumran. On the Essenes, Qumran, John the Baptist, and Jesus.* Grand Rapids, MI: Eerdmans.

Steinmann, A. E. 2009. When Did Herod the Great Reign? *Novum Testamentum* 51.1: 1–29.

Stemberger, G. 2010. Sadducees. In *The Eerdmans Dictionary of Early Judaism*, ed. J. J. Collins and D. C. Harlow, 1179–81. Grand Rapids, MI: Eerdmans.

Sterling, G. E. 2013. "A Man of the Highest Repute": Did Josephus Know Philo's Writings? In *Studia Philonica Annual* 25, ed. D. T. Runia and G. E. Sterling, 101–13. Atlanta, GA: Society of Biblical Literature.

Stern, E. (ed.). 1993. *The New Encyclopedia of Archaeological Excavations in the Holy Land, Vols. 1–4.* New York: Simon & Schuster.

Stern, E. (ed.). 2008. *The New Encyclopedia of Archaeological Excavations in the Holy Land, Vol. 5, Supplementary Volume.* Jerusalem: Israel Exploration Society.

Stern, M. 1980. *Greek and Latin Authors on Jews and Judaism, Edited with Introductions, Translations and Commentary, Vols. 1–2.* Jerusalem: Israel Academy of Sciences and Humanities.

Stiebel, G. 2014. Military Equipment. In *Gamla III: The Shmarya Gutmann Excavations 1976–1989, Finds and Studies, Part 1 (IAA Reports, No. 56)*, ed. D. Syon, 57–107. Jerusalem: Israel Exploration Society.

Stiebel, G., and J. Magness. 2007. The Military Equipment from Masada. In *Masada VIII: The Yigael Yadin Excavations 1963–1965, Final Reports*, 1–94. Jerusalem: Israel Exploration Society.

Talmon, S. 1997. A Masada Fragment of Samaritan Origin. *Israel Exploration Journal* 47(3–4): 220–32.

Talmon, S. 1999. Hebrew Fragments from Masada. In *Masada VI: Yigael Yadin Excavations 1963–1965, Final Reports*, 1–149. Jerusalem: Israel Exploration Society.

Tcherikover, V. 1972. Hellenistic Palestine. In *The World History of the Jewish People, Volume Six: The Hellenistic Age. Political History of Jewish Palestine from 332 B.C.E. to 67 B.C.E.*, ed. A. Schalit, 53–144. New Brunswick, NJ: Rutgers University Press.

Tcherikover, V. 1999. *Hellenistic Civilization and the Jews*. Peabody, MA: Hendrickson.

Thackeray, H. St. 1927–1928. *Josephus, The Jewish War, Vols. 1–3* (Loeb Classical Library). Cambridge, MA: Harvard University Press (reprinted 1997, 2006).

Tomson, P. J. 2017. Sources on the Politics of Judaea in the 50s CE: A Response to Martin Goodman. *Journal of Jewish Studies* 68.2: 234–59.

Tov, E. 2004. *Scribal Practices and Approaches Reflected in the Texts Found in the Judean Desert*. Leiden: Brill.

Tov, E. 2008. *Hebrew Bible, Greek Bible, and Qumran, Collected Essays*. Tübingen: Mohr Siebeck.

Trigger, B. G. 2006. *A History of Archaeological Thought*. New York: Cambridge University Press.

Tristram, H. B. 1866. *The Land of Israel: A Journal of Travels in Palestine, Undertaken with Special Reference to Its Physical Character*. London: Society for Promoting Christian Knowledge (second edition).

Trivedi, B. J. 2002. What Disease Killed King Herod? *National Geographic News* (January 28); http://news.nationalgeographic.com/news/2002/01/0128_020128_King-Herod.html (accessed September 7, 2016).

Tzafrir, Y. 1982. The Desert Fortresses of Judea in the Second Temple Period. In *The Jerusalem Cathedra 2*, ed. L. I. Levine, 120–45. Detroit, MI: Wayne State University Press.

Underhill, H. W. 1967. Dead Sea Levels and the P.E.F. Mark. *Palestine Exploration Quarterly* 99: 45–53.

VanderKam, J. C. 2000. Jubilees, Book of. In *Encyclopedia of the Dead Sea Scrolls, Vol. 1*, ed. L. H. Schiffman and J. C. VanderKam, 434–38. New York: Oxford University Press.

VanderKam, J. C. 2001. *An Introduction to Early Judaism*. Grand Rapids, MI: Eerdmans.

VanderKam, J. C. 2004. *From Joshua to Caiaphas, High Priests after the Exile*. Minneapolis, MN: Fortress Press.

VanderKam, J. C. 2010. *The Dead Sea Scrolls Today*. Grand Rapids, MI: Eerdmans.

VanderKam, J. C., and P. Flint. 2002. *The Meaning of the Dead Sea Scrolls: Their Significance for Understanding the Bible, Judaism, Jesus, and Christianity*. San Francisco: HarperSanFrancisco.

de Vaux, R. 1973. *Archaeology and the Dead Sea Scrolls, The Schweich Lectures 1959.* London: Oxford University Press.

Vermes, G. 2011. *The Complete Dead Sea Scrolls in English.* New York: Penguin.

Vilnay, Z. 1973. Costigan and His Tombstone. In *The Judean Desert and Dead Sea,* ed. Z. Ilan, 418–19. Ein Gedi Field School: Society for the Protection of Nature in Israel (in Hebrew).

Vörös, G. 2013. *Machaerus I. History, Archaeology and Architecture of the Fortified Herodian Royal Palace and City Overlooking the Dead Sea in Transjordan. Final Report of the Excavations and Surveys, 1807–2012.* Milan: Edizioni Terra Santa.

Vörös, G. 2015. *Machaerus II. The Hungarian Archaeological Mission in the Light of the American-Baptist and Italian-Franciscan Excavations and Surveys. Final Report, 1968–2015.* Milan: Edizioni Terra Santa.

Wacholder, B. Z. 1989. Josephus and Nicolaus of Damascus. In *Josephus, the Bible, and History,* ed. L. H. Feldman and G. Hata, 147–72. Leiden: Brill.

Warner, R. 1972. *Thucydides, History of the Peloponnesian War.* Harmondsworth, Middlesex, UK: Penguin.

Wassen, C. 2005. *Women in the Damascus Document.* Atlanta, GA: Society of Biblical Literature.

Webster, G. 1998. *The Roman Imperial Army.* Norman: University of Oklahoma Press.

Woolf, Greg. 1998. *Becoming Roman: The Origins of Provincial Civilization in Gaul.* Cambridge: Cambridge University Press.

Yadin, Y. 1963. *The Finds from the Bar-Kokhba Period in the Cave of Letters.* Jerusalem: Israel Exploration Society.

Yadin, Y. 1965. *The Excavation of Masada 1963/64.* Jerusalem: Israel Exploration Society.

Yadin, Y. 1966. *Masada: Herod's Fortress and the Zealots' Last Stand.* New York: Random House.

Yadin, Y. 1971. *Bar-Kokhba, The Rediscovery of the Legendary Hero of the Last Jewish Revolt against Imperial Rome.* London: Weidenfeld and Nicholson.

Yadin, Y. 1993. Judean Desert Caves: Cave of the Letters. In *The New Encyclopedia of Archaeological Excavations in the Holy Land, Vol. 3,* ed. E. Stern, 829–32. New York: Simon & Schuster.

Yadin, Y. 1999. The Ben Sira Scroll from Masada. In *Masada VI: Yigael Yadin Excavations 1963–1965, Final Reports,* 151–225. Jerusalem: Israel Exploration Society.

Yadin, Y., J. C. Greenfield, A. Yardeni, and B. A. Levine (eds.). 2002. *The Documents from the Bar Kokhba Period in the Cave of Letters. Hebrew, Aramaic, and Nabataean-Aramaic Papyri.* Jerusalem: Israel Exploration Society.

Yadin, Y., and J. Naveh. 1989. The Aramaic and Hebrew Ostraca and Jar Inscriptions. In *Masada I: The Yigael Yadin Excavations 1963–1965 Final Reports,* 1–68. Jerusalem: Israel Exploration Society.

Yaffe, S. 1973. The Climate of the Dead Sea. In *The Judean Desert and Dead Sea,* ed. Z. Ilan, 44–46. Ein Gedi Field School: Society for the Protection of Nature in Israel (in Hebrew).

Yavor, Z. 2010. The Architecture and Stratigraphy of the Eastern and Western Quarters. In *Gamla II: The Architecture, The Shmarya Gutmann Excavations, 1976–1989 (IAA Reports, No. 44),* ed. D. Syon and Z. Yavor, 13–112. Jerusalem: Israel Antiquities Authority.

Zerubavel, Y. 1995. *Recovered Roots: Collective Memory and the Making of Israeli National Tradition*. Chicago: University of Chicago Press.

Zias, J. 1998. Whose Bones? Were They Really Jewish Defenders? Did Yadin Deliberately Obfuscate? *Biblical Archaeology Review* 24.6: 40–45, 64–65.

Zias, J. 2000. Human Skeletal Remains from the Southern Cave at Masada and the Question of Ethnicity. In *The Dead Sea Scrolls Fifty Years After Their Discovery, Proceedings of the Jerusalem Congress, July 20–25, 1997*, ed. L. H. Schiffman, E. Tov, and J. VanderKam, 732–39. Jerusalem: Israel Exploration Society.

Zias, J., and A. Gorski. 2006. Capturing a Beautiful Woman at Masada. *Near Eastern Archaeology* 69.1: 45–48.

Zias, J., D. Segal, and I. Carmi. 1994. Addendum: The Human Skeletal Remains from the Northern Cave at Masada—A Second Look. In *Masada IV: The Yigael Yadin Excavations 1963–1965, Final Reports*, 366–67. Jerusalem: Israel Exploration Society.

INDEX

IMAGE CREDITS

Map 1. Ancient World Mapping Center, University of North Carolina at Chapel Hill (www.unc.edu/awmc).

Map 2. Ancient World Mapping Center, University of North Carolina at Chapel Hill (www.unc.edu/awmc).

Fig. 1. From Netzer 1991a: front dust jacket; by permission of Hillel Geva and the Israel Exploration Society.

Fig. 2. From Hurwitz 2014: 1; by permission of Hillel Geva and the Israel Exploration Society.

Fig. 3. Courtesy of Győző Vörös.

Fig. 4. From Ben-Tor 2009: 18, fig. 9; by permission of Hillel Geva and the Israel Exploration Society.

Fig. 5. Photo by Jodi Magness.

Fig. 6. From Foerster 1995: Pl. XIII; by permission of Hillel Geva and the Israel Exploration Society.

Fig. 7. From Hurwitz 2014: 22; by permission of Hillel Geva and the Israel Exploration Society.

Fig. 8. From Netzer 2001: 98; by permission of Hillel Geva and the Israel Exploration Society.

Fig. 9. Courtesy of Gwyn Davies.

Fig. 10. Photo by Jodi Magness.

Fig. 11. Photo by Jim Haberman.

Fig. 12. Photo by Jodi Magness.

Fig. 13. Photo by Gabi Laron, Hebrew University of Jerusalem; by permission of Hillel Geva and the Israel Exploration Society.

Fig. 14. Photo by Gabi Laron, Hebrew University of Jerusalem; by permission of Hillel Geva and the Israel Exploration Society.

Fig. 15. Photo by Gabi Laron, Hebrew University of Jerusalem; by permission of Hillel Geva and the Israel Exploration Society.

Fig. 16. Photo by Jodi Magness.

Fig. 17. Photo by Jim Haberman.

Fig. 18. From Ben-Tor 2009: 76; by permission of Hillel Geva and the Israel Exploration Society.

Fig. 19. From Netzer 1991a: xvi; by permission of Hillel Geva and the Israel Exploration Society.

Fig. 20. Courtesy of Todd Bolen / BiblePlaces.com.

Fig. 21. Photo by Jodi Magness.

Fig. 22. From Ben-Tor 2009: 42, fig. 35; by permission of Hillel Geva and the Israel Exploration Society.

Fig. 23. From Ben-Tor 2009: 31, fig. 23; by permission of Hillel Geva and the Israel Exploration Society.

Fig. 24. From Ben-Tor 2009: 73, fig. 68; by permission of Hillel Geva and the Israel Exploration Society.

Fig. 25. Photo by Jodi Magness.

Fig. 26. Courtesy of Todd Bolen / BiblePlaces.com. Credit: Matt Floreen / www.mattfloreen.com.

Fig. 27. From Stern 1993: 718; by permission of Hillel Geva and the Israel Exploration Society.

Fig. 28. Photo by Jodi Magness.

Fig. 29. Reconstruction by Leen Ritmeyer ©.

Fig. 30. Reconstruction by Leen Ritmeyer ©.

Fig. 31. Photo by Jodi Magness; by permission of the Israel Museum, Jerusalem.

Fig. 32. Photo by Jim Haberman.

Fig. 33. From Netzer 2001: 117; by permission of Hillel Geva and the Israel Exploration Society.

Fig. 34. Photo by Jodi Magness.

Fig. 35. Photo by Jodi Magness.

Fig. 36. From Netzer 2006: 83, fig. 20. © Mohr Siebeck Tübingen, 2006, by permission of Mohr Siebeck.

Fig. 37. Photo by Jodi Magness.

Fig. 38. Photo by Jodi Magness.

Fig. 39. From Porat et al. 2015: xv, Ill.5; by permission of Hillel Geva and the Israel Exploration Society.

Fig. 40. Photo by Jodi Magness.

Fig. 41. Photo by Jodi Magness.

Fig. 42. Photo by Jim Haberman.

Fig. 43. From Netzer 1991a: 305, Ill. 488; by permission of Hillel Geva and the Israel Exploration Society.

Fig. 44. From Hurwitz 2014: 85; by permission of Hillel Geva and the Israel Exploration Society.

Fig. 45. From Hurwitz 2014: 52; by permission of Hillel Geva and the Israel Exploration Society.

Fig. 46. From Hurwitz 2014: 83; by permission of Hillel Geva and the Israel Exploration Society.